Nathaniel West

Daniel's Great Prophecy

The Eastern Question. The Kingdom

Nathaniel West

Daniel's Great Prophecy
The Eastern Question. The Kingdom

ISBN/EAN: 9783337135140

Printed in Europe, USA, Canada, Australia, Japan

Cover: Foto ©Lupo / pixelio.de

More available books at **www.hansebooks.com**

BY

Rev. Nathaniel West, D. D.

כתב אמת

PUBLISHED BY
THE HOPE OF ISRAEL MOVEMENT.
A. C. Gaebelein, Supt.
E. F. Stroeter, Sec'y.
128 Second Street, New York City.
1898.

COPYRIGHT, 1898,
BY REV. NATHANIEL WEST, D.D.

Three errors there are that forever are found
    On the lips of the good, on the lips of the best;
But empty their meaning, and hollow their sound,
    And slight is the comfort they bring to the breast.

So long as man dreams of a time in this age,
    When the Right and the Good will all evil subdue;
For the Right and the Good war ever will wage,
    And ever will Evil the conflict renew.

So long as men hope that Mammon will live
    Like a bride with her lover, united to worth;
For her favor, alas, to the mean she will give,
    And Virtue possesses no title to earth.

So long as man thinks that to mortals a gift,
    The Truth, in her fulness of glory will shine;
For the vail of the goddess no mortal may lift,
    And all that men do is to guess and divine.
                                    SCHILLER.

PREFACE.

The Book of Daniel was written to prefigure, in outline, the course of history from the Babylonian exile to the second coming of Christ, and to reveal the age of millennial glory "underneath all heavens," following that event. It, therefore, exhibits the character of our own times, as part of the "Times of the Gentiles," which is really the title of the whole book. As in the prophet's day so in ours the kingdom of God is in conflict with the kingdoms of the world; and, as in our Lord's day, is assaulted by all the forces of evil, the assailants seeking to snatch it away by violence. A contemplation of both civil and ecclesiastical events, during the past five years—not to speak of the whole century—only confirms the truth that the same policies that governed the empires and religious establishments of the ancient world, in their official life, and continuously since the introduction of Christianity, exist in our own day, and demonstrates the fact, made clear in Daniel's pages as elsewhere in both Testaments, that the World-Power remains essentially unchanged, notwithstanding its nominal profession of Christianity, and will do so till overthrown by the coming of the Son of Man.

It was a consideration of the events current in our own day, and viewed in the light of the "sure word of prophecy," that induced the writer, though in the midst of much mental and physical suffering, to gather up some results of his past labors, and with the impressions received from recent events present them in a series of articles, to the editors of " Our Hope," who generously allowed space for their publication in the Monthly, devoted to the movement in behalf of Israel, not alone in New York, but in both hemispheres. That movement, based upon the recognition of the fact that the divinely established distinction between Jews and Gentiles, nationally, is a standing one in the New as well as Old Testament history; that there is yet a glorious future for the ancient people of God; and that the turning of Israel to their own Messiah,"even Jesus," strikes the hour of His appearing to them. and brings the emancipation of the nations from the politics and power that now enthral them, meets my decided approbation as it wins my heartiest sympathy. To enlist a deepened interest in an enterprise so worthy of support, and so ably conducted by the scholarly and self-denying editors of " Our Hope," and encourage the study of Daniel's book in its relations to Israel, the nations, and the kingdom of God, also led to the exposition of the prophecies here given, and the offer of them to the Monthly just named. A general desire on the part of the readers, to see the exposition in book form, is the reason of the present volume.

The book of Daniel consists of twelve chapters—as we have it—of which five are historical, viz., i., iii., iv., v., vi., and seven are prophetical, viz., ii., vii., viii., ix., x.-xii., each a distinct prophecy, yet all organically one. It is with the prophetical part, alone, the exposition has to do; and the object has been, not to give the tedious and oftentimes painful processes connected with the study of the text—a thing impossible in a space so brief, and withal uninteresting to the majority of readers—but the results of the processes, in a popular and intelligible way, and so assist the understanding of the prophetic contents scope and aim of the book, and its relation to all prophecy. These predictions set forth, by means of symbols and their interpretation, the political and religious struggles of the Jews with the empires of the world, and the outcome for both, in greater clearness, definiteness and unity, than are seen in all other prophets. They were designed to be a book of comfort and hope for the Jewish people, supporting their Messianic expectations, and also a warning to the kingdoms of the world. Their scope extends beyond the times of Antiochus Epiphanes. B. C. 175-164, and beyond the times of Titus, A. D. 70, reaching to the second coming of Christ and the millennial kingdom. They pertain less to the contemporaries of the prophet than to the generations following. They span all that remained of the Old Testament time, and the whole

New Testament also. The "Last Things" in them are the end of our age, the Antichrist, the great tribulation, the second advent, the resurrection, the deliverance of Israel, the destruction of the Antichrist, the judgment of the living nations, and the kingdom of God in victory. These are called the *Eschata*, the things that pertain to the End of our Age.

The amount of labor done in the critical and exegetical study of the book in our generation has been very great; much of it virulent and unscientific. The defense has been both scientific and triumphant. It is impossible to give even a summary of the bibliography. The writer has spared no pains to make himself acquainted with the latest results of the modern criticism, as far down as to 1897, including the polychrome edition of Daniel by Professor Kamphausen, and his formal attack upon the book, previously issued. It is a comfort to know that the book still remains an anvil on which all hammers are shattered. We may admit a Maccabean editorship, without any difficulty, even as we admit an editorship of our English Bible. This is very remote from saying that the book is a Maccabean composition, or half and half so. In the light of all criticism, we still agree with Hengstenberg that "to refer the composition of the book to Maccabean times will remain false so long as God's word remains true; therefore, to all eternity." And with Sir Isaac Newton we can say that "to reject Daniel's prophecies is to reject the Christian religion; for this religion is founded on his prophecy concerning Christ," a statement ridiculed by Dean Farrar who first distorts the words of Newton, then holds them up to false construction and rebuke. And we can repeat with approval the words of Pusey that "the book of Daniel is especially fitted to be a battlefield between faith and unbelief," and that "the book is either divine or an imposture," no middle ground possible. And self-commending are the recent words of Rupprecht, to any unprejudiced mind familiar with the criticism, "The modern criticism of Daniel's book is, in its spirit, un-Christian, immoral, and unscientific." The "advanced knowledge of the book," as professed by such writers as Kuenen, Wellhausen, Kamphausen, and Cornill, or even by a Bevan and Behrmann still later, and imitated, second-hand, by Farrar, leaves untouched the solid learning and arguments of an Auberlen, Keil, Volck, Wolf, Caspari, Orelli, Oswald, Pusey, Tregelles, and later still, of a Tiefenthal, Herzfeld, D'Envieu, Dornstetter, Düsterwald, Atzberger, and others, of like mature judgment and profound attainments. Unless the book of Daniel is genuine and authentic, the whole New Testament eschatology falls to the ground. For, as Westcott has well said, "No writing of the Old Testament had so great an influence in the development of Christianity as the book of Daniel," and even Cornill is obliged to confess that "hardly another Biblical book has exercised so controlling a power over all subsequent time, and, to-day, we still stand under the influence of ideas and views which the book of Daniel was the first to throw into the development of the religion of Israel;" he might have also said, "of the religion of Christ!"

It is customary to appeal to the fact that certain evangelical scholars, like Delitzsch, Kahnis, and others, have conceded to the critics the Maccabean origin of the book of Daniel, or at least a portion of it. The appeal is worthless. Jerome tells us "the whole church woke up in the fourth century to find itself Arian." The Middle Age found it Papal. In the last century Oxford and Cambridge, Berlin and Heidelberg, were chief nurseries of Deism and Rationalism. England, France and Germany assailed the Word of God on every side. And as for our own times, it was Delitzsch, who, notwithstanding his concessions, denounced the Higher Criticism as "Bible-hating, history-manufacturing science." Even a Hitzig called it "an abomination of desolation." Gess, conceding the Maccabean origin of Daniel's book, yet adds, "It is impossible to excuse the writer of it from the charge of pious fraud." Kuenen, the master-mind of all the critics, when approaching death, ordered the suppression of every unsold copy of his greatest work, and the reimbursement of his publishers from his estate. At the close of a long life of critical labor, De Wette, a leading spirit in his day could say in sadness,

> "I lived in times of doubt and strife,
>   When child-like faith was forced to yield,
> I struggled to the end of life,
>   Alas, I could not gain the field!"

But there are scholars, as well as scholars, whose words are not to be set aside by the sneers of second-hand imitators of unbelieving criticism. It is Kaulen who testifies, "After the most thorough investigation I am certain that the writer of the Book of Daniel shows a most intimate personal acquaintance with the palace of Nebuchadnezzar and the affairs of the Babylonian court and empire, and that the book was written in the time of the exile." In like manner Lenormant: "The more I read and reread the Book of Daniel, the more I am struck with the truth of the tableau of the Babylonian court traced in the first six chapters, and of the ideas special to the time of Nebuchadnezzar. Whoever is not the slave of preconceived opinions, denying the supernatural, must confess when comparing the chapters with the cuneiform monuments, that they are really ancient, and written at but short distance from the events themselves." And as to the prophetical part, the words of Düsterwald state the simple truth concerning the false criticism. "The foregone denial of the supernatural—that is, of God in prophecy—underlies every denial of the genuineness and authenticity of these predictions. Once admit that ii., viii. and ix. reach beyond Antiochus Epiphanes and into Roman times, then it is not possible to deny the supernatural, or that here is true prediction of remote events. That our Lord and His apostles so interpreted these prophecies admits of no doubt. When, therefore, the opposers of their genuineness and authenticity assail these predictions as apocryphal, for the sake of maintaining their working rule, we can reply to them that solely in the interest of their science they assail Christ Himself, and usurp His place as the interpreter of prophecy and the heaven-sent Teacher of the Church." We need not fear. The Book of Daniel has survived every attack upon it for two thousand years, and will to the end. "The violence of modern criticism," says D'Envieu, "has only reproduced, under the show of learned strategy, the old assaults in the first years of our Christian Era."

In a few pages, the results of a study of the difficult problem of the "Seventy Weeks," are given. Since the publication of my work, "Studies in Eschatology," the whole subject has been reviewed in the light of volumes not then accessible. The whole history of their interpretation has been carefully gone over, from 200 years before Christ to the present time; (1) the pre-Christian period, ending with our Lord's Olivet discourse, A. D. 33; (2) the period of the first two Christian centuries, including both Jewish and Christian interpretation, ending A. D. 190; (3) thence to the close of the fifth century, A. D. 490, from Clemens Alexandrinus to Ammonius; (4) the middle-age period to A. D. 1250, from Severus to Aquinas; (5) thence to the sixteenth century, or reformation times; (6) thence to the present time. The independent conclusions, previously reached, have all been confirmed. In this vast field of inquiry nothing has been left undone by Reusch who has given the Patristic interpretations, or by Calovius who has given the Mediæval,or by Rohling who has given the Modern, or by Fraidl who has reviewed carefully all these labors, or by D'Envieu who has supplemented them. Time has added nothing, not even through the Higher Criticism, beyond what the ingenuity of men devised during the first four centuries. In general the four categories into which the various interpretations fall are (1) that Messiah appeared within the seventy weeks, the destruction of Jerusalem, A. D. 70, being the end of the 70th week; (2) that Messiah appeared near the end of the 69th week, and was cut off in the middle of the 70th, the end of the 70th being the transition of the gospel to the Gentiles; (3) that the two Little Horns are the same, and the seventy weeks ended with the times of Antiochus, B. C. 164, a view most vigorously repelled by the church; (4) that the Messiah appeared at the end of the 69th week, that the interval of the Roman times of the Gentiles lies between the 69th and 70th weeks, and that the seventieth week is the last—Antichrist's week—a view held by the ablest exegetes of the first three centuries. Delightful is the view held by Raymund Martini, A. D. 1350, and by Solomon Levy, "a born Jew," that "Prince Messiah" is not Cyrus, nor is " Messiah cut off " Onias III., but that " Gabriel to Daniel, and Gabriel to Mary, prophesied of the same Messiah, even Jesus Christ;" that Daniel, influenced by the Messianic hope and deliverance of Israel which Isaiah seemed to connect with the return from Babylon, supposed the time of the hope might be at the close of "Jeremiah's seventy years," and that, as Gabriel had already in vii. fixed the time of the second advent, so did he fix the time of the first in ix., and led the prophet to look out into the "Times of the Gentiles" to find both advents; and specially that Messiah *must* come between the completion of the second temple and its destruction by Titus.

The one satisfactory result of the whole study has been to see how certainly the ablest church exegetes, in early times, contended, and successfully, that the 70th week is the Antichrist's week, at the end of the "Times of the Gentiles." The Interval between the third and fourth weeks was hidden from their eyes, and has remained undetected till the present time.

No apology is needed for another work on the book of Daniel, nor ever will be. I hold it to be unassailable that our Lord had the whole book of Daniel, and especially the vision of judgment, at His second coming, Dan. vii., directly in His mind when He uttered His great Olivet discourse concerning the end. And I hold to be indisputable by any mind not warped by false criticism, that the oracle in Dan. xii: 4, 8, foretelling the study of Daniel's book in the "Time of the End," refers not only to its study in Maccabean times, B. C. 168 to 164, at the end of the third prophetic empire, but to the "Time of the End" of the fourth, in its divided state, i.e., to our own times and the immediate future. That oracle belongs to the great concluding prophecy in x.-xii. concerning the "Warfare Great," whose climax is the solution of the "Eastern Question." And because this concluding prophecy, x.-xii., is but the expansion of what is given in the closing part of ix., it involves the study of the "70th week," therefore of the "70 weeks;" and since x.-xii. is again but the expansion of what is given in viii., as viii. is the expansion of vii. and ii., therefore the oracle, xii: 4, 8, predicts the intense study of Daniel's whole book, and the understanding of it, as a sign of the end of our age. This renders all apology for such study unnecessary and justifies the interest felt to-day in Israel's destiny, and its relation to the victory of the kingdom of Christ.

In order to keep the unity and aim of the book before the mind of the reader, the exposition is woven around the central theme of the book, viz., that the kingdom foretold by the prophet cannot come to victory "underneath all heavens," until the second coming of the Son of Man. A further help to enable the reader to grasp the contents of the prophecies is to remember that all the matter of the predicted history falls under these seven rubrics—the Jews, the Four Empires, the Two Little Horns, the Seventy Weeks, the Warfare Great, the Messiah at both Advents, the Kingdom.

As to the study of the Jews, the histories by Edersheim, Milman, Adams, and Josephus, Stanley's Jewish Church, the books of the Maccabees, Conder's Judas Maccabeus, and Latin Kingdom of Jerusalem, Besant and Palmer's History of Jerusalem, and Le Strange's Palestine under the Moslems, will be found all-sufficient. As to the four empires, Rawlinson's Seven Great Monarchies, and his Herodotus, with Flint's, and Hegel's Philosophy of History, and Cox's Syria and Egypt, tell all that is needed. As to the chronology, Clinton's Fasti Hellenici still holds its place as authority. As to the geography of the book of Daniel, the Ancient Atlases by Kiepert, and Kampen, give all the four empires, the Diadochian kingdoms, and spread in full the storm centre of the Eastern Question. A summary of universal history, crowded with dates and events, and unsurpassed for accuracy, is provided by Plætz, eleventh edition, and is the leading text-book in all the German gymnasia.

A late writer of much ability, dismayed at the aspect of Christendom, and little anxious as to the inspiration of God's Word, or the old faith, proposes the doctrine of "our spiritual conceptions," and of "evolution spiritually," as the quickest way to bring in the golden age and the triumph of the kingdom of God. Hypothetically, he says, "If the world, the flesh, and the devil are at war with righteousness, once for all, that we must look to convulsive overthrow for its establishment—to some millennial transition waited for so long in vain, and hidden so thoroughly out of sight in the events around us." Again, "No matter how many convulsive changes and millenniums religion may promise itself, we see that they do not come. Our Christian faith, amid all its prophetic gleams, has traveled a weary way in which nothing has been gained save in the slowest manner." If this is not "pessimism," it is hard to tell what is. The statement is historically untrue. The rapid extension of Christianity in the early ages is one of the best established facts of history. The rapid extension of missions since the close of the last century, and of the translation of the Bible into almost all languages, are not less so. And as to "spiritual evolution" in the "scientific sense," the gradualism of a Darwin, Lyell, Huxley, and Spencer, repudiating all catastrophe and cataclysm, what else but "slowness" is the progress through interminable stages? The whole "pessimism" rests on the denial of miraculous intervention which accomplishes more in one hour than preceding centuries could achieve. It is precisely by means of "convulsive overthrow," after long yet imperfect development, the kingdom of God comes to victory. Nowhere has the Scripture assigned to the church universal triumph in this age, before the Lord comes. On the contrary, the law of apostasy and degeneration runs parallel with the law of advance, and only by "convulsive overthrow," in the final crisis, is the antagonism solved. Such is the Bible teaching. The apostle Peter has discussed and determined conclusively the whole question in 2 Pet. iii: 2-15. For a teacher of the truth to be oblivious of this, is a calamity as great as for a minister of state not to know the constitution of his country.

To one point I desire to call special attention. It is remarkable how the critics and the commentators have failed to see that by the words, "the Scripture of truth," Dan. x: 1, is meant nothing less than Daniel's book, and not the unwritten book of "God's providence," or of the "divine decrees," or the "Old Testament." Orthodox interpreters have been blinded here, and every sharp-sighted critic, without exception, persistently evades the true interpretation, aware of its destructive force against the false theory of the book if once the fact is admitted. The admission of that fact forces the alternatives, either the writer of the book of Daniel was a guilty forger, whose crime can never be excused by "the custom of his times," or Daniel, the prophet of the exile, was its author.

The chapters on the Type and Antitype, the Transition-Section, the Great Interval, in xi: 39, 40, the Antichrist's Last Campaign, and the concluding Summation—not published in "Our Hope" for want of space—appear in the present volume. Some sections, also, omitted from the other chapters for want of space, are here supplied.

This little volume is sent forth with the earnest prayer that God will bless the "Truth" of Daniel's book to the souls of all the "Wise" who, as the "Time of the End" draws near, will study it with diligence, and find it a light to their understanding and a bulwark to their faith and hope. It is well to remember that the kingdom of God is battling still with the "Ten-horned Beast," whose head was wounded by advancing Christianity, but whose wound is now being healed by its social and political de-christianization. With Israel's recovery the Gentile dominion passes away. The Beast dies.

May the prophet's word be a stimulus to work and pray for Israel's conversion and restoration, and the hastening of that day when, through "convulsive overthrow," an "End" will be put to the Gentile politics and power that disgrace our present age! May the "Kingdom" soon come in victory, and God's will "be done on earth as it is in heaevn!"

NATHANIEL WEST.

Clifton Springs, March, 1898.

TABLE OF CONTENTS.

CHAPTER I.

General Introduction.— Character of the Book of Daniel; World-Power; Scope of the Book; Daniel's Mission; Character of Daniel; The Thesis.

CHAPTER II.

Daniel, Chapter II.— Israel's Place in History; Babylon's Place; The Fundamental Prophecy; Law of Prophecy; The Colossus; Impact of the Stone; Rationalism; "The Days of those Kings;" The Rolling Stone; False Interpretation; The True; Honor to Daniel and Glory to God.

CHAPTER III.

Daniel, Chapter VII.— Critical Question; Vision of the Four Beasts; The Fourth Beast and its Horns; The Little Horn; Vision of the Judgment of the Horn and the Nations; Ancient of Days; Son of Man; Overthrow of Kingdoms and Sultanates; Chiliasm; The Kingdom given to the Saints; Time of the Judgment, Place of the Judgment; The Ten Horns; The Criminality of modern World-Powers; Their Doom.

CHAPTER IV.

Daniel, Chapter VII., continued.— The Little Horn; His Names, The Great Tribulation; Witness-bearing; The Ancient of Days; The Judges in the Judgment; Angels; Books Opened; Complete Retribution; The Son of Man; Effort to evade the Chiliastic Doctrine of the Book; The Monarch of the Fifth Empire; The Kingdom and the People of the Saints.

CHAPTER V.

Daniel, Chapter VIII.—"Time of the End" of the Third

Empire; The Kingdom not mentioned; Date of the Vision; Place of the Vision; The Vision itself; The Eastern Question; The Ram and Rough Goat; Cyrus and Alexander; Antiochus Epiphanes; Vision of Horror at Jerusalem; Angelic Dialogue; Apparition of a Man; The 2300 Evening-mornings; Interpretation of the Vision; Time of Fulfillment; Vain Efforts to identify the two Little Horns; Similarities and Dissimilarities; Grounds of the same; Purpose of the Vision.

Chapter VI.

Daniel, Chapter IX.—The Seventy Weeks; General Remarks; Place of the Prophecy; Occasion of it; The Prophecy itself; Its correct Translation; Covers the Prayer; Exposition of the Seventy Weeks; Their Sub-distribution; The two Intervals; No Year-day Theory in Daniel; The Seventieth Week; The Four Great Ideas of World-view, World-history, World-judgment and World-chronology; The Interpretation sure; The Secret disclosed; The Reasons of the False Interpretation; The Jews as Reckoners of Time; Gentile Confirmation; The Jurisdiction of the Seventy Weeks over all New Testament Prophecy; It fixes absolutely the Timepoint of the Second Advent.

Chapter VII.

Daniel, Chapters X.-XII.— One Prophecy: The Theme, the "Warfare Great;" The Eastern Question; Nature of the Revelation; Date of the Prophecy; Place and Time of the Vision; Occasion of the Vision; The Vision itself; The Christophany; The Persons in the Scene; The Effect of the Vision; Prostration of the Prophet, and Flight of his Companions; The Recovery of the Prophet; The Comfort; Israel under the guardian Care of Angels; Daniel's Book, a "Scripture of Truth;" Warning against the false Criticism of this Book.

Chapter VIII.

Daniel, Chapters X.-XII., continued.—Chapter xi., 1-35."Tsaba Gadol," the "Warfare Great;" The Chapter assailed as a

Spurious Production; Reply; Geography of the Prophecy;
The Eastern Question; Division of Chapter; The Persian
Succession; The Greek; The Diadochian Kingdoms; Ptolemies and Seleucids; The Intervals in the Prophecy; Wars
of Syria and Egypt; Antiochus Epiphanes; Campaigns
against Egypt; Campaigns against Palestine; The Maccabean Tribulation; The Martyr-Roll.

CHAPTER IX.

Daniel, Chapters X.-XI., continued.— Chapter xi., 36-45:
The Transition-Section; Various Views; True View of the
Type and Antitype; Place of the Great Interval between
the Ends of the Third and Fourth Empires; Photograph
of the Antichrist; The Antichrist's last Campaign, and
World's Last Battle; " Time of the End;" The Three
Greater Powers in the Field; Occupation of Egypt; Inva-
sion of Palestine; The Great Tribulation; Michael standing
over the Jews; Angelic War in Heaven; Universal War on
Earth; Joel's Picture of the Scene; Zechariah's; Isaiah's;
John's; The Blood-Bath; The Preparation of the Nations
for the Struggle; The Military Budgets of Russia, Germany,
Austria, France, Italy; The Causes; The " Ever-recurring
Law; " The Eastern Question, and its Solution.

CHAPTER X.

Daniel, Chapter XII.— Conclusion of the Prophecy; Defin-
ition of the Time; Intervention of Michael; The Great
Tribulation; The Deliverance of the Jews; The Resurrection
of the Holy Dead; Splendor of the Risen Saints; Life
Everlasting; Completion and Authentication of Daniel's
Book; Study of the Book in the " Time of the End;" The
Epilogue; The Higher Criticism; Perplexity of Daniel; Its
Solution; First Dismissal of the Prophet from the Scene;
Extension of the " Time of the End;" The 1290 and 1335
Days; The Blessed Time; Second Dismissal of the Prophet;
The Promise of the Prophet's Resurrection; Christ, Glory,
the Kingdom, the End—Our Hope.

Chapter XI.

Summation, Objections, Conclusion; General Teaching of Daniel's Book; The Passing away of all Kingdoms and Empires; Resumè of the Main Features of Daniel's Book; The Design of the Judgment of the Nations; God's Name Sanctified, His Will done on Earth as in Heaven; Connection between Eschatology and the Messiah-doctrine; Objections to Daniel's Doctrine; Reply; The Sequence of the Kingdom in Victory upon the Second Advent; Curiosities of Opposite View; Character of the Millennial Kingdom; Reign of the Saints on the Earth; Jerusalem the Centre of the New Age; Christ present in His glory; The Kingdom of " the 1000 years; " The Vastness of the Idea of the Kingdom; False that the Kingdom of Christ is not here now; False that it comes to victory before He comes; Science demands a Millennial Age; Use and Abuse of Prophecy; Chiliasm indestructible; Testimony of the Writer; Parting with the Prophet.

THE FOUR EMPIRES.

From B.C. 606 to Second Coming of Christ.

Caps.					
II. Collossus. Stone Kingdom.	1 Chaldean. Gold. B.C. 606.	2 Medo-Persian. Silver. 538	3 Græco-Macedonian. Brass. 334	4 Roman. Iron. Clay. B.C. 25	Toes
VII. Beasts. Son of Man Kingdom.	1 Chaldean. Lion. B.C. 606.	2 Medo-Persian. Bear. 538	3 Græco-Macedonian. Leopard. 334	4 Roman. Monster. B.C. 25	Horns
VIII.		2 Medo-Persian. Ram. 538	3 Græco-Maced. Goat. 331	Antiochus 175-164	2300 Trib.
IX.		2 Medo-Persian. Chronology, etc. 538	3 Græco-Macedonian. 331	A.D. 70	1260 / 1260 Trib. (Interval 1897 already.)
X–XII. Second Advent Kingdom.		2 Medo-Persian. Successors. 538	3 Græco-Mac. Successors. 334	(Interval 1902 already.)	2300 / 1260 / 1260 Trib.

Oriental. Occidental.

(19)

"The prophets of the Old Testament in a marked and special manner looked forward into the future. They personated and expressed the Hope of Israel and the Kingdom of God. Standing on their lofty watch-towers, and looking to the farthest horizon, they saw events unseen by ordinary men, and spoke of things to come long after the generations they served had passed to the tombs. They were the first in antiquity to perceive that the old East was dead. They celebrated its obsequies in advance of the dissolution they saw to be inevitable. They were the tragic chorus of the awful drama that was unfolding itself in the Eastern world. As kingdom after kingdom passed away, they sang the funeral dirge of each. There can be no question that the book of Daniel, containing the first mention of the great idea of the succession of the ages and of the growth of empires and races, is the first outline of the philosophy of history."

Dean Stanley.

DANIEL'S GREAT PROPHECY.

Chapter I.

"By the rivers of Babylon, there we sat down; yea, we wept when we remembered Zion. We hanged our harps upon the willows in the midst thereof. For there they that carried us away captive required of us a song; and they that wasted us required of us mirth, saying, sing us one of the songs of Zion! How shall we sing the Lord's song in a strange land? If I forget thee, O Jerusalem, let my right hand forget her cunning! If I do not remember thee, let my tongue cleave to the roof of my mouth, if I prefer not Jerusalem above my chief joy!" Psalm cxxxvii: 1-6. Such is the pathetic lamentation of a sweet but sorrow-smitten minstrel of Israel, expert in song and skilful with the harp telling the grief of his people in the hour of their humiliation. The holy temple, the sanctuary of God and central shrine of Israel's worship, had disappeared in flame and smoke. Divine judgment had destroyed the "city of the Great King." The temple vessels, and the people, had been borne away captive into Babylon to grace the triumph of a heathen ruler. The instrument in God's hand for the execution of this judgment was Nebuchadnezzar, the crown-prince of the Chaldean empire. Three times he came as a conqueror and took Jerusalem; the first time, B. C. 606, deporting Daniel and his companions; the second time, B. C. 598, Ezekiel and a larger number; the third time, B. C. 587, burning the city, and completing the captivity. To celebrate the anniversary of his conquest and the consolidation of his empire, he erected a golden image of himself upon the plains of Dura, summoned a State concert, and at the sound of his royal band of music, demanded universal homage to his person, on pain of death for refusal. Seventy years the Jews were delivered to the Chaldean power. At such a time the Lord raised up "Daniel the Prophet" to foretell the course and doom of all Gentile empires, and the final triumph of the chosen people and of the kingdom of God. In connection with certain miraculous events of his time, the Book of Daniel makes known to us the divine communications he received, unveiling the whole future down to the second coming of Christ. Its religious and polititcal importance are recognized by all the world. It tells that the " Lord's song" will first be sung by Israel "in the land of Judah," when Israel has returned to faith in Christ, and all Gentile kingdoms have been overthrown. Isa. xxv: 1; xxvi: 1-21; Dan. ii: 44; vii: 13, 25-27.

The canonicity and inspiration of the book of Daniel are established by testimonies more numerous and varied than can be claimed for any other sacred writing. They come from the pens of inspired prophets and historians, and from the whole body of Jewish literature subsequent to the close of Old Testament prediction. Chaldæan, Persian, Greek and Roman authors have confirmed its statements. Centuries have verified its prophecies. The lips of Christ, Peter, Paul, John and the evangelists, have borne witness to its truth. The entire New Testament is effulgent with its eschatology. The early church teachers, with rare devotion, applied themselves to search diligently and understand its contents, and held it aloft as a shining proof of the Christian faith. Schoolmen and reformers studied it with deepest interest. Jews, Christians and Mohammedans, Catholics and Protestants alike, have vied with each other to explore its mysteries. From B. C. 534 to A. D. 1898, through 2,400 years, more than ten thousand volumes have been written as a tribute to its worth and world-wide significance, and, in our generation, the monuments of Assyria, Babylon, Persia, Armenia and Egypt, have united to do it honor. Holy men to-day realize the fact that in this book was concealed a sun of surpassing brilliance, whose light should burst forth in the "Time of the End" and irradiate with its splendor the eyes of all whose blessedness it is to seek it. And yet, no book of the Bible is more distasteful to the unbelieving criticism of our times, nor does it find enemies more dangerous than many who profess to be defenders of the truth, degrading its dignity and value to the level of mere apocryphal production. Its offence is the manifest presence of the supernatural in every page. It claims to be a faithful chronicle of events transcending the possibilities of all ordinary occurrence, a revelation also from heaven, and, in large part, a word spoken by angels. In it we read histories the most marvelous, and prophecies whose far-sightedness outstrips the utmost reach of human genius, forecast and sagacity. It provides the most brilliant confirmation of the inspiration of the prophets. It discloses the only true philosophy of history, unveils a procession of the ages, publishes an almanac of time and sets before us a moving panorama of marching empires and of rising and falling kingdoms, covering already nearly 2,500 years. It foretells a hundred events, three-fourths of which have been fulfilled. It supports its omniscient predictions by omnipotent deeds placed alongside of them as pledges of their accomplishment, the supernatural in the one case, the proof of it in the other. In an honest mind unswayed by prejudice and false science it compels belief. Its grasp is the grasp of the Almighty.

Great moral and dogmatic truths are guaranteed by miracles speaking to the eyes, concerning the true God, the true religion, the true people of God, and the world's destiny, confronting all the idolatries of the nations. Like a blazing headlight cast across the centuries and illuminating the whole track of time, shines the announcement that human history is the result neither of chance nor fatality, nor of man's will alone; that the events of nations and the actions of men, although the product of their own free will, are yet pursuant to a predetermined plan of God, Most High, who " removes and sets up kings, gives wisdom to the wise and knowledge to them that understand; who reveals secrets, knows what is in the darkness, and in whom light dwells;" that history has an appointed goal to which it must attain, and that the rise, rule and revolution of empires, their apogee, decline and fall, have already been decreed and recorded, and must eventuate according to the will of God. In the most solemn manner, it emphasizes the truth that God, Most High, is "Governor among the nations," greater than Bel, Nebo, Istar or Merodach, or all the gods of the heathen, a Power superior to all the "Powers," a "Power, not ourselves, that makes for righteousness," and walks through history: that while rewarding the good He punishes the evil; that for every crime committed by nations, governments or men, for every wrong abetted or inflicted, for every unrighteous deed, for every policy of pride and greed, of selfishness, oppression of the poor and the weak, for every indifference to distress, for every act of cruelty and ambitious lust of territory, wealth and supremacy, Justice will exact a righteous retribution; and that the one consolation left to sufferers amid all the complications that perplex the diplomacies of nations, retard the relief of unavenged humanity, and try the patience of God's children, is the deep conviction that such will be the case.

No sublimer moral truth ever passed the lips of any writer. What the Greek tragedy attributed to blind 'Justice" standing behind every scene, and to "Necessity" behind Justice, the prophet describes as the work of a free, intelligent and overruling Power, "God Most High," omnipotent and irresistible. Wickedness may seem to triumph for a time, and the prayer of outraged and enslaved communities meet only disappointment, but, sooner or later, judgment must strike the guilty.

Nor is it as an abstract proposition this great truth is asserted, but is illustrated as a concrete fact in history, by the rise and fall of empires, states and kingdoms, on whose sepulchres the one epitaph stands written, "*Dead for Want of Righteousness!*" That is the lesson of the book, a theodicy that justifies the ways of God, vindicates His long-suffering and discipline, His last destructive stroke, and the setting up of His own kingdom where the "will" of God shall "be done on earth as it is in heaven." National sin must be punished, the governments of earth must be destroyed, and the nations judged, in order to their salvation. Not monarchs, nor empires, but "*The Heavens do rule!*" God alone is the ground of the universe, and His righteousness, truth, mercy and holiness, His will and His judgments, are the establishment of His throne. Might does not make right, but the nature and will of God. Right is not the enactment of the State. The maxims of expediency and selfish interests are not law. The will of princes, cabinets and counsellors is not the measure of obligation. The right of rule rests not on human conquests, nor is the power to rule the creation of a people. God alone is the ground and source of all. Such the doctrine and the lesson of the book.

Among the things that excite our curiosity and arrest our attention, as we read the book, are the metallurgy and zoology of its predictions, representing four great empires in succession—two Oriental, the Babylonian and Medo-Persian; two Occidental, the Græco-Macedonian and the Roman. The representation is made first by means of specific metals, gold, silver, brass and iron, mixed with clay; next, by four wild beasts, the lion, bear, leopard and an untamed ten-horned monster, or megatherium. The second two are again represented by two domestic animals, the ram and rough goat. A colossal statue of human form, bright and terrible, its head gold, its feet iron and clay, stands erect as the symbol of *the whole organized political power of the world in unity,* including its various governments and policy, its material strength built upon the products of the mines, its laws of degeneration, disintegration and division; in short, the entire development of the world-power, through a succession of empires, the last of which survives in its fragmentary state until the Lord comes. The whole symbol is a picture lesson and divine programme of the world-power advancing systematically and organically in definite periods of time to a goal fixed in the counsel of God, that goal *the absolute destruction of all Gentile governments, politics and power, and the erection of the kingdom of God on their ruin.* The prophet would have us write the date B. C. 606 over the head of the statue, and the second coming of Christ; the "Stone," at the end of its toes. During the time between these dates the Colossus stands unoverthrown, and on prostrate Israel's breast the Gentiles exercising the sovereignty of the whole earth. At the end of the times of the Gentiles, whose length is that of the statue, its fate is to be struck on the toes by the Stone from heaven, the mountain of God's holiness, grinding the statue to powder, the wind of judgment blowing away its dust, "like the chaff of the summer threshing floor." "*Sic transit gloria Mundi.*" The God of heaven, at such a time, sets up a kingdom, the fifth in succession, unsucceeded and indestructible.

As to the inner spirit, essence, nature and life of the world-power, it is symbolized by that of the four predacious beasts, whose ethics are those of the jungle, viz.: the physically "fittest to survive," the Rob Roy ethics of

> "The simple plan
> That he may take who has the power,
> And he may keep who can,"

the motto for one the same for all, "Arise, devour much flesh!" This is further illustrated by the action of the two domestic cornute animals, butting and rebutting one another. The stronger devour the weaker, in every case for selfish interests and increase of power. Governed by savage, sensuous, impure, sinful and brutal impulses and passions, it perpetuates its right of rule over man by military violence, plunging horns, teeth and iron heel, into every tribe or people that opposes. In short, the whole world-power, from first to last, is constitutionally beastly and metallic, and continues so down to the end of its existence, and this notwithstanding the progress of the nations in culture and civilization, and in spite of every influence of Christianity upon it. It cannot be otherwise, for selfishness and jealousy are its inner principles. Down to the end of Gentile rule, the motives and the policies that actuated Sennacherib, Nebuchadnezzar, Cyrus, Alexander and Cæsar—heathen motives—are the back-lying springs of action that will govern the whole world-power, and every form of it, whether "I the King" or "We the people." Never can the religion of Jesus Christ celebrate a universal victory under the whole heaven until the heaven-descending "Stone" grinds to powder the proud Colossus, and the Son of Man annihilates in person the last anti-Christian ruler. The life of all the first three beasts passes into the fourth, more terrible than all before it, even in its divided ten-horned state, grim with iron armament, while among these separate horns and kingdoms an eleventh arises, plucking up a " Dreibund " in its way, thus himself becoming "an 8th" "stouter than his fellows," acquiring the power of all the rest, anti-Christian to the core, the persecutor of the saints of God, and bent on universal empire. That is the last picture of our modern culture and so-called Christian civilization, a picture " Modern Progress " is determined not to believe, but which God is determined it shall believe, when its haughtiness is laid low, its loftiness bowed down, and its books of sorcery, like those of Diana-worshippers at Ephesus, are given to the flame. The fate of the persecuting Horn, the last representative of Gentile progress, science and culture, and that of his kingdom, and of the whole world-power, is destruction. On their grave rises in beauty and glory, the kingdom of God.

Wonderful prediction which hatred of its truth makes men deny, and refer the whole to the dream of a disappointed Maccabean Jew, the guilty forger of the book in Daniel's name 400 years after Daniel's death! Wonderful beyond imagination! The prophet traverses the march of world empires and kingdoms from his own time to the end of our present age, the second coming of Christ. He foretells the conduct of the world-power, and illustrates its madness by the mania of Nebuchadnezzar and the doom of Belshazzar. Running down the centuries he introduces us to Cyrus, Cambyses, Darius, Xerxes, Artaxerxes, to Alexander and his successors, the struggles of Egypt and Syria for Palestine, the campaigns of Antiochus Epiphanes. He foretells events in the history of Berenice, and of Cleopatra, the mother of all the Cleopatras and sister of the Greek Antichrist. He brings us to the rise of the Roman empire on the ruins of the republic in Cæsar's time, when the " dregs of Romulus " were all that remained, its subsequent bipartition, its fragmentary tenfold state still later, and apart from which the mediæval and modern history of Europe is without explanation. He exhibits the last Antichrist, and his allied powers, as the summit of world-development. By a law of prophetic retrogression, he returns from the final goal to predict the birth of Christ, His death, the destruction of Jerusalem and its temple by Titus, the desolation of the land and fate of the Jews during the sequent times of the Gentiles. Advancing again to the end, he describes in brief the scenes of the last seven years of our present age, the Antichrist's proper week. Two advents of Christ he predicts, the one in humiliation, the other in glory. He forecasts the conflict of the Jews with the world-power along the whole line of their sad dispersion, the final triumph of the former and the total ruin of the latter at the second coming of Christ, and the victory of the kingdom of Christ over all the earth, when One mightier than Cyrus shall bid His ancient people return to their land, and One greater than all the Joshuas, Zerrubbabels, Ezras and Nehemiahs, of the Old Testament shall lead them back.

As to the mission of Daniel, it was, in many respects, like that of Joseph and Moses at the court of Egypt, and again like that of Paul to the Gentiles. He was a "chosen vessel" ordained of God to bear "His name before Gentiles and kings, and the children of Israel,"—not only to take part in the great events of the Babylonian and Persian empires, but to represent in person, to the kings who ruled them, God's ancient people and the true religion; to fortify the captives by miracles and prophecies, confound the heathen wisdom and idolatry, and maintain the truth concerning the coming Messiah and His Kingdom. To disobey the orders of the court with absolute impunity, and yet maintain his position in spite of the king and the satraps, to defy the sword, the flame and the lion's den, and compel decrees in favor of "God Most High," this was the privilege of the prophet and his three companions. The wise men of the world-power, the Magi of the East, believed that they alone had wisdom and had derived it from their gods, whose images and temples towered high over all heathendom. The powers of the world believed that they acted independently of Jehovah. The God of Israel, for them, was no more than Moloch or Astarte, the tribal deity of nomads, less civilized than themselves—powers who imagined that they governed the world according to their will, and that the future was in the hands of them and their gods. It was Daniel's mission to dissolve this delusion, and prove to them that they were but instruments in the hand of "God Most High," who ruled the whole course of history according to His own will, that the whole future lay before Him like a map prepared by His own hand, and that He who knows the future must be the Ordainer and Disposer of all events, a Power personal, intelligent, all-wise, holy, and the Almighty whom neither the kings nor the nations could resist without punishment. It was in the mission of Daniel to humiliate, shame, and abase the pride of all world wisdom and world power, and exalt the God of Israel. By such means could he prepare the vast peoples of the Old World for the coming of Messiah and His Kingdom, and break into pieces the confidence they reposed in the idols of their worship. By such means he introduced into the ancient literature those Messianic expectations which foretold the overthrow of all Gentile religion, politics and power, the conversion of the nations, the passing of the sovereignty of the earth to the people of God, and the fact that a descendant of the royal line of David would one day atone for the world's transgression, and, still further, preside over the restoration of Israel out of all lands where they had been scattered. Thus did he humble the pride of Babylonian and Persian kings and reduce to shame the wisdom of the wise.

The wonder is that this book began to be written by a young man eighteen years of age, a captive at the court of Babylon, and hostage for the good behavior of the vassal king of Judah; a youth of royal blood and a holy celibate for the kingdom's sake. Before he reached his majority he reproduced and interpreted the monarch's dream, and because of his piety, learning, genius and fear of God, grew to become the prime-minister and master of the magi in the realms of Babylon and Persia. By the banks of the Euphrates, Ulai and Tigris, he talked with angels and received visions from God. A hundred years he lived contemporary with the kings of Assyria, Babylon, Media, Persia, Greece and Rome, and the last four kings of Judah. He personally knew Jeremiah, Ezekiel, Joshua the High Priest, and Zerubbabel, prince of the house of David. In Babylon and Shushan he met the royal magnates of the heathen world. He was contemporary with the Greek sages Anaximander, Xenophanes, Parmenides and Pythagoras. He studied "Moses and the Prophets," and like Joseph and Moses could decipher Egyptian obelisks and read Assyrian and Babylonian texts with greater ease than can any of our modern archæologists. He loved Jerusalem, the temple and the Holy Land. The woes of his nation touched his heart and the desolation of Zion melted his eyes to tears. Although, by his own influence, the edict of Cyrus was procured for the release of the captives, yet as an exile, he chose to remain at the court in Babylon in order the more to promote their interests. He pursued his mission, trusting in a faithful God. With what eyes his associates looked upon him we are at no loss to know. In his person, he was fair of countenance, well-favored, the admiration of Ashpenaz, Melzar and Arioch, the object of their tender regard. In his demeanor, he was courteous, dignified, deferential, reverent and respectful. In his character, abstemious, serious, devout, courageous, unblemished in his private life and incorruptible in public office, a pattern of righteousness, holiness, wisdom, prayer and faith—full of the fear of God—a favorite with all. In his attainments, he was skilled in all learning "ten times better than all the magicians and astrologers" that served in the king's realm, the envy of the satraps who sought to destroy him. What angels thought of him we know. Gabriel could address him as a man full of holy desires, "a man greatly beloved." What the prophets of his time thought of him we know. Ezekiel could speak of him as worthy to stand beside Noah and Job because of his righteousness. The queen-mother of Belshazzar could call him " a man of excellent spirit, and knowledge and understanding," full of "the spirit of the holy Gods." The prince of Tyre knew of him as " the wisest of men " long before the Delphic oracle, so-called Socrates. The Jewish historian of later days held him in the highest estimation. It is Josephus who says, "he was one of the greatest of prophets, honored during his life as well by kings as by the people, and after his death the inheritor of an everlasting remembrance." The Synagogue could say, " If the wise men of all nations were placed in one scale and

Daniel in the other, Daniel's scale would descend and the scale of the others go up into the air." Illustrious man, superior to all the kings of the earth, inferior to no prophet that ever arose before or after him! The lions in their den stood silent at his presence and bowed their salutations to him! A centenarian, he entered the tomb, dismissed to his rest by an angel from heaven, and all that remained of the mortal part of a man so great " sleeps " to-day " in the dust of the earth " at Shushan, one of the capitals of ancient Persia. He received a promise that one day his body should rise again, transfigured into glory bright as the firmament's glance and gleaming as the stars forever and ever. In presence of such a history, mission and life, it seems profane to speak or even think of our own.

In view of what is yet to follow, and in place of a refutation of modern false criticism, not possible here to be made, I assume at the outset, (1) the genuineness and authenticity of the book of Daniel; (2) its Messianic character; (3) its eschatological scope; (4) that its five great prophecies are one prophecy, and that its miraculous narratives were intended to be pledges of their fulfillment; (5) that the Medo-Persian empire, viz.: that of Cyrus, is the second, and the Roman empire is the fourth of the four prophetic empires in the Colossus, this fourth one now divided into the separate and independent kingdoms of the modern European state's system, and destined to pass away; (6) that by the term " kingdom " is meant both a reign and a realm, and on this present earth; (7) that the fulfillment of so much already of what Daniel foretold is a guarantee that the rest will be accomplished. And our thesis is this, that the Fifth Kingdom to rise on the ruins of all the rest is the Kingdom of Christ in immediate and universal victory, and which (1) never yet has so arisen, (2) never can, and (3) never will so arise, till the second coming of the Son of Man in the clouds of heaven, to put down all Gentile politics and power, and introduce His universal reign of righteousness and peace. Herein, I afford occasion for the taking of offence without, however, giving any, by our modern church-wisdom which, instead of studying the book of God, invents a new revelation for His benefit, removing far from the heart of the church the hope that should lie nearest to it, and assigning to the church a mission nowhere assigned to her in the Scriptures—an invention which apart from the revelation God has given, the empirical proofs of nineteen centuries have shown to be false, and the error of which nineteen more, should they come, would only redundantly confirm. This attitude, however, is a necessity, while any offence taken on its account is a mere contingency. The unity, harmony, consistency and organic self-interpretation of the Scriptures are the evidence of their infallibility and a bulwark of defense confronting every human theory. The "sure word of prophecy" is not darkness, but a "light shining in a dark place, unto which we do well to take heed." And the certitude we seek is assured by the fact that "no prophecy of the Scripture is of any private interpretation (of what God's mind is), nor came in old time by the will of man, but men spake from God, being borne along by the Holy Ghost."

"It is undoubted that in the remarkable human form of the Collossus, seen by the Chaldean king, and interpreted by Daniel, the history of mankind, especially of the world-power in its imperial forms, and the kingdoms derived from it, has been unveiled, from Daniel's time to the second coming of Christ and the establishment of the Millennial reign. The best and most learned investigators of the Scriptures, to-day, are unanimous herein, viz., that the first empire, the head of gold, is the Babylonian, the silver is the Medo-Persian, the brass is the Græco-Macedonian, the Iron is the Roman, and the clay feet and toes the modern European States-system, including Syria, Egypt and Greece. We have only to wait till Jesus Christ, the Corner-stone of His church, and now the Top-stone in heaven, shall come and destroy the dynasties of this world, and bring His own kingdom to victory everywhere."— Mühe.

Chapter II

The proof of our thesis found at the close of the previous article, rests on a clear understanding of Israel's place in history, and on the structure of Daniel's book. Israel, the nations, the kingdom of God, are its themes. Our standpoint is 600 years before the first advent of Christ. Daniel's people, the Jews, are the key of the whole interpretation. "*Salvation is from the Jews,*" not from Assyrians, Babylonians, Egyptians, Persians, Greeks or Romans. The great design of the creation of the Hebrew race from Abraham's loins was Israel, the bearer of the true religion, and standing in contrast with the entire heathen world, and, by virtue of the covenant with David, the banner kingdom also, a holy, royal, priestly, prophetic and Messianic people, charged with the mission of bringing salvation to all mankind. Their polar antagonism, therefore, to all other peoples sunk in idolatry was constitutional by God's appointment. For this reason Israel's history becomes the pivot of all other history and Israel's destiny decides the destiny of the world. In Egypt the Hebrews grew to be a distinctive people; Sinai was the birthplace of their nationality and of their covenant with God, a covenant in which He pledged to them universal dominion upon conditions of their loyalty, faith, love and obedience to His commandments. As a code He gave them the Ten Commandments with judicial and ritual institutions. Under David and Solomon they reached the height of their national glory. After the disruption of the kingdom of Solomon, they remained free from foreign invasion till the eighth century before Christ, save the single instance of the invasion of Judah by Shishak, king of Egypt, B. C. 949. In the eighth century came the Assyrians striking them successively till the Ten Tribes were carried away captive and Samaria was overthrown, 722. Next followed the Babylonian rod, Judah borne into exile, 606-587, her temple burned and the city of Jerusalem destroyed. Nothing could arrest the downward step of apostasy, even though the prince was a pious politician, faithful as Hezekiah or Josiah, and the prophet courageous as Isaiah or Jeremiah. The might of sin was stronger than the law, inborn depravity more potent than the prophet's appeal. Sacrifices were vain offerings to God—a "smoke in His nose," unendurable. Seven times apostate from their own Jehovah, their realm and royalty passed into Gentile hands. The Babylonish exile saw the visible kingdom of God, the only organized kingdom of God on earth, blotted out from the map, the independent political existence of the Jewish nation forfeited forever until the "Times of the Gentiles" should close and Israel's kingdom once more be restored in glory greater than at first, as part of Messiah's kingdom, established in victory under the whole heaven. This the goal of all prophecy, concerning the Jewish people, God's "choice forever," and the whole burden of Daniel's book.

When Daniel wrote, the historical situation was deeply significant. In spite of the light of nature, the whole world was wrapped in spiritual gloom. The period preceding the exile, B. C. 606, had been one of sanguinary conquest, and Babylon sat on the waters of the Euphrates as mistress of the nations. Six different languages were spoken in the Euphrates Valley—the centre of the world's literature, commerce, trade, art, science, religion and military pride and glory. All nations and tribes were ruled from here. Palestine was in her hands, the princes of Judah beneath her feet, and, to the mind of the Babylonian king, the capture of the holy city and possession of the temple vessels was a victory over Israel's defeated tribal God, Jehovah. With the conquest of Judah Nebuchadnezzar's empire was now consolidated, and he deemed himself "King of Kings" and "Lord of Lords" over the whole earth. True, indeed, a movement in Media and Persia seemed to forebode disaster, and Greece and Rome were lifting their backs high on the western horizon. And what might the *future* bring? Is Jehovah defeated forever? The exile-time was a time of reaction and revolution. It troubled the monarch's thoughts,

If Israel and the nations have succumbed to Babylon's might, may not Babylon herself succumb to the nations? And will Israel be captive forever and Gentile sovereignty sway a sceptre that is eternal? The sleep of the monarch was troubled in "the second year" of his reign.

At such a time Daniel enters into history, B. C. 606, a captive at the centre of all world movements. God causes the Babylonian king, as He did Pharaoh, Alexander and Pilate's wife, to "dream a dream," the dream of the great monarchy image, in chap. ii., and also to forget the dream. This dream and its interpretation are the *fundamental prophecy* of all the prophecies in the book of Daniel. All else is supplementary to this. Chapter vii. repeats and enlarges this, under new symbols, in order to bring out *something new* in the development and character of each of the four empires. Chapter viii. repeats again the second and third empires, in yet other symbols, again to develop *something new*. Chapter ix. returns to the fall of Babylon under Cyrus and runs on with a chronological scheme to the same "end" as in ii. and vii., and typically shadowed in viii. Chapters x.-xii. revert once more to the second empire and run on to the same "end" as before. The same law of advance to the goal or end, of return and advance again to the same end, that we find in the different series of sevens in John's apocalypse, we also find here. The future is too complex to be represented in one series of visions, the end too great to be displayed in one revelation. The *something new* requires a return to begin again, a cyclical movement, to make a new race, to the end, till all that God intends to reveal is given. It is the mode of evolution in all prophecy concerning the End. So it is here. The first series is found in chap. ii. The "End" is the end of the "Times of the Gentiles." The goal is the destruction of all Gentile sovereignty, all Gentile politics and power, the restoration of the kingdom of Israel and the triumph of the kingdom of God, the kingdom of Christ, over all the earth.

We are ready now to see the proof of our thesis, given at the close of the previous article. The monarch's dream is in ii: 31-35, the interpretation in ii: 36-45. The point of chief interest is the *Impact of the Stone* on the toes of the statue or image, i. e., the destruction of the Gentile World Power to which Israel is now subject in every nation under heaven, and has been since the crown passed from the head of Zedekiah and Gentile sceptres have ruled God's ancient people. The prophet reproduces and interprets the forgotten dream of the king. Coming to the explanation of the "toes" of the statue, he says, " And as the toes of the feet were partly of iron and partly of clay, the kingdom (the fourth) shall be partly strong and partly broken. And whereas thou sawest iron mixed with clay, *they* (the toes, i. e., the kings of the ten kingdoms) shall mingle themselves with the seed of men, but they shall not cleave one to another (royal and political alliances will be broken) even as iron is not mixed with clay. And, *in the days of those kings*, shall the God of heaven set up a kingdom which shall never be destroyed and the kingdom shall not be left to other people, but shall break in pieces and consume *all these kingdoms*, and it shall stand forever. Forasmuch as thou sawest that the stone was cut out of the mountain without hands, and brake in pieces the iron, brass, clay, silver and gold, the great God hath made known to the king what shall come to pass hereafter, and the dream is certain, and the interpretation is sure.'

Among the secrets of the future, the prophet, therefore, reveals (1) the total destruction of the statue, i. e., of the politically organized Gentile power, and the substitution of the Kingdom of God in the stead of all earthly kingdoms, forever, and (2) that the time of this world crisis is " hereafter," even " in the days of those kings," the toes, therefore, in the last days of the " kings," who are the heads of the separate and contemporaneous " kingdoms " into which the fourth, or Roman, empire will be divided. By the iron he means the hard and strong imperial, and by the clay the weaker, more plastic, and popular, element in human governments, seeking vainly to combine and cohere in political unity; absolutism repelling popular freedom, and constitutionalism, and reversely the latter the former; mixed monarchies, where the popular will wars against the imperialism of crowns and defies the will of the crown; a state of political insecurity and instability. By the mingling of the kings with the seed of men, royal alliances and intermarriage of royal houses to strengthen dynastic interests, is meant. By the "Stone" cut out from the mountain without hands, and falling upon the toes of the statue, is meant the descent of Jesus Christ from heaven in judgment to smite the kings of the earth and dash the nations in pieces. By the fall of the statue, the destruction of the whole world power is signified, and by the stone becoming a "mountain" filling the whole earth, is meant the world-embracing, universal, indestructible and everlasting kingdom of Christ, set up in victory, on this present earth. on the ruins of all existing governments, in the last days of the last kingdoms into which the old Roman territory will be divided.

Rationalistic dislike of supernatural and far-reaching prophecy attempts to show that the book of Daniel was composed in the days of Antiochus Epiphanes, B. C. 175-164, nearly 400 years after Daniel was dead, and that the "Ten Toes" represent not any contemporaneous kingdoms to be formed out of the Roman empire, but are ten individual successors of Alexander the Great—ten kings, not contemporaneous, but in line. Still more, those "kings" do not mean "kingdoms," and that the fourth empire in the statue is not the Roman but the Graeco-Macedonian. Words need not be wasted. Hereafter we shall see that the book of Daniel was composed by Daniel during the Babylonian exile, and under the reign of Cyrus; that the fourth empire is the Roman, and that the "Ten Toes" are co-existing kingdoms formed out of it. Furthermore, in prophecy the terms "kings" and "kingdoms" are convertible. The "kingdoms" are represented in the persons of their kings, and the kings represent their kingdoms. The Four Beasts are called both "kings" and "kingdoms," Dan. vii: 17. The Ten Toes are also called both "kings" and "kingdoms," in the same verse, ii: 44. "Kings" and "kingdoms" are identical in ii: 38, 39. The vain attempt to exclude the Roman empire from the statue, and so exclude the birth of Christ from the development of the prophecy; further on, His crucifixion, the destruction of Jerusalem, and the future overthrow of all Gentile power, is well understood in modern times.

The question as to the *time point* of the impact is vital. The prophet nowhere teaches that this impact occurs at the junction of the knees with the thighs of the statue, where the Roman empire first comes into view, in contact with the Greek, anterior to the birth of Christ. Moreover, the first advent is not symbolized anywhere in the statue. We meet it nowhere till we reach chap. ix. The stone's impact does not occur at the first advent. The words " the God of Heaven shall set up a kingdom " are indeed the Old Testament basis for the New Testament designation, the "kingdom of Heaven," which John the Baptist and Christ preached as "at hand" and "come" in their day. This affords, however, no proof that the *impact of the stone* occurred then. It is true that the " kingdom of Heaven " was set up on its spiritual side, at the first advent, in the birth, life, death, resurrection and ascension of Christ, and in the outpouring of the Holy Spirit, and preaching of the gospel, and is the same kingdom that will yet be set up in its outward visible glory as a world-wide sovereignty " under the whole heaven," when Gentile politics and power become as " the chaff of the summer threshing floor." But it is not true that it is to the first advent the prophet's eyes are directed in the vision of the stone's impact. It is not the beginning of the fourth empire under Augustus we have here, but its *end*, and in the *last* days of the ten toes or separate kingdoms into which it is then divided. Such division did not exist in the days of Augustus, nor of Tiberius, nor of Diocletian, nor of Constantine, nor even in the days of Theodosius when the final division east and west was made. The tenfold division of the empire into separate and independent kingdoms follows the work of the Goths, Vandals, Huns and Heruli, in the sixth and seventh centuries, just prior to the emergence of Mohammed, and the mediæval and modern kingdoms as now existing, are not the last arrangement of the toes. The stone could neither strike the toes before they were formed, nor, having struck them and turned them to "chaff," allow them to survive, like England, France, Germany, Austria, Italy, Greece, Turkey and the rest. " No place is found for them." The work of the stone is not smooth, gentle, evangelical and peaceful rubbing, but perpendicular fracture, pulverization, judicial grinding, atomization, an attending wind of judgment blowing the chaff, dust and powder of all Gentile politics so far out of sight as never to be seen any more. Clearly, therefore, by the words "*in the days of those kings,*" is not meant "in the days of those *four empires,*" as Jerome would have it, nor "in the days of *one* of those four," as his perplexed commentators would turn it, but in the *last days* of the *fourth,* divided into ten separate, contemporaneous and independent kingdoms.

The efforts of *post*-millennialists to break this exposition are vain. Nothing is clearer than that the empires symbolized in chaps. ii. and vii. are the same, and therefore the "end" in each the same, viz., the end of the fourth divided empire. Indisputable is the fact that the "ten toes" and the "ten horns" represent the same kings and kingdoms, and that the destruction of the one is the destruction of the other. Conscience, honesty, truth, cannot otherwise hold. Therefore, again, nothing is clearer than that the *days* here mentioned as the days of the toes (ii: 44) are the "1260 days," or "time, two times and half a time," of the horns in vii: 25, i. e., the last 1260 days of the 70th week of Daniel, as seen in ix: 27 and xii: 7. Post millennialists have no option here. With pre-millennialists they firmly hold that Daniel has unfolded not merely the future, like other prophets, but has given the date of the first advent of Messiah, then the crucifixion and next the destruction of Jerusalem, followed by the times of the Gentiles, Dan. ix: 26, Luke xxi: 24, and closed by the restoration of Israel and overthrow of Gentile governments. They admit that the prophet has given us not merely the time-point for the setting up of the Messianic kingdom in humiliation, as a kingdom of the cross, viz., the first advent, but also of the setting of it up as a kingdom of the crown, in glory at the second, and that he has taken off the dark veil that obscured the future and unrolled to the eyes of His people the whole pathway of their sorrows, their glorious end and the doom of their oppressors. They admit more; they admit that he has connected all this with a scheme of chronology in chap. ix. which locates the time-point of the final deliverance at the close of Gentile times, and at the close of the last half of the 70th week. Misfortune, indeed, immense and protracted, that for so many centuries this 70th week should have been regarded as immediately succeeding the 69th, therefore as following the birth of Christ. But now that this great error has been destroyed, and the 70th week shown to be the Antichrist week at the end of our age, the last ground of objection is removed. The "ten toes" being "ten kingdoms" and "kings," and their last days being the days preceding the impact of the stone, who is Christ in judgment, it follows that "the days of those kings" are the last "1260 days" of the 70th week of Daniel. They are still future to us and have nothing to do with the first advent.

But conclusive beyond all is the New Testament light upon the whole question. On all hands it is admitted that the "ten horns" of the beast in Rev. xiii. are identical with the ten horns of the beast in Daniel vii., and that there. as here, "1260 days" are the days assigned as the last days of the fourth empire. And as the horns are the toes, and both are the kings, it follows that "*these kings*" in Dan. ii: 44 are precisely the "*ten kings*" in Rev. xvii: 12, *whose alliance with the Antichrist or little horn of* Dan. vii. endures 1260 days, and *whose destruction with him is the work of the Son of Man, the Stone, Jesus Christ, at His second coming.* The impact of the stone is, therefore, at the second advent and was not at the first, and the kingdom set up as a result of that impact is not yet established in the form predicted, nor can be till the Lord Himself comes.

It is true that nothing is said or seen in chap. ii. of the Antichrist, the Son of Man, or the clouds of heaven, for the simple reason that it is Nebuchadnezzar's dream the prophet interprets and to the heathen king God made no revelation of the Antichrist, the Son of Man, the second advent or of Israel's deliverance, but only of the course and doom of Gentile kingdoms and power. It is in the next vision where the symbols are changed in order to bring out *something further and new* that we meet these things. Chap. ii. is the fundamental and general vision. All that follows is supplementative and more minute unveiling. Such is the law of progress in divine revelation. As the tree branches and buds, so also does prophecy.

The impact of the stone is eschatological. All that is said of the first coming of Christ in the book of Daniel is found in chap. ix., viz., that His birth should occur at the close of the 69th of the seventy weeks there foretold and His crucifixion precede the destruction of Jerusalem. Neither in ii., vii., viii., x.-xii., is the first advent revealed.

One further point, by both pre- and post-millennarians. The idea of rolling has been introduced into the text. They speak of the "*rolling stone.*" By post-millennarians this is done to evade the chiliastic doctrine, the doctrine that the kingdom cannot come to victory over all the earth till Christ comes. Prejudiced by early education, false teaching and the declamation of good men, trained to spiritualize the prophecies and deny to Israel a national future, or a millennial age on this present earth, after our own, and before the final new heaven and earth, they must find some way to break the force of the stone's destructive impact, and make the "days of these kings" mean 2,000 years at least, if not 20,000 more! The stone "rolls," and the "rolling" is an evangelical process, peaceful, missionary and full of music and love, with now and then some transient friction by way of occasional wars and rumors of war, with here and there a famine, earthquake or pestilence, which, however, only assist the rolling. The grinding is gradual, caused by the progress of Christianity, education, culture and civilization. By religion, better politics, vespers, ethics and love, human governments, especially those of Christian Europe and the United States, will become more Christian, and society be redeemed and reformed sociologically from the evils that now afflict it. The Stone comes in contact first of all with the knee-joints of the Colossus, "rolls" gently down the iron legs, increases in size by aggregation of molecular atoms, or individual saints, and converts the world-power to a nominal Christianity, so that kings, cabinets, parliaments, congresses, nations, all profess to be Christians—massacres, murders, wars and crimes, mammon, selfishness, greed and oppression, to the contrary notwithstanding—swells to a "mountain" before the toes are reached, and so "fills the whole earth." Strangely enough the Colossus is dwarfed down gradually, the chaff constantly flying, and yet it is all the time standing. The filling of the whole earth, which is posterior to the impact, is made anterior. "Broken to pieces" means glued together, and "smote" means "roll." "No place found for them," means that the kingdoms still exist as such, in a Christian form or under a Christian name. Sudden, perpendicular and chaff-making impact is displaced by gentle cycling from knee to ankle-joint and instep to toe, the statue still standing! The word "together" is strangely overlooked, and "one after another" put in its place. The result is, that the prophet is made to tell Nebuchadnezzar that Gentile politics and power will not pass away, but, at the first coming of Christ, a "Stone" will begin to "roll," and keep on "rolling" for two thousand years, and that in the midst of the millennial age massacres, aided and abetted by "Christian powers," will shame those of pagan times, and so the "kingdom" will come to victory, the world be converted, Israel saved, all nations blessed, while the "Stone" rolls on, side by side with the "concert of Europe," the "Balance of Power," and the "Integrity of the Ottoman Empire."

It is a customary method, among our ordinary expounders of Daniel's book, to represent the impact of the Stone in the following way: "These empires have all passed away, already, and the kingdom hewn out of the hard quarry of sin-petrified humanity by divine grace, has already been established in the Christian church. During her history empires and thrones have risen and fallen, and nations have rushed to arms and swept, as with a tornado of blood, the surface of the earth, then gone to rest, but the kingdom stands. Age after age the arrows of ridicule and scorn have been shot at its subjects, the artillery of infidelity has attacked its strongholds, the sharp-shooters of wit and genius have sallied forth against its unwary hosts, and every description of opposition has been leagued against the Lord and His Anointed. But the kingdom stands." Thus, *after* "*all* these empires have passed away" and "no place is found for them," they *still exist*, and (to quote another word) "the armies of the Lord press on to victory!" The Stone is rolling still from the "qaurry" across the imagined plain in order yet to reach the Toes of the statue—nonexistent yet existing. Sobriety might well enquire whether a little grammar, logic, and study of Daniel's book, might not have spared the public exhibition of a rhetoric so self-contradictory and amusing?

The most common defense of this presentation is to say that by "kingdoms" in the statue only heathen kingdoms are meant, and, as a matter of fact, the prophecy in large part has been already fulfilled. The misfortune of that answer is two-fold, (1) that three of the empires—Babylon, Medo-Persia and the Greek—had passed away *before* the "Stone" was born, and that instead of striking the fourth, the fourth struck it, and laid it in its grave, and that now, though ascended to heaven, it cannot descend from the mountain till the last days of divided Roman empire; and (2) that it is precisely on Christian toes and Christian horns the "Stone" falls, and it is Christian kingdoms, so-called, that are ground to powder. The impact of the Stone is a judgment not on heathenism, but on Christendom, after the gospel has been given to all nations. It smites the "Christian Powers" that be, in order to make room for the Kingdom of Christ.

Some pre-millennialists introduce the "rolling," but in order to show "two stadia" in the kingdom set up. These they call the "Kingdom of the Rolling Stone," and the "Kingdom of the non-Rolling Mountain," the one dating from the first advent, the other from the second. By this means two separate functions are assigned to the "Stone," (1) that of "rolling" for 2,000 years or more, (2) that of impact at the end of these years. All this springs from the fact that the time of the first advent is assumed as the "time of the days of these kings," which it is not. Even on the supposition that the Stone rolled *on a plain*, what impression could it have on the statue? None! The moment it strikes the toes the statue falls. The stone does not "roll" after its contact with the toes. The church-period does not follow the impact, but precedes it. The toes are the *end* of the fourth empire. It is true that Christ's kingdom makes progress in this age by extension of the gospel, but the church period and the progress of Christianity are precisely two things that nowhere enter into the visions of Daniel. No "woman" is seen in his perspective as in John's. He has nothing to do with the development of the church. Israel as a nation, the nations, the kingdom in victory, are his themes. He predicts the first advent and the crucifixion simply as events in Israel's history, laying the ground for the destruction of Jerusalem by Titus and the dispersion of the Jewish people into all lands, until the time comes for their restoration. His eyes are directed to the end of Gentile times. He sees the Kingdom of Christ set up in victory over all the earth, and Israel's kingdom restored, only upon the ruins of all Gentile politics and at the second coming of Christ. The fact is, that neither Nebuchadnezzar nor Daniel saw any "rolling," or horizontal or circular motion of any kind, but simply a perpendicular impact upon the toes, a tottering statue, a fall tremendous, a cloud as of chaff, a driving wind, and the Kingdom of Christ at once filling the whole earth. "When Thy judgments are abroad the inhabitants of the earth will learn righteousness." Moreover, how the same "Stone" could "roll" toward the four points of the compass at once and fill the whole earth is inconceivable. It is only as a standing and self-expanding stone this universality could be achieved. The impact itself will be universal. The effect of that impact will be the same. *Everywhere the kingdom will come.* The judgment of the nations is in order to the salvation of the nations. Nor will it require ages to set up the kingdom of Christ on earth at His coming. The idea of long continuity through ages long is not found in the Hebrew verb, translated "became," i. e., "became mountain" (ii: 35). It is the same verb found in the words "and man *became* a living soul." Gen. ii: 7. It denotes here a fact accomplished at the time of the action.

And such was the view of the holy prophet who spake by inspiration of God. He humbled the monarch's pride by teaching that Israel's God was not defeated because Israel had been delivered, for sin, to Gentile hands, but still lived as "God most High," a Revealer of secrets, Almighty to save, righteous in punishing sin, yet watching in love His people; that, one day, Gentile power should perish forever, and the kingdom of

God be set up in victory everlasting from pole to pole. The rise and fall of successive empires, of which the fourth is the Roman, was shown to the monarch, the far "end," the doom of man's governments, the establishment of the government of God, and on this present earth, when God's will shall be "done on earth as it is in heaven." Then God's people, heirs of the kingdom, will be free from the despot's chain, and humanity cease to groan beneath a burden no power but God's could remove. So preached the great pre-millennial prophet of the exile in the ears of the king of the greatest kingdom on earth, a doctrine whose teaching to-day the church dishonors. To the monarch it came as a message from God by the mouth of a seer who declared that "the vision is certain and the interpretation is sure." It impressed the soul of the king. It brought glory to God; to Daniel, great honor, abundant gifts, a seat in the gate of the king, as primate of all the realm and master of all the wise, and to Daniel's friends, dignities next to his own.

May the vision be soon fulfilled!

And such was the view of this prophecy taken by great church teachers in early times, of whom two remain unsurpassed, the one, Irenæus the Great; the other, his greater disciple, Hippolytus, the first saying, "At the end of our age the Stone will strike the statue," and "Jesus Christ is the Stone;" the second saying, "At the end of our age the Stone grinds to powder the kingdoms of this world." Nor will the prophecy admit of any other interpretation.

' Imperial powers must sink when virtue fails,
And selfishness with pride alone prevails;
He argues ill who from its fortune draws
The goodness or the badness of a cause;
Success on merit does not always wait;
Remember, too, old Babylon the Great!
Through prosperous crime the ancient empires fell;
Ambition, bloodshed, guilt, their funeral knell;
Unerring law, with its resistless force,
Mapped out for each its swift and downward course;
A ruling power defined their years, their pace,
The road that led to judgment and disgrace;
Were not events by Him, Most High, controlled,
How could their certain order be foretold?
How could the prophet sing of future doom,
Or in the present read the age to come?"
—Crell.

Chapter III.

DANIEL, CHAPTER VII.—THE FOUR BEASTS.

A critical question of importance confronts the student of this prophecy, and involves the veracity of the whole book of Daniel. A word, therefore, is necessary as to Daniel's historical reliability, with which his prophecies are so intimately connected. The date of the vision and its writing are said to be in "the first year of Belshazzar, king of Babylon," ch. vii: 1. Modern criticism denies the existence of any such king, even as it denies the existence of " Darius the Mede," ch. ix.: 1 The absence of the special name Belshazzar from ancient history has caused many to identify him with Evil-Merodach, the son and immediate successor of Nebuchadnezzar, B. C. 561, inasmuch as Daniel represents Belshazzar as the " son" of his "father" Nebuchadnezzar, and his sucessor, v: 2. 22. According to this view the date of the prophecy is B. C. 561, or, 23 years before the fall of Babylon, 538. The third year of Belshazzar, the year of his sacrilegious feast, and death (v: 1-30) was, therefore, B. C. 559, or 21 years before the capture of the city; his successor, " Darius the Mede," being Neriglissar, B. C. 559. Daniel, therefore, is wholly wrong, historically, in 5: 22; 6: 28; 7: 1; 8: 1; 9: 1; since Belshazzar, the son of Nebuchadnezzar, like Darius the Mede, is unknown to history, and no death of any such king occurred when Babylon was taken. Belshazzar's feast and death were Evil-Merodach's feast and death, 21 years before the Chaldean power passed away. So runs the criticism, other views also having been advanced to account for the same supposed difficulty, viz., that Belshazzar is a myth, like " William Tell," or Shakespeare's " Merchant of Venice," the fabrication of a Maccabean Jew, besides many others still.

The testimony of the Babylonian cylinders of Cyrus and Nabonnaid, and the annalistic tablets of the time, have successfully repelled this assault on Daniel's credibility. The name Belshazzar has been discovered under the form of "Bel-sar-usur," the "Ha-bal-sarru" of the Chaldean army, the "Vice-king" and "eldest son" of Nabonnaid, the last king of Babylon, who reigned 17 years, B. C. 555-538, this "son" being co-regent during the last three years of his reign, i. e. three years next preceding Babylon's fall, 538. The monuments still further establish the facts that to "Bel-sar-usur" was entrusted the defence of Babylon in 538, while his father Nabonnaid took the field in Accad and was defeated by Cyrus, the same year. The Greek historians, Herodotus and Xenophon, both support the statement of Daniel that Belshazzar met his death at that time in the midst of revelry, an "impious young king." Assuming, therefore, the identity of Belshazzar with Bel-sar-usur, the reliability of Daniel is confirmed and the true date of the vision in ch. vii. is B. C. 541, the third year before Babylon's fall. All the statements of Daniel are in perfect harmony with this. It must be noted that Daniel nowhere affirms that Belshazzar was the "immediate" son or successor of Nebuchadnezzar, nor that he was "the last king of Babylon," nor does he deny that he was the son of Nabonnaid, nor that Nabonnaid was the "last king." He calls him "son" of Nebuchadnezzar, as does also the imposing Queen-Mother, in the banquet, v: 2. 22. Nebuchadnezzar is called his "father." In Semitic languages no word exists for "grandfather" and none for "grandson." The term "Ab," "father," denotes semitically all ancestors, as when Abraham is called the "father" of the Jews, and the term "Ben," "son," all descendants, as when Jesus Christ is called the "son" of David, and "son" of Abraham. Belshazzar was indeed the son of Nabonnaid, and at the same time semitically and in popular usage, the "son" of Nebuchadnezzar, i. e. his grandson. The Queen-Mother was his grandmother, the mother of the wife of Nabonnaid, the widow of Nebuchadnezzar, whose daughter Nabonnaid married, thus gaining his title to the throne. The title "king" was given to Belshazzar when co-regent with his father, as was the case with Nebuchadnezzar himself. Dan. i: 1. Professor Sayce, like others, has misinterpreted some inscriptions, and conceded to the critics their assault, yet reserving the right to "change" his opinion "on better information"—a wise reserve in view of the just words of Delitzsch, that "Assyriologists have made many false readings of which they may well be ashamed."

The inscription on the great Cyrus-Nabonnaid Cylinder closes its account of the capture of Babylon thus,—beginning with *Col. iii: line 6.* "In the month Tammuz Cyrus came and fought a battle. * * * The men of Accad broke out into insurrection. On the 14th day the soldiers of Cyrus took Sipara without a stroke of the sword. Nabonnaid fled. On the 16th day Ugbaru (Gobryas) and the army of Cyrus came to Babylon, without fighting. In the month Marchesvan (November B. C. 538), on the third day, Cyrus came to Babylon, proclaimed peace, and made Ugbaru (Gobryas) governor. On the 11th day of Marchesvan Ugbaru had, * * * *And the King died. From 27th Adar to 3d Nisan there was mourning in Accad.*" The "King" was no other than Bel-sar-usur, since Cyrus spared Nabonnaid and made him governor of Carmania. The Inscription is indisputable. It calls Bel-sar-usur the *"first-born son,"* and leaves him in command of Babylon, while his father is in the field, in Accad. It calls him *"King,"* his father still living. It makes him co-regent, and the actual ruler in the city of Babylon, after his father's crown was lost. It narrates the capture of the city on the 3d and his death on the 11th. The inscription is defective in places, but we are left to infer that the King's death was the result of wounds inflicted during the night of the capture. Daniel says "he was slain," i. e., struck fatally with the sword. The monument says he "died" —was killed. And yet this part of the Inscription, giving the *title* and *death* of Belshazzar, is deliberately suppressed by Kamphausen, the editor of "Daniel" in the polychrome Bible of the Critics,—when quoting the lines immediately preceding the notice of the death! Das Buch Daniel, p. 25-28. The Inscription was published by Rawlinson 1854, Pinches 1882, Schrader 1880, 1890, Hommel 1888, Düsterwald 1893, and by many more. All Assyriologists are aware of it.

And now for the prophecy itself. In ch.ii. the monarch of Babylon had dreamed and seen a four-metalled colossus. Here, in ch. vii, Daniel "dreams a dream," and has " visions of his head upon his bed "—" visions of the night," vii: 1. The spirit, even when the brain sleeps, has a faculty in which sensible objects can be represented as if seen by the bodily eyes. Seven tableaux pass before him, the first five relating to four beasts successively rising from a storm-tossed sea, vii: 1. 4. 5. 6. 7.,the last two to the judgment of the Fourth Beast and its Horns, vii: 8. 13. Each is introduced by the wonder-word "Behold!"—"I saw and behold!" In ancient times animal forms were used by Oriental monarchs to symbolize their empires, as Assyrian and Babylonian excavations show, and history as well, and in the history before us we learn how God employed such forms to represent the different successive phases of the "World-Power," in all time, and so unveil to the prophet its future course and its end. Ch. vii. furnishes the decisive confirmation of the truth of our thesis, viz.,that the kingdom of Christ can never come to victory over all the earth until the second coming of the Son of Man.

The vision of the Fourth Beast marks an unparalleled advance in the mode of prophetic representation, by introducing a solemn assize, in which " One like a Son of Man " comes with clouds, to destroy the last Antichrist and all Gentile polities and power, and to erect a fifth and universal monarchy " underneath all heavens." It is the high-point of Old Testament eschatology. There is nothing like it anywhere else in all the prophets. It is paralleled only by the scenes in the Revelation given of God to Christ, and by Him through His angel to John. As a picture of the advent it is without a peer in the Old Testament, transcending all other representations by its solemnity, sublimity, and majesty, its dramatic power and its terror. It enters more largely than any other scene into New Testament prophecy, and forms the basis of all the New

CHAPTER VII.—THE FOUR BEASTS.

Testament representations of the End. Twenty-one out of twenty-eight massive verses are here given to the fourth, or Roman Empire, seventeen of these to Christ and the Antichrist. It means that the subject is of infinite moment.

The prophet beholds four empires emerging, one after another, out of the billowy sea of the heathen world. The surging waters are an emblem of the heathen nations in tumult. The Beasts correspond to the metals in ch. ii., and in the order of their appearing. The strength and swiftness of the Babylonian empire and its ferocity are represented by a *Lion* with eagle's wings. The loss of its plumage denotes the cessation of its conquests, and its change of posture from that of a beast to that of a man, and the gift of "a man's heart," the moral effect produced by the recovery of the Chaldean king from his seven year's mania. Dan. iv: 16; 25-37; 34-37. The *Bear's* elevation, lifting itself with its paw "on one side," marks the superiority of the Persian to the Median element in the Medo-Persian empire of Cyrus. The "three ribs" in its mouth are his conquests of Susiana, Lydia and Asia Minor, while the command, "Arise and devour much flesh," denotes the carnivorous voracity of the Bear and the future conquests of Babylon and Egypt. In the *Leopard* or *Panther* the "four wings" represent the celerity of Alexander's conquests in every direction, and the "four heads" the partition of his empire into the four kingdoms of Syria, Egypt, Macedonia and Asia Minor.

The "Fourth Beast" is that which attracts the prophet's special notice; a Beast, dreadful, exceeding strong, terrible, with iron teeth, devouring, breaking in pieces, stamping, diverse from all the rest. "Ten horns," the symbols of kings and their kingdoms together, surmount the head of the Beast, among which an "eleventh" rises, having "eyes like a man," denoting its intellectuality and human personality, and a magniloquent mouth blaspheming. Uprooting a triple alliance that stands in its way, it acquires the power of all the horns, because "stouter than its fellows." Three years and a half it persecutes the "saints of the Most High," the Jewish people, changing their festive times and ritual laws, subjecting them to great tribulations. At the end of this period a Judgment scene breaks in, and terminates the mad career of the Horn. Thrones are placed, (not cast down) in the heavens immediately above the earth, for judges to sit upon, in the midst of which the "Ancient of Days" (Hattiq Yomin), the "bedayed" one, sits, venerable to behold, arrayed in white vesture, "white as snow and the hair of his head like the pure wool." Pavilioned in flame, streams of fire proceeding before Him, ten thousand times ten thousand angels attending, He presides over the heavenly Sanhedrin come for judgment. "The Judgment sits and the books are opened." The effect of the judgment is stated. The Beast, the personal Eleventh Horn, who, by acquiring all power, had become the whole Beast in his own person, is taken and slain, and his body given to Tophet, the burning flame. The rest of the Beasts survive a brief season, after their dominion is taken away, and are destroyed. But this is not all. Though God the Father, the "Ancient of Days," presides, yet "Another," to whom "dominion and glory" are given, i. e., the right to judge, rule and receive the honor, as well as the kingdom, suddenly appears in the midst of the scene. "I saw in the night visions, and behold, One like a Son of Man came with the clouds of heaven, and came to the Ancient of Days, and they brought him near before Him. And there was given to him dominion, and glory, and a kingdom, that all peoples, and nations, and languages, should serve Him; His dominion is an everlasting dominion which shall not pass away, and His kingdom that which shall not be destroyed." It is the "Parousia" of Christ we have here, the second advent of the Son of Man, to whom the Father has committed all judgment, that all men should honor the Son even as they honor the Father. John 5: 22. 23. It is Israel's Messiah, the Christian's Lord, who executes the judgment willed by the Father upon the World-Power and its last representative, the antichristian Horn. A *Double-scene* is here, a scene in two acts, v. 9-12, and v. 13, 14, in order to bring out prominently the fact that it is by the Father's will the Son is made the Judge of all mankind, and by His incarnation, death, resurrection and ascension, has acquired the right to judge and reign eternally.

The prophet was impressed and perplexed by the solemn vision, and "would know the truth of all this" that he had seen, "the truth of the *fourth beast*" especially,"and of the ten horns," and yet more especially " of the other that came up, before whom three fell," " the horn that had eyes, and a mouth speaking very great things, and whose look was more stout than his fellows." He is intensely curious and particular in his specifications. An angel explains. After briefly describing the all-conquering character of the Roman empire, (7: 32) he says, " And the Ten Horns thou sawest out of this kingdom (the Roman) are Ten Kings that shall arise, and another shall arise after them, and he shall be diverse from the first ones, and shall subdue three kings. And he shall speak words against the Most High, and shall wear out the saints of the Most High, and think to change times and laws. And they (the saints) shall be given into his hand until a time, two times, and the dividing of a time (1260 days). But the Judgment shall sit, and they (the Ancient of Days, the Son of Man, the angels) shall take away his Sultanate to consume and destroy it to the end." (vii: 24-26.) And now comes the grand announcement of the outcome and goal of the prophecy, the companion-piece precisely of that in ch. ii: 44, viz., "And the kingdom, and the Sultanate, and the greatness of the kingdom underneath all heavens, shall be given to the people of the saints of the Most High, whose kingdom is an everlasting kingdom, and all Sultanates shall serve and obey Him"(vii:27). Here,the "kingdom" is set up on earth by the "God of heaven," at the second coming of the Son of Man in the clouds, to destroy the last Antichrist, and demolish all Gentile politics and power. Here is found the much-despised "Chiliasm" (Pre-millennialism), indestructible as the truth and throne of God! As face answers to face in water so Dan. vii: 27 answers to Dan. ii: 44, an invulnerable demonstration that the kingdom of Christ cannot come to victory, nor "God's will be done in earth as it is in heaven," until the second coming of the Son of Man. He who denies this denies the text of the prophet, the Word of God, spoken and interpreted by an angel of God, a vision and interpretation written by inspired hands at the time they were given (7: 1), and like all else in Daniel's "book," authenticated as the "Scripture of Truth," and with the closing revelation commanded to be sealed as a perfect word, a light and a lesson for the "wise" in the "time of the end." (xii: 4, 9, 10.)

Great and solemn as is this vision, it is not, however, a vision of the last judgment which occurs at the close of the millennial age, and brings the "new heaven and earth." It is the Messianic judgment, placed by all the prophets at the end of our present age, when Gentile Times expire and new-born Israel's times begin in the kingdom of God on earth. Territorially, the vision covers, not all the planet, but only the sphere of the empire of the Fourth Beast, viz., the old Roman territory from the Euphrates to the British Isles, and from the Danube and Rhine to the cataracts of the Nile. And even here, in this vision, it is not the whole picture of the end that is given, but a section only and limited to the tribulation and high-point, or crisis, of the "Day of Lord" when the Son of Man appears in the scene. To other prophets the task was assigned, as to Moses, Isaiah, Joel, Ezekiel, and Zechariah, to develop other events occurring at this time, but to Daniel alone the painting of this one solemn portrait of the "Ancient of Days" and the "Son of Man." Each inspired artist executed the task committed to his hand, each painting his work on separate canvass then laying aside his pencil and brush and passing into the peace of God. A total view of the "end" requires a combination of the events in all these separate pictures, arranged in their order and relations, on one great canvass of the future, a task reserved for John, with further developments and the final finish of all. It is thus that the "kingdom" announced at the close of the last 1260 days of Daniel's 70th week (Rev. x: 7) in the ringing notes of the seventh angel (xi: 15) and cheered by a voice from heaven, because of Israel's conversion (xii: 10, 11), is seen to be one and the same "kingdom" with that in Dan. ii: 44, and vii: 27, the "kingdom" in Matth. xxv: 34, and to which the holy apostle John—thanks to his pen!—has given the name of "the thousand years." Rev. xx: :1, 6. It is announced in the distinctest terms, and painted in the brightest colors, as the millennial kingdom on earth, introduced by the pre-millennial coming of the Son of Man in the clouds of heaven. Rev. xiv: 14; Matth. xiii: 36-43. If "Chiliasm" has been made a name offensive to so-called "Orthodoxy," it is only because God's Word has first been made offensive to interpreters whose spiritualizing processes and evolutionary civilization dislike the picture of the end as given in the Scriptures. What we have here in Dan. vii. is

I. The *Time* of the Judgment. It is at the "end" of the 70th week in Dan. ix. 26, 27, the close of the Times of the Gentiles, the end of the last 1260 days of the Antichrist's persecuting reign as lord of ten monarchies in one, and the holder of Jerusalem, yet coming quickly to his own "end" with none to help him. Dan. xi. 45; Zech. xiv: 1-5; Rev. xiv: 14-20; xix: 11-21. It closes the horn's career, Dan. vii. 21, 22. The final conflict terminated by this judgment includes the "Day of the Lord upon all nations," preceded by that fatal spell when the powers that be and society at large, as in Noah's day, shall be intent on architecture, commerce, trade and all domestic pleasure, singing the siren song of "Peace and Safety," as did the false prophets of old, unconscious that "sudden destruction" is near. 1 Thess. v: 3; Jer. viii: 11, 15, 16; xiv: 13; xxiii: 17-30. That will be the Concert of Europe and the world! The political hypocrisy of the time will betray itself in this, that while affecting arbitration of international disputes, new ambitions, new international complications, and new oppressions and aggressions will be devised, the whole world arming for war. Joel xiii: 9-11. The alliances of Christian governments with those that are anti-Christian, for the sake of gain, the extension of territory, wealth and power, the oppression of the weak by the strong, the spectacle of massacre allowed by Christian nations, the hollowness, the treachery to treaties and to covenants, the concert of Christian powers in a code of international authority, founded neither on the principles of justice nor of humanity, but on the will of the strongest, and violated in the interests of the strongest, will so affect, disgust

and exasperate mankind, that, once more, as in the days of
Robespierre and Voltaire, Christianity itself will be scouted in
the circles of the learned, and by the masses, and the very
foundations of civil, social and religious order be broken up.
Protestantism can no more accuse Popery. At such a time
the " Little Horn " will come, and run his career unchecked
by anything " withholding," 2 Thess. ii: 6-12, till checked by
the counter-coming of the Son of Man. That second coming
is the glorious, visible and public Parousia of Christ—His
appearing in the clouds of heaven, as the vision shows, for
both judgment and salvation, its one time-point, the close of
the Great Tribulation. It is the same time-point as in Matt.
xxiv: 29, 31; 40-44; xxv: 1; 2 Thess. i: 6, 7; ii: 1-8; Rev.
xi: 15-17; xix: 11-21, and prior to which heaven receives and
retains Him on His Father's throne. Acts 3: 19-21, (R. V.)
It is the high-point in the "Day of the Lord" which begins
before the Advent and continues after it, the Day "in the which"
the Lord comes, and not before it: Matt. xxiv: 42, 44, 50;
Luke xii: 39, 46; xvii: 30; Acts xvii: 31; Rom. ii: 16; 2 Thess.
i: 10; 2 Tim. i: 18. As in all prophecy, so here, Judgment
and Salvation go together, "as it was in the days of Noah,"
and "of Lot," and the "coming out of Egypt."

The New Testament fills in the details unmentioned in
Daniel's vision, viz., those of international war and strife. The
kingdoms will have prepared for themselves the instruments
of their own destruction. The logic of the situation will have
caused already an effort to reintegrate the jarring nations into
one vast empire, as the best solution of the problem of government, a world-empire free from Christianity and bound alone
to a religion of humanity, in which the world's last leader will
be the chief object of worship, the world's new Messiah. The
temporary realization of that scheme with all its wickedness,
will provoke the last heaving of the nations and call into being
the " Day of the Lord." Supernatural terrors will break in on
the new order of things, more void of order than all preceding
times. " Heaven, earth, sea and the dry land will be shaken."
Hagg. ii: 6, 7. It will be a time of tribulation and anguish, of

slaughter and gloom, and of persecution of God's saints, a time when the sickle, the flail, the fan, and the fire, will do their work, a time when the harvest is ripe, and the vintage so full that the vats overflow, "because the wickedness is great." Joel iii: 13. The struggle for supremacy will bring the "War of the Great Day of God Almighty," Rev. xvi: 14, when the horn prevails against the saints and seeks to build his new empire on the destruction of all Christianity in human governments, and on the extirpation of the Jews. To that, the kingdoms of this world will come, till the Lord comes to destroy their power. Then, what Daniel saw in vision will become a fact in history, the nations gathered together against Jerusalem, the last Antichrist playing his last desperate game against the Holy City. Then, "the Son of Man shall come in His glory and all the holy angels with Him, and He shall sit on the throne of His glory, and before Him shall be gathered all nations, Matth. xxv: 31; Zeph. iii: 8; Zech. xii: 2; xiv: 1-5; Ps. 1: 1-6. The reintegration and the rule, the fact that Gentile politics and power, nominally Christian, have come to anti-Christianity for the sake of gain, and the powers that be have conspired to give their strength to the Beast, not only against Rome, Rev. xvii: 13-16, but Jerusalem, Rev. xiv: 20, and to shed the blood of God's saints, will precipitate the last phenomena. "Woe worth the day!" Nature herself will shudder, and sun, moon and stars refuse to look on the butchery, and through the darkness that shrouds the hour the flash of the Advent will kindle the sky, and glare on the concert of crime below, and earth's monarchs, magnates and millionaires, her statesmen and diplomatists, the commanders of her armies and fleets in all waters—all the great, rich and mighty, bond and free—will "call on the rocks and mountains to hide them from the face of Him who sits upon the throne, and from the Wrath of the Lamb; for the great day of His wrath is come, and who shall be able to stand?" Rev. vi: 12-17. The sixth apocalyptic seal contains the vision and judgment in Dan. vii. All the prophets look to the "end" and to the second coming of Christ. All look to the "seventh trumpet" and to the "seven vials," the last of which ends the kingdom of the Horn. Dan. ix: 27; Rev. xix: 11-21.

II. The *Place* of the Judgment. So far as the "thrones" are concerned (vii: 9), it is aerial, in stormy and fire-lit clouds, overhanging the earth, and visible to all. "The heavens declare His righteousness, for God Himself is Judge." Ps. l: 6. The diurnal rotation of the planet on its axis will make the visibility a universal necessity. "Every eye shall see Him." Rev. i: 7. But, so far as the special vision in Dan. vii. has to do with the destruction of the Antichrist and his empire, and Israel's deliverance, the judgment is localized to the Holy Land. Dan. xi: 45; xii: 1. Geographically and topographically the place is defined by Moses as "the land," Deut. xxxii: 43; by Asaph as "Zion," Ps. l: 1-6; by Isaiah as "the land of Judah," "this mountain," and "Jerusalem," xxv: 7; xxvi: 1; xlvi: 13-16; by Zephaniah as "Jerusalem," iii: 8-17; by Joel as the "Valley of Jehoshaphat," and the "Valley of Decision," iii: 11-16; by Zechariah as "Jerusalem," where all nations are gathered, and as the "Mount of Olives which is before Jerusalem on the east," where the Lord's "feet shall stand in that day," xii: 2-8; xiv: 1-5; by Ezekiel as the "Valley of the Passengers," the "Overim" or "Crossers-over," "on the east of the sea,' the Mediterranean,—the great transit route across Palestine from Carmel to the Jordan, i. e., the "valley of Megiddo," and "Plain of Esdraelon," Ezek. xxxix: 11; Judg. iv: 7; v: 19; Zech. xii: 11; by Daniel as the "Mountain of the Beauty of Holiness between the seas," i. e., Moriah in Jerusalem, between the Mediterranean and Dead Seas, where the mosques of Omar and El Aksa now stand amid the cypress trees, Dan. xi: 45; xii: 1; and by holy John as "Armageddon," Rev. xv: 15, 16. These designations cover Galilee, Samaria, Judea, the whole of Palestine now held by the Turk, as the centre of the final struggle between the Jews and the Antichrist seeking to hold the land as his own, and make the Holy City the capital of his new empire. The last military station of the "Horn" is at Jerusalem, his last encampment the Holy Place where once Jehovah's temple stood. What scenes occur here at this time when the "Powers" fight their last fight, and Gentile politics go down to the dust, may be read in Zech. xii: 2-9, and xiv: 1-5. In Palestine, the final conflict between Judaism and New Born Israel, and between Christianity and reinvigorated Islamism, in short, the decisive battle between the religion of Christ as a power sought to be crushed and all other false religions, and between the sceptre of Christ and all other sceptres, will be waged. And He who ascended from Olivet in a cloud will return in clouds to Olivet. And where once "the kings of the earth stood up and were gathered together against the Lord and His Anointed" (Acts iv: 24-27), they shall be gathered again, but in a rôle reversed. The Holy Land, so many times invaded by the kings of the earth during 4,000 years, and winning for itself the title of "the battlefield of the kingdom of God," shall once more, and for the last time, become the local centre of the closing struggle in the fortunes of the ancient people of God. "In that day, Judah shall fight at Jerusalem," Zech. xiv: 14, and "the Lord shall defend the inhabitants of Jerusalem, and he that is feeble among them shall be as David, and the house of David as God, as the angel of the Lord before them." Zech. xii: 8. It is then "Michael" stands up for the Jews. Dan. xii: 1; x: 13; Rev. xii: 7. "And the Lord shall go forth and fight against those nations as when He fought in the day of battle. And His feet shall stand in that day on the Mount of Olives, which is on the east before Jerusalem. And the Lord, my God, shall come; all the holy ones with thee!" Zech. xiv: 1-5; Isa. xxiv:21-23; Ps. l: 1-6. And so it shall be that "when the enemy invades the land like a flood, the breath of the Lord shall be as a rushing stream against him, and the Redeemer (Israel's Goel) shall come to Zion, to the converts from apostacy in Jacob, said the Lord." Isa. lix: 19; Rom. xi: 26; Isa. lxvi: 5; Rev. xix: 11-21; xiv: 1-5; Acts iii: 19-21 (R. V.)

III. The *Parties* in the Judgment. Already mentioned in general, it is necessary still to speak of them in particular. They are (1) the Fourth Beast, (2) the Ten Horns or Kingdoms, (3) the Little Horn, (4) the Ancient of Days, (5) the

Angels, (6) the Son of Man, (7) the Saints of the Most High, or the People of the Saints of the Most High. With the New Testament development of this vision by our Lord, in His assignment of the Christian church to her place alongside of Israel, in Daniel's perspective, we have nothing here to do. Matth. xxiv: 4-15; xxv: 1-30. Daniel's apocalypse is wholly for the Jews, a purely Old Testament one. We have, however, to do with our Lord's development of Rome in the same perspective, given to John in the Revelation by the Lord Himself through His angel. The Church is not here, although the period covered by the horns is the church-period, and constitutes almost the entire interval of the Roman "Times of the Gentiles" which Daniel locates, as we shall see, between the 6cth and 70th week of the seventy weeks in ch. ix. The parties in Daniel are the above-named. In the judgment of the living nations, Matth. xxv: 31-46, and which includes the judgment here in Dan. vii., "these my brethren" answer to "the people of the saints of the Most High,"—the 144,000 in Rev. xiv: 1-5

As to the "Fourth Beast," a word will suffice. Everything said previously concerning the fourth empire is here applicable. It is the Roman empire, whose first emperor was Augustus, and identical with the bloody, persecuting beast in Rev. xiii: 1-18, and xvii: 1-18, and involves its whole history.

As to the "Ten Horns." Everything said previously concerning the "Ten Toes" is applicable here, since both are identical. They are neither ten Ptolemies, nor ten Seleucids, the successors of Alexander, nor ten Cæsars, nor ten provincial governors of the empire in Nero's time, but are ten separate, independent and contemporaneous kingdoms with their kings, in Europe, Asia and Africa, formed within the limits of the old Roman territory, East and West, in the last days of their existence. Nevertheless, it is one of the most remarkable phenomena in all history, that, for 1,300 years, last past, twenty-six catalogues of the kingdoms formed in the Western empire, each catalogue covering a half century, show the number "ten" as that to which these kingdoms, as imperial powers, have, with few exceptions, uniformly gravitated. While this is true, and true to-day, that Great Britain (including Egypt), part of Germany, France, Spain, Portugal, Austro-Hungary, Italy, Greece, Turkey, and part of Russia, occupy the territory of the old empire, yet good reasons exist for holding that a further distribution will be made, by the sword or by diplomacy, in the time of the "end."

Among these are the facts (1) that the ten toes are identical with the horns, and both with the ten horns in the Revelation by John; (2) that the toes, therefore the horns, lie not in the western territory of the empire alone, but in the eastern as well; (3) that in John they appear discrowned, quasi-kings, whose power has gone to the Beast for a time and special purpose, i. e., Rome's destruction; (4) the impossibility of showing, now, which of all the kingdoms of Europe, Asia and Africa the final ten will be. Concede to Preterism and Presentism all they affirmatively claim and can demonstrate validly from history: that Nero was an Antichrist, the Pope another, the one a pagan, the other an ecclesiastic, and also, that, while the Papacy is Western Antichrist, Islam is Eastern, the one ruling as "Vicar of Christ," the other as "the Shadow of God," still to Futurism must be allowed the unconquerable answer that the harlot, Rome, the horns and little horn, exist till Christ comes to destroy them, and the Jews wage their last conflict with the last Antichrist, in times immediately preceding the second advent. Therefore, the final distribution of the kingdoms is still before us. Remarkable is the statement of Hippolytus, Bishop of Rome, in the second century, that the ten kingdoms will be "discrowned" and become "democracies" at the end of our age, a conclusion he reached solely from Dan. ii: 42, 43. So Theodoret: "In the time of the end ten kings shall arise and one, who will subdue all, be the demiurge of all wickedness." Jerome's statement is, "We teach, therefore, what all our ecclesiastical writers have delivered to us, that, in the end of the world (age), when the Roman power shall be destroyed, ten kings shall arise, who will divide the empire among them, and an eleventh shall come, who will uproot three, which having been done, the other seven will submit their necks to the victor's yoke. This is the common interpretation by all ours."

It is worthy of note that one of the types of the last Antichrist (Antiochus) rose out of territory now occupied by the Sultan, while another (Nero), rose out of territory now occupied by the king of Italy. The dividing line, between East and West, ran ideally, north and south, through Belgrade, cutting the Mediterranean sea in two, extending to Tunis in Africa, thence projected to the desert, Constantinople the capital on one side, Rome on the other. Apart from this, and the kingdoms formed in the western half, mediæval and modern European history has no explanation. The breaking up of the western half was completed by the Barbarian irruption upon it, from the third to the sixth century, and the formation of the kingdoms just prior to the rise of Mohammed. The breaking up of the eastern half, and its conquest by Mohammed II., was effected in 1453, when Constantinople was taken, and the Turk camped on the Bosphorus. Whatever the final distribution of the ten kingdoms, it is certain they will represent the whole culture and civilization of Europe, Asia and Africa in all its degrees, within the limit of the old united empire; their conflicting religions, different tongues, and governments practically discrowned by the Antichrist, their mutual rivalries and jealousies, ambitions and enmities; their international commercial system the mammon-sceptre of the last itmes; their apostasy from truth and righteousness, from freedom, humanity and justice; their anti-Christianity, bloodshed and crime. All the questions that now agitate them, in their struggle for the mastery,—Pan-Hellenism, Pan-Slavism, Anti-Semitism, the integrity of the Turkish empire, the competition of the " Christian Powers " for control of the trade of the East, their relation to the weaker and oppressed peoples, race antagonisms, their policies, and, in spite of Christianity, their selfishness and sinfulness—will continue till the Lord comes to " dash them in pieces," and make them " as the chaff of the summer threshing floor."

IV. The Duration of the Judgment. This is nowhere defined in the Scriptures, unless we take the close of the Great Tribulation or end of the last 1260 days of the Horn's career as its commencing point, and the close of the 1335 days, as its concluding point: Dan. vii: 25; xii: 12. Two months and a half exhaust the period. In a wide sense the "Day of the Lord" which begins before the advent and continues after it, is called a "Day of Judgment," and during it the last Seals are opened, the Trumpets sounded and the Vials poured with all their terrible phenomena. But the final Judgment on the Horn and his allies, and the final stroke on all Gentile politics and power begins with the Advent itself, and must close before the "Blessed" time. Swift and severe, it will be a "short work in righteousness," shaking together "heaven, earth, sea, dry land and all nations" (Hagg. ii: 6, 7; Heb. xii: 26, 29), for the Lord will "finish the work and cut it short in righteousness; because a short work will the Lord make upon the earth," Rom. ix: 28—" sudden destruction," 1 Thess. v. 3. The supernatural phenomena which precede, increase, intensify and melt into the "Day of the Lord," will reach their culmination with the Advent itself. And, as Zechariah informs us, Joshua's long day—"neither day nor night"—will be repeated in the final crisis. Zech. xiv: 6, 7. The kingdom of the Horn will be "consumed and destroyed unto the end." Dan. vii: 26.

The solemn thing here is that the "ten horns" are all Christian kingdoms which have become politically, in their governments, apostate from Christianity, and represent a civilization of culture and mammon, and a policy of crime at war with moral righteousness. They are the "Powers" of a hardhearted military Christendom, politically dechristianized, the very "horns" in John's apocalypse and, in their last state, allies of the Antichrist in the persecution of God's saints. And to such an outcome present signs are not wanting. The championship, by Christian governments, of anti-Christianity, even of an empire historically organized to shed Christian blood; the championship of a power whose chief sits at the Golden Horn as the "Shadow of God," "Lord of two continents," and "Kings of Kings," to whom "Allah" has committed the rule of the world, an Antichrist, a hater of Christians, open rejecter of Christ as the Saviour of the world; an impostor who denies the deity of Christ, and the divine and eternal relation of the "Father" and the "Son," whose ritual is the stated massacre of God's saints, whose reward for massacre is a sensual paradise, whose alternatives to all mankind are the "Koran or the Sword,"—is enough to make the "fury" of God rise in His face. Since the world began, no greater crime has been committed—save the crucifixion of Christ—than the introduction of this organized anti-Christian power, in 1856, into the family of civilized and Christian nations by the so-called "Christian Powers" themselves, at a cost of 300,000 lives and 300,000,000 of money, and in the face of gigantic massacres whose atrocities made the blood of mankind run cold. And all the more unutterably guilty have been the "Powers," since the subsequent massacres in 1860, 1876 and 1894-1897, in south-eastern Europe, Crete, Greece, Armenia, with the slaughter of 130,000 Christians, and a total since 1822 of 162,000, and the destruction of the homes of 1,000,000 sufferers, and the agonies, tortures and dishonor of mothers, daughters and babes, have been allowed by the "Powers" to pass unavenged—Russia now consenting—all the "Christian Powers" shelling with their fleets (1897) defenseless Christians fighting to secure their freedom from the Turks! Immeasurable, save by God Himself, is the unforgotten crime of Christendom, since, shamelessly as openly, by "concert of the Powers" the championship of the "integrity of the Ottoman Empire" is justified by the doctrine of the "Balance of Power," the "Peace of Europe," the "Interests of Bondholders," and the "Necessities of Commerce and Trade," in short, "Business Interests" which England's Premier has told the world are "paramount to mere religious feeling and to all considerations of mere humanitarian sentiment!" A compact such as this, by the so-called "Christian governments" of Europe, which hereby prove themselves to be a federation of stock-jobbing companies of royal birth, intermarried, wearing crowns on their heads and backed by standing armies and fleets, ruling the world, is enough to excite universal anarchy and revolution, and is a challenge to God to vindicate His Word.

These lines are not forgetful of Papal massacres in history, outstripping far the pagan. Nor do they decide the question whether the last anti-Christian "Horn" shall be an apostate Pope as many have supposed, or a Sultan as still others think, or "some other man." It is enough that the "Ten Horns" have already been formed, though not in their final arrangement. The "what withholdeth" or "hinders" the appearing of the last Antichrist in God's counsel, is the politically organized Gentile power, or combination of civil powers professedly Christian, ordained of God "not to bear the sword in vain," but to execute justice, to repress crime, conserve in righteousness the civil and social order, and promote the triumph of the kingdom of God. False to this high trust, their right of existence is forfeited. When once it is evident that these "Powers" are instruments of oppression and persecution, leagued to promote injustice, despotism, inhumanity, and every evil work in the name of Christianity, and bent chiefly on self-aggrandizement, increase of commerce, trade, wealth, extent of territory, and supremacy each over the other, the result can only be an insurrection of the more and more educated masses, a reaction against both Christianity and the civil order, and an explosion of universal revolution. It is then the "foundations will be destroyed," the "let" removed, and the last Antichrist appear. Christendom will be responsible for it, and the penalty of her treason against the law of God, the Gospel of Christ, and the common principles of natural justice, will be the righteous annihilation of all Gentile politics and power, in the midst of unparalleled tribulation and distress. It is the lesson of the book of Daniel, as of all the prophets, and of John's apocalypse. It is, moreover, the very word of Christ. To modern rulers thus leagued, under the common sceptre of mammon, and to all the world's financial strength, God has said, "Your covenant with death shall be disannulled, and your agreement with hell shall not stand." Isa. xxviii: 18. As a party in the judgment the kingdoms are marching to their last division and their doom, and calling for their last leader. The "Horns" need a master and will find one "in the time appointed." "Bondholders" hungering after "dividends," and the Governments in partnership with them as their police, must reckon with Him to whom God will "divide" a portion with the great, and he will "divide" the spoil with the strong, and the last "Concert of Europe," when the "kings and princes, and the chief captains, and the rich, and the strong" shall invoke the rocks and the mountains to "fall" on them and hide them "from the face of Him that sitteth on the throne, and from the wrath of the Lamb." Rev. vi: 15-17. Broken shall be the whole "commercial system" of the world, now ruling all governments and nations. Ezek. xxvii: 1-36; Rev. xviii: 1-24; Isa. xxiv: 1-2. Then the Horn will be judged, and the colossus become "as the chaff of the summer threshing floor." A new age will heave into history, and the "Kingdom" come. Truth will spring out of the earth and Righteousness look down from heaven, and here on this present earth, as in heaven, God's will shall be done. It is the vision we have been considering, and the Vision is true, and the interpretation sure.

"When the Son of Man shall come in His glory, and all the holy angels with Him, then shall He sit upon the throne of His glory; and before Him shall be gathered all the nations; and He shall separate them one from another as the shepherd separates the sheep from the goats. And He shall set the sheep on His right hand. but the goats on the left. . . . Then shall He say to them on His right hand, Come, ye blessed of my Father; inherit the kingdom prepared for you from the foundation of the world. . . . Inasmuch as ye did it unto one of *these my brethren*, even the least, ye did it unto me. . . . Then shall He say unto them on the left hand, Depart ye cursed into everlasting fire, prepared for the devil and his angels. . . . Inasmuch as ye did it not unto one of *these least*, ye did it not unto me. And these (on the left) shall go away into everlasting punishment, but the righteous (shall come) into life everlasting."— Our Lord.

Chapter IV.

DANIEL, CHAPTER VII. (CONTINUED).—THE LITTLE HORN, THE GREAT ASSIZE.

As to the "Little Horn," in vii. 8, 11, 20, 21-26, it is evident that he is the chief party among all the criminals arraigned in the judgment. Like the rest, he is a king, the head of a kingdom, both symbolized in one. Bad as the rest have been, this one is worse, transcending them all in his crimes. The hostility of all the ancient empires to Israel is here. The principles, policy, selfishness, pride and antichristianity of all the horns find here their highest expression. He is the product of his times. Little at first, yet he mounts to greatness among his fellows, his first achievement, the subversion of "three kings" who stand in his way, vii: 24. He differs from the rest, having "eyes," the symbol of wisdom, science and circumspection, and of craft and cunning withal, a "mouth" and "voice" arrogant against the Most High, vii: 11, 25, and a "look" stouter than that of his fellows, vii: 20. He "makes war with the saints," and for three and a half years "wears them out," and "prevails" against them, "changing their times and laws," vii: 21, 25. He is "slain, destroyed, his body given to the burning flame," and his "dominion consumed and destroyed to the end," vii: 11, 26. In all these reports he is "diverse" from the rest," vii: 23, 24. If his rise is rapid, his reign is short and his ruin complete.

The different names under which he is known are many. He is "the prince that shall come on wing of abomination, a desolator," ix: 26; the concluder of a treaty or "covenant" with the masses of the Jewish people, for "one week," and breaker of the same, permitting their ancient worship, then causing it to cease in the middle of the week, ix. 27; one who sets up "the abomination" that causes desolation, foretold by our Lord, Matt. xxiv. 15; "that wicked" in Isa. xi. 4; the "enemy that invades like a flood," Isa. lix: 19, and whose end is in the "overflowing," Dan. ix: 26. 27; He is "the King" who comes to his end at Jerusalem with "none to help him," Dan. xi. 36. 45; he is Paul's "man of sin," to whom the apostle applied the title given by the Maccabees to his prototype—"sinful man," a "root of sin," 1 Macc. i. 10; ii. 62; 2 Thess. ii. 3., He is "the Antichrist" of John, 1 John ii. 18; the personal "beast" that "ascends out of the bottomless pit," wars with the saints and slays the "two witnesses" of Christ, Rev. xi. 7, 3; "Apollyon," the destroyer, Rev. ix: 11; the "beast" in Rev. xiii: 5, to whom Satan gives his "power, throne and great authority;" a mysterious person, of whom it is said that he once "was" on this earth, but "is not" now, yet "shall ascend out of the abyss," "be present," then "go into perdition, Rev. xvii. 18, a very "son of perdition;" a "lawless one," whose coming is with all the "energy of Satan," and "with signs and lying wonders, and with all deceit of unrighteousness for them that perish," teaching "the lie" that both Christ and Christianity are a fraud, 2 Thess. ii. 9-12, and whom "the Lord Jesus shall slay with the breath of His mouth, and destroy with the brightness of His coming," 2 Thess. ii. 8. As by plucking up "three" of the Ten Horns, he thereby became "an eighth," so is he described again as "an eighth" in Rev. xvii. 11, one who stands out above all his fellows in bad pre-eminence, as not only a "Beast" and a "Devil," but as a "God," sitting "in the temple of God" in Jerusalem, "showing himself that he is God," the self-exalting "opposer" of God, 2 Thess. ii: 4; Dan. viii: 11; xi. 36, but is a "Man" whose secular and anti-Sabbatic monogram is "666," the number of his name," Rev. xiii. 18. Such the "Little Horn" Daniel saw in vision—a Satanic re-appearing military leader, atheist, antichrist and supreme imperial ruler of the last times, in whom, by consent of the Horns, is vested the whole power of apostate governments in Europe, Asia and Africa, within the limits of the old Roman territory; himself and his allies the destroyers of Rome, Rev. xvii. 12-18, and whose last campaign, following Rome's destruction, is his invasion of the Holy Land where he comes to his end, Dan. xi. 40-45; Rev. xix. 11-21.

And complete will be the retribution, unto ages of ages. There is an eternity in justice, and the protest of right against wrong, of innocence and weakness against oppression, and the call for long-delayed satisfaction, are immortal. No law or prescription exempts from doom the nominally Christian yet actually dechristianized nations and governments of the earth. It is not possible that the Horn and his hosts shall be victorious in the "War of the Great Day of God Almighty." Such victory would be out of harmony with the epoch of Judgment, the law of righteousness, the destiny of Israel, and the entrance of the kingdom of God. The time has come for the Son of Man to overturn all Gentile power and crush the Horn in whose brain now floats the empire, forever. Foredoomed to everlasting punishment is the entire host of antichristianity with their blaspheming prince at their head. Israel's victory is assured. The overthrow of the Antichrist and his hosts before the Son of Man is tragic. The hissing thunder bolt, the lightning, the bedazzlement, the shock, the brimstone as at Sodom, the darkness as in Egypt, the driving hail-stone a talent's weight, the earthquake dividing the mountain, the vertigo, the reeling as when Saul fell from his horse, the plague, the panic, the prayer to the rocks, the mutual slaughter, these will be effective, the symbols of a severer and longer punishment. How insignificant the armies of the earth, and impotent the vain eruptions of the horn "in that day!" Man plays a small part in such a scene. In such a crisis, freighted with loss to all Gentile power, and with victory to God's people, lies the "Progress of the Nations," the "Peace of the World," and the "Triumph of the Kingdom of God." It scandalizes the diplomacies of courts, and mocks the coalition of kings.

This Horn is the Hero of the "Great Tribulation" foretold not only by Daniel, vii. 25; xii. 1, but also by Moses, Deut. xxxii. 36-43; Balaam, Numb. xxiv. 23, Isaiah, xxvi. 13-21, Jeremiah, xxx. 7, our Lord, Matth. xxiv. 15-21 (and parallels), by Paul, 2 Thess. i: 6. 7; ii: 8-12; and fully pictured by John, Rev. iii: 8. 9; vi: 9-11; vii: 14; xi: 2, 7; xii: 6. 12. 14. 17; xiii: 1-18; xiv. 12; xx. 4. It will be a tribulation sorer than any yet preceding under Manasseh, Antiochus. Nero, the Caliphs and Popes, or Sultans of modern days, a time of world-wide trial and sore temptation for the people of God, a time of suffering, death and martyrdom for Jesus' sake, a time " such as never was since there was a nation, even to that same time," Dan. xii: 1, " such as never was since the beginning of the world, no, nor ever shall be," Matth. xxiv: 21. By such intense expressions, so indescribably solemn, and full of faithful warning, we learn the unparelleled importance of this epoch for the Kingdom of God. It is the crisis of the Kingdom of Christ in its final struggle with the apostate powers of the earth, and with the kingdom of Satan under the lead of the last Antichrist. Nor are the indications of its approach obscure. " Coming events cast their shadows before." When the so-called " Christian Powers," the " Horns" in their present distribution, are in concert with antichristianity for the sake of gain, and Mammon sways the sceptre over moral righteousness, and national churches, the stalled stipendiaries of the State, have become a salt that is savorless, powerless to compel their rulers to enforce justice, or defend the inalienable rights of man grounded in his personality, or protect the saints of God from massacre, when the kings and rulers of the earth and Christian governments panoplied for war, are partners with Mammon in orgies of blood for selfish ends, binding oppression on the necks of the poor, seeking by force to wrench from the weak their lawful possessions, the heart steeled to human sympathy, the ear deaf to every appeal for help, and conscience dead, it is only a step or two till Sin comes to its height, and Sin's last leader must appear. International politics will generate events subversive of all existing international relations, and create new alliances and new combinations leading up to the final crisis no summer sunshine nor pleasing landscape in nature can avert. The " Day of the Lord " will steal in like a thief, and the " Great Tribulation " come. Viewed from a human standpoint, it can only be the necessary evolution of modern statecraft, a Nemesis the apostate powers have vainly hoped to avoid. From the Divine standpoint, it means the Judgment of the world.

God's true people everywhere will be called to their best witness-bearing and most honored trial of their patience and faith in behalf of Christ. Intensity of suffering, however, will not avail to divert them from their fidelity. As in Manasseh's day, in Maccabean times, in Nero's day, in Moslem and Papal times, and as in Bulgarian, Armenian and Cretan times, so, once more, will their steadfast love, their endurance and martyrdom only prove that He who calls them to such a trial has "counted them worthy of the kingdom of God," 2 Thess. i. 5. The patriot's consecration of his life as an offering on the altar of his country will be more than surpassed by that ardor of love for Christ which will make His saints "rejoice" even to be "killed all the day long" for His sake, and to "glory in tribulation," Rom. viii. 36. "Here is the patience of the saints." "Here are they who keep the commandments of God" in opposition to the orders, and "hold fast the testimony of Jesus" in opposition to "the lie," of the Antichrist, Rev. xii: 17; xiii: 10; xiv: 12. Divine grace supports their souls with strength according to their day, and confirms their faith by rich promises of glory and honor made to the overcomer, by the example of Christ, the memories of the past, the sealing of the Spirit, the election of God and the certain knowledge that the Coming of the Lord is near. The sweetest of all the notes they will sing is this:

> "Oh, what, if we are Christ's,
> Is earthly shame or loss?
> Bright shall the crown of glory be
> When we have borne the cross."

As to the "Ancient of Days," literally "One ancient in respect of Days," older than all the late-made gods of the heathen, transcending all time, He is "Jehovah" Himself, the Eternal, in the absolute Unity of His essence, God. It is He, according to Old Testament representation, who constitutes the Judgment (1) by descending from heaven to earth, (2) by placing the thrones, (3) by seating the judges upon them, (4) by opening the books. The white garment denotes His majesty, rank, holiness, righteousness; the white hair His antiquity, even Eternity; the throne of enveloping flame His avenging justice; the revolving wheels of fire the rapidity of His advancing judgments, and the stream of radiating flame the persistence of His judicial activity till His strange work is done. It is said, He " did sit," but only after He " came," vii: 9, 22. This is of first importance for the interpretation, as we shall presently see. It was not needful to say that the "Ancient of Days" came " in clouds " since that is the Old Testament view of the descent of Jehovah to judge the nations and His people. He is always spoken of as "coming *down*" in glorious epiphany with fire-flame and " in clouds," and attended by "angels," Exod. xix: 16; Ps. xlvii: 6; Zech. ix: 14; Isa. xxvii: 13; Exod. iii: 2; xix: 18. " He bowed the heavens also and *came down*," Ps. xviii: 9-15. He " *came down* on Mount Sinai," Exod. xix: 16-20. He " rideth into Egypt on a swift cloud," Isa. xix: 1. " Our God shall come and not keep silence: a fire shall devour before Him," Ps. l: 1-5. The same is said of Jesus Christ in the New Testament, 1 Cor. iii: 13; 2 Thess. i: 7-10; Matth. xxiv: 30; Rev. i: 7; xiv: 14. Here, in Daniel's vision, it is God the father, the " Aged One," who first descends, and constitutes the judgment in the cloud-region overhanging the earth. He " sits " in flame and storm.

As to the Judges who sit on the thrones, the vision is silent, because the New Testament church was not yet a fact in history, although there is enough in the Old Testament, elsewhere, to indicate who some of the Judges are, Ps. l: 5. It is in the New Testament, however, we learn without mistake who the co-assessors are. In the Revelation to John which developes the Judgment-Scene in Daniel, the Second Coming of Christ is placed under the Seventh Trumpet and after the Sixth Vial, at which time the resurrection of the holy dead occurs, Rev. xi: 15-17; xvi: 15, 16, therefore before the judgment upon the Antichrist, the Beast. It is immediately before the final slaughter in the valley of Jehoshaphat, "outside the city," the reaping of the holy living ones by holy angels, and the rapture of the saints, occur, just before the Seventh Vial is poured out, Rev. xiv: 14-16, 17-20. It is therefore at the close of the Antichrist's 1260 days the Advent occurs. The same representation is given in 2 Thess. ii: 1-3, and in Matth. xxiv: 29-31, 40, 41; xxv: 1. In Daniel the same order of events is seen. The resurrection of the holy dead at the Second Coming of Christ occurs at the close of the last 1260 days, the end of the "Great Tribulation," Dan. xii: 1; vii: 13. Then, just prior to the last stroke of judgment is the "gathering" of God's saints by angelic ministry, Ps. l: 1-5; Matth. xxiv: 29; 2 Thess. ii: 1; 1 Thess. 4: 14-18. Clear, therefore, it is that the co-assessors in the "Great Assize," Dan. vii: 9, are the *Risen and Glorified Saints*, since the "thrones" on which they sit in Rev. xx: 4, are the same "thrones" Daniel saw in vii. 9. Paul declares "the saints shall judge the world," 1 Cor. vi: 2, his authority being the text in Dan. vii: 9.

As to the Angels, the whole angelic world is here as "executors" of the Judgment by the Son of Man, Jude 14. 15. Their innumerable number is given as 10,000 times 10,000 and thousands of thousands," Dan. vii: 10; at the very least 204,000,000, but more, since the extent of the multiplication is impossible, "a multitude that no man can number," Rev. v: 11; vii: 9; Heb. xii: 22, because of the indefinite terms "thousands of thousands." All these, seen standing before the throne, wait on the "Ancient of Days" to minister judgment on the allied millions of the "Horn," "angels of might." 2 Thess. i: 7. Already they have reaped the righteous, and now stand ready to reap the wicked, and "take out of the kingdom all things that offend and them that do iniquity," Matth. xiii: 41. Gabriel is there, and Michael is there, erect for Israel in the last crisis, Dan. xii: 1; Rev. xii: 7, and Raphael, Israfil, Ithuriel and Uriel standing in front of the light of the sun, Rev. xix: 17. Over against the wailing concert of Europe the embattled hosts of God will stand, ready to make the last charge with " lightnings and thunders," " hailstones a talent's weight," " snares, fire, brimstone and a horrible tempest, the portion of the wicked," and turning the swords of the wicked " against themselves," will approve the righteous judgment of God. Solemnly they will intone the words, " Righteous art Thou, O Lord, who wast and shall be, because Thou hast thus judged; for they have shed the blood of saints and of prophets, and Thou hast given them blood to drink!" Rev. xvi: 5, 6. "Fowls of the air, come, gather yourselves together to the supper of the great God, that ye may eat the flesh of kings and of captains, of mighty men, of horses and riders, free and bond, small and great!" Rev. xix: 17, 18. This is apostate Christendom's cup!—blood for blood, massacre for massacre, the righteous judgment of God, the end forever of bloodshed and war!

The solemnity of the scene is augmented by the fact that " the Books were opened," Dan. vii: 10. These " Books " are the records of the crimes of the Horn, the Beast and his allies, the sins of the ten confederate kingdoms of the last times in Europe, Asia and Africa, and the sins of which they are heirs at law, the sins of misgovernment, the sins committed against the saints of God. Wherever else the Judgment will strike so far as this particular scene is concerned, it strikes the nations of Christendom within the limits of the old Roman territory ruled by the Horn. They are the records of the living nations, of the kings, judges and rulers of the earth, Ps. ii: 10, who have taken counsel against the Lord and His Anointed, Ps. ii: 2,—the books, papers, files of their Gentile cabinets, their concert and their ruptures, their treaties and diplomacies, their guilty apathy, procrastination and venality when action was demanded in vindication of the right, their deeds, words, joint-notes, protocols and scheming policies, the motives of all supporting or opposed to the Horn. They are the archives, angel-kept, wherein are registered the noon-day iniquities and secret midnight work and devices of the " Powers," whose conduct paved the way for the " Great Tribulation," and made imperative a judgment to punish, in order to save, the nations and rescue the kingdom of God from extinction. The whole history of the Last Times is here: the encouragement of anti-christianity for the sake of gain, the coalition of Christian governments with the guilds of Mammon against justice, truth, religion, humanity and liberty; their covenants made and broken; their rivalries and envies, highway robbery and rapacity; their greed of gold and lust of supremacy; their defiance of Christian sentiment and of every appeal to virtue; their despotism, pride, misgovernment, duplicity, oppression of the weak and guilty trade with the strong,—and most of all, their shedding of innocent blood. All are here recorded with a pen unerring. No injustice is forgotten, no massacre or devastated homes, no crimsoned fields strewn with the upturned faces of the dead. Nor is the name of one who took part in producing such scenes, or consented to the wrongs that begat them, misspelled, or the place of his residence misread. The whole apostasy of Christendom, the Horn's loud-mouthed arrogance and the words of the cry, "We will not have this man to reign over us," are written in the "Books," and judgment by the records must pass on the kingdoms whose boast was their Christianity, culture, civilization. Such the solemn scrutiny.

Our Lord's description of the separation of the nations gathered against Jerusalem, and the decision that fixes the destiny of their individuals, according to their conduct toward converted Israel in the tribulation, leaves little doubt that the "throne of His glory" at that time will overhang the Mount of Olivet, facing Jerusalem, where the delivered Jews will be gathered nearest to Himself. Geographically, northward toward the mountains, on the right, the "righteous," while southward, on the left, through the valleys of Hinnom and Jehoshaphat, and toward the Dead Sea, the "wicked," will be congregated. The scene in Matth. xxv: 31-46, is but the development of the scenes in Joel iii: 12-17; Zech. xiv: 1-5.

As to the "Son of Man" (Bar Enash), to whom the "Ancient of Days" commits this judgment, modern criticism has attempted to show that the expression, "One like a Son of

Man," imports no more than a figure of speech, " personified Israel," or " the personified people of the Saints"; at best the abstract " idea " that the kingdom of the Saints will be humane in contrast with the beastly kingdom of the Horn. By such means the doctrine of the literal, personal Advent of Christ to gather His Saints, redeem Israel, destroy the Antichrist, judge the nations and introduce the millennial age, is sought to be set aside, and His Second Coming declared a spiritual one, already a fact in history. This dust is easily swept away. The word " like " in no way denies a proper personality, but simply states in what form the object seen in the vision appeared to the Seer. So the Chaldean king saw " four men " walking in the furnace, and " the form of the fourth was like to a Son of God," Dan. iii: 25. In the one a human, in the other a superhuman or Divine personality is seen, and these two are one. Our Lord's identification of Himself under the most solemn adjuration before the supreme council of his nation, with the " Son of Man " in this vision, and as " coming in the clouds of heaven," Matth. xxvi: 63-67, and again as the " Son of Man," to whom the " Father hath committed all judgment," John v: 22, 23, and the whole New Testament use of this phrase when dealing with the " Last Things," Matth. xvi: 27; xxiv: 30, 31; xxvi: 64; Acts i: 9-11; Rev. i: 7; xiv: 14, rebukes sufficiently this assault on the vision which is the Old Testament source of the title . The glorious person who appears in the scene is none other than the son of Mary, son of David, son of Abraham, the incarnate, crucified, exalted Son of God, Israel's own Messiah, the Redeemer of the world and Judge of all mankind.

The Sanhedrin and the whole Jewish nation so understood it. Before the Lord made use of the title the " Book of Enoch " called Messiah " Bar Anani," the " Son of a Cloud." The Targum of Jonathan called Him " Bar Nibli," the " Son of a Cloud." Jacchides said, the " Son of Man in the clouds is Messiah our Righteousness." To the question, who is Bar Enash (the Son of Man), Rabbi Simeon answered, " He is Messiah of whom it is said, He came with the clouds of heaven." It was to Him, a frail man, yet begotten by the Holy Ghost and born of the virgin, Jehovah said, "Sit thou at my right hand," Ps. cx: 1. David's son was David's Lord, God and Man, two natures in One Person forever! It is He who comes to judge the Horn, the nations and the world, and deliver Israel from the grasp of the last Antichrist,— their own "Kinsman-Redeemer" and royal "Brother" according to the flesh.

Post-millennialists have undertaken to show that the Judgment-Scene here "has nothing to do with the Second Advent." They take their stand on the preposition "*to*" in the verse, "One like a Son of Man came with the clouds of heaven, and came *to* the Ancient of Days, and they (the clouds) brought him near before Him," vii: 13, and maintain that what is here meant is the *Ascension* of Christ in clouds "to" the Father at the close of His First Advent and ministry. By this means it is hoped to destroy "the doctrine of the pre-millennial coming of Christ." It is clearly seen that the "Kingdom," as predicted, comes to victory on the earth and is given to the Son, vii: 14, and the Saints, vii: 27, only after the Son has "come with the clouds of heaven," and that, if by this coming the Second Advent is meant, the doctrine of the pre-millennial advent of Christ is irrefutable as the word of God. The effort, therefore, is to show that by the expression, "came to the Ancient of Days," is meant the *Ascension* from the Mount of Olives, A.D. 33, and that the kingdom of the "1000 years" dates from that event. The argument is as plausible as the ignorance of biblical prophecy is palpable. As already stated, Old Testament prophecy always represents "Jehovah," the absolute God, as "*coming down*" from His throne far above all heavens to the cloud region overhanging the earth, to hold Judgment. It is He who "descends" and makes the fire-lit thunder-heaps His throne. The peculiarity of the amazing Scene in Dan. vii: is this, that neither the name "Jehovah," nor the name "God" is employed, but that two parties, the Father, or "Aged One," *i.e.*, the "Ancient of Days," and the "Son of Man," who by His relation to the Father is also the

Son of God, appear in the same Judgment at the end of the 1260 days of the Horn's career, vii:25, 27; xii: 7. The vision assumes the incarnation or birth of Christ foretold in ix: 25, His crucifixion in ix: 27, and His ascension to the Father's throne, from where, long concealed, He now appears revealed. It is the Second Advent of Christ that is first made known to Daniel, since only then is the kingdom given to Israel. Though using the phrase, "Ancient of Days, the prophet remains true to Old Testament representation—rather the vision does—and presents the Father as first of all descended to Judgment in clouds overhanging the earth, angels attending. The new thing Daniel beheld was the entry of " One like a Son of Man " into the same scene, also coming with the clouds of heaven, and coming " to " where the Ancient of Days was already seated, viz., over the earth, both angels and clouds bringing him " near before Him." And this in order that then and there " dominion " involving judgment might be given to the Son, and a " kingdom " besides. It was needless to tell a Hebrew that this coming " to " where the " Aged One " sat was the *Return* from heaven to earth of a " Son of Man," born of woman, and previously exalted to the highest, even the heavenly throne. The preposition " to " is a perfectly correct text, and so far from teaching the Ascension of Christ, is absolutely indispensable to establish the fact that here the Second Advent is meant. Such the way the Holy Spirit taught Old Testament saints the great truth that by the Father's will the " Son of Man " exalted to heaven, should return to judge the world. If in the New Testament the " Aged One " is not seen in the Advent visions, it is because the " Son of Man " was already in the world, and appealed to this very vision, saying, " The Father judgeth no man, but hath committed all judgment to the Son," and " hath given Him authority to execute judgment also, because He is the Son of Man," John v: 22, 27. "Behold, He cometh with clouds and every eye shall see Him," Rev. i: 7. Therefore does the " Chiliastic doctrine " stand, impregnable as the truth of God, confirmed by the mouth of Christ Himself, and by both Testaments.

What we have here, therefore, is the glorious King of the Fifth Kingdom to succeed all others, and be succeeded by none. In prophecy, kingdoms are defined by the titles of their founders. "The great Beasts are four kings that shall arise," vii: 17, Nebuchadnezzar, Cyrus, Alexander and Cæsar. "The ten Horns are ten kings that shall arise," vii: 24, the monarchs of the last days. "The little Horn is another that shall arise after them," vii: 24. So does the "Son of Man" appear in the vision as the *Founder of the Fifth Kingdom*, the successor of the four, a kingdom universal over all the earth, unsucceeded and everlasting. It is the Kingdom of the "Son of Man" in victory at His Second Coming. All the solemn scenery surrounding the "Ancient of Days" surrounds the "Son of Man." It is the *Monarch of the Fifth Empire* we have here, who comes in the clouds of heaven. seated in royal splendor and solemn pomp on the "throne of His glory," Matth. xxv: 31, angels His escort, encircling flame His illumination. Flashes of glory alternate with blackness of midnight, attended by trumpet, storm, fire and deep-rolling thunder. It is as a Warrior and Judge that Daniel sees Him. He comes, not to consume the nations, but the wicked among them, who know not God nor obey the gospel of His Son, to smite the Antichrist, destroy the Horns, their governments and dynasties, wipe out all Gentile politics and power, make the Colossus as "the chaff of the summer threshing-floor," and set up His own kingdom in righteousness and peace, wide as the world, all crowns on His head and on the heads of His saints. It is what we have in Psalms ii: and lxxii:, and in the thrilling group that ends with "Old Hundred!"

As to the last party named in the Judgment-Scene, they are called the "Saints," with whom the Horn "makes war," vii: 21, 25, the "Saints of the Most High" who receive the kingdom, and possess the kingdom forever, even forever and ever," vii: 18, 22, the "People of the Saints of the Most High," to whom is given the kingdom and the greatness of the kingdom, not in a super-earthly or celestial sphere, but "underneath all heavens," vii: 27. Incontrovertibly, these are Daniel's people, the Jews, whose land the Horn has invaded, and who have suffered under the Antichrist during the Great Tribulation. It is their fortunes the prophet foretells, their relation to the world-power from the time of their captivity till the Son of Man comes. For them, pre-eminently, this Old Testament apocalypse was given, forecasting their sinful and weary way, and the glorious end of the election of God, xii: 1. They are New-Born Israel of the last times, " delivered" when the Son of Man comes, the converts from apostasy in Jacob, saith the Lord, Isa. lix: 20; Rom. xi: 26. Their holy dead have already been raised from their tombs, and made co-assessors with Christ on His throne. To the holy living, reserved in God's counsel to be the local and sustaining center of the Messianic Kingdom in victory on the earth, and whose "reception" is to be as "life from the dead" to the nations, Rom. xi: 15, and their "fulness" the greater "riches of the Gentiles," xi: 12, " the kingdom and the greatness of the kingdom under all heavens" is given. Under Christ, they lead the world. The Gentile Powers have had the "Times of the Gentiles," and answered for their conduct. Israel's times in the kingdom now begin, the world a witness of the difference of administration in the new and better age from that which obtained in the age just buried with its crimes. It means that, by the will of God and the gift of the Son of Man, earth's sovereignty shall pass to the hands of God's ancient people, the kingdom be restored to Israel, and all the promises to Abraham and his literal believing seed be at last fulfilled. The "gifts and calling of God" to them are irreversible, a boon their own apostasy could not invalidate, Rom. xi: 29, the gift of primogeniture, the gift of the land, the gift of their mission to be the bearer of the promises and collective mediator of salvation to the world. Their elect remnant was the nucleus of the church. Their elect remnant augmented to fullness, shall be the nucleus of the Kingdom in the coming age. Their gathering, last struggle, conversion to Christ, regeneration by the Holy Spirit and political establishment in their own land as a "righteous nation," and their transcendent blessing to the nations are guaranteed by the covenant, promise and oath of God, and by a hundred most decisive scriptures in both Testaments, Ezek. xxxvi: 24-28; xxxvii: 21-27; Zech.xii: 10-14; Rom. xi: 25, 33; Rev. vii: 4-8; xi: 3, 7, 13, 18, 19; xii: 10, 11; xiv: 1-5. Whatever expansion the New Testament gives to the idea of the "Saints" as heirs of the kingdom,—and it does widen the term to embrace all who have Abraham's faith, whether Jews or Gentiles,—still the contrast, nationally and politically, between Jews and Gentiles is a standing one, while earth endures. Spiritually one body in Christ, yet economically in God's purpose and plan the contrast remains for David's sake, for Abraham's sake and for Israel's sake, "of whom Christ came, who is over all, God blessed forever," Rom. ix: 5. To deliver them, baptize them with a fresh aspergence of Divine grace, give them the victory and establish them in glory and honor in the kingdom, the "Son of Man," their own "Brother" and ours, will appear in the clouds of heaven.

And this has ever been the one interpretation of the best Hebrew Doctors in all ages of the world. "The time will come," said David Kimchi, "when Jacob shall prosper and be redeemed and exalted, though now he is scattered and very low, and a wonder to the nations. When the nations are gathered against Jerusalem, God will give to Israel the victory." So the renowned Rabbi Solomon Isaac: "The time will come when Jacob shall overcome the Horns of the nations that scattered him, and be exalted to dominion in the kingdom." So Aben Ezra teaches that "the Judgment in Daniel is the Judgment of the living nations when Israel shall be avenged, as Moses taught in Deut. xxxii: 39-43; Zech. xiv: 1-5. The nations will then believe what they do not now. At last, they will recognize the truth that Israel shall see deliverance, a people smitten for their sins, they will say that the stroke fell on Israel for their benefit." So Abarbanel, saying, "God will not only give to Messiah but to Israel a portion with the great, even to Israel the wealth of the nations that have afflicted him, and who will assail him in the last days." The Targum of Jonathan is no less explicit: "Israel shall see the kingdom of Messiah, and from subjection to the nations the Lord shall deliver him. He shall see the punishment of his enemies, and be satisfied with the booty of kings." Such are the " People of the Saints of the Most High," to whom the kingdom will be given " underneath all heavens,"—even New-Born Israel turned to repentance and faith, and beholding their long-rejected King, the " Lord Himself from heaven." Nor will a greater day have ever greeted the nations than this, " when the Lord will take away the reproach of His people from off all the earth," Isa. xxv: 8, and " Israel shall blossom and bud, and fill the face of the world with fruit," Isa. xxvii: 6.

Involuntarily we turn to that beautiful scene of the Sun-clothed Woman in Rev. xii: 1-6, the daughter of Zion bringing forth "a manly child to rule all nations" in the time of the great tribulation, "a nation born in a day." Isa. lxvi: 5-9; Rev. iii: 26-28; Rev: xii: 5. The symbol gives the whole history of the Jewish church at both advents, as is the case with other symbols. She appears as the mother of Messiah —her seed, persecuted by Satan, yet sheltered—her Son caught away to the throne of God. She appears also as the mother, in the End-time, of the manly child, persecuted again, and sheltered, her manly son, national Israel, exalted " to rule the nations" when Gentile power is overthrown. She is clothed in New Testament light and the glory of the Lord, which was not the case when she bore Messiah. She is dressed here in her eschatological attire, according to the representation in Isaiah, "Arise, shine forth, for thy light is come, and the glory of the Lord is risen upon thee!" Isa. lx: 1. In the tribulation she is sheltered 1,260 days, the remainder of her believing seed in the field, persecuted by the Antichrist. The twelve stars are plainly the symbol of Israel, at last victorious and crowned. That the "moon under her feet" signifies the old dispensation, passed away, is admitted; but is there not something deeper still in the symbol? Will not her victory be a victory over the Crescent of Islam as well as over Judaism, in the last times? Can we say that Israel's triumph over the Ottoman power is not here included by that divine Spirit who sees the end from the beginning? and that the overthrow of both Judaism and Mohammedanism is not here intended? That such will be the fact is beyond all question. Nor can we deny that the symbol is put in direct connection with Michael's standing for the Jews in the tribulation when the Turkish power must pass away and Palestine be restored to the Jews by the interposition of their own Messiah. It is the time when the horns that have exalted themselves against Israel are judged, and the Antichrist meets his doom. Great will be the day! Dr. Döllinger has made the impressive remark, that "the symbol of the Sun-clothed Woman is one of the most beautiful in the Apocalypse, and of wider significance than most suspect." May not that "wider significance" be the inclusion of Islam's overthrow? the crescent under the feet of the daughter of Zion? the manly child victorious over Gentile power?

"Allah! perchance the secret word might spell;
If Allah be, He keeps His secret well.
   What He has hidden, can we hope to find?
Shall God His secret to a maggot tell?

The Koran! Well, just put me to the test;
Lovely ld book, although in error drest,
   Believe me, I can quote the Koran too;
The unbeliever knows the Koran best.

And do you think that unto such as you,
A maggot-minded, starved, fanatic crew,
   God tells the secret, and denies it me?
Well, well, what matters it, believe that, too."
—Omar Khayyam.

Chapter V.

DANIEL, CHAPTER VIII.—THE EASTERN QUESTION. RAM AND GOAT.

Chapter viii. contributes another striking proof of the truth of our thesis, viz., that the kingdom of Christ cannot come to victory over all the earth until the Second Coming of the Son of Man. Precisely here in this vision we look in vain to find the "*Kingdom*" which constitutes the goal of Daniel's predictions and the final triumph of the ancient people of God. The fulfillment of the prophecy lies historically in pre-christian times, a century and a half before the birth of Christ. At the same time its typical "meaning," as an organic and mediating link in a complex chain of prophecy having one end in view, points to higher fulfilment in the far "Time of the End," and is in harmony with the visions in chap. ii. and vii. This is confirmed by the fact that though, first of all, the "*Time of the End*" denotes the near horizon at which the prophet looks, viz., the close of the third empire, B. C. 165, it yet reaches to the "*Last Indignation*" of God against the Jewish apostasy, viii: 19, an "End" not yet apparent in history, and which comes alone with the destruction of the last Antichrist, the Horn in vii: 8, and "prince that shall come" in ix: 27, and the wilful and atheistic "King" in xi: 36, 40-45. Just because the "Time of the End" in the present vision was historically B. C. 168-165, no mention is made of the "Kingdom" as set up at that time; a fact that throws the mind forward to the close of the fourth empire to find it. Here, as everywhere else, even from the very first prophecy in chap. ii, it becomes clear that no part of Daniel's predictions can be fully understood or interpreted, without a knowledge of the whole. The fulfillment of the prophecy in chap. viii., concerning the Horn that afflicts the Holy People, points to a higher fulfillment in future days when the Jews will no longer be apostate, but a people whose apostasy is "finished," and "sins" sealed, a "righteous nation" forever. Then the kingdom comes with the "last end of the indignation," viz., the close of the Great Tribulation.

As chap. vii. was supplementary to chap ii., so chap. viii. is supplementary to both. Great space was given to the affairs of the fourth empire, the Roman, in chap. ii. and vii., while only four verses had been given in both to the second and third empires (ii: 32, 39; vii: 5, 6), the Persian and the Grecian. The vision, therefore, in chap viii., treats more largely of these, yet rapidly runs over them in order to reach the "Little Horn" of the third. Henceforth the whole interest of the book of Daniel circles round Messiah and His relation to those Two Horns, and to the Jews. As the Horn in chap. vii. is the last Gentile oppressor of Israel, viz., the Antichrist, still future to us, so the Horn in chap. viii. was the last Gentile oppressor in pre-christian times, viz., Antiochus Epiphanes, at the close of the third empire. As in chap. vii. all the introductory predictions led up, *as* introduction, to the Horn there, in like manner all in chap. viii. to the Horn here. The one important purpose of all such introductions in every chapter is to show that amid all changes of empires Israel remains indestructible, that the continuity of the Hebrew race, without a kingdom, outruns all kingdoms; that Babylon, Medo-Persia, Greece and Rome may pass away, but Israel lives, and that he is scarce less than demented who can doubt that, in the end, Israel's Kingdom will rise on the ruins of every other. The period covered by chap. viii. is that section of the "Times of the Gentiles" from the capture of Babylon, B. C. 538, to the death of Antiochus Epiphanes, B. C. 164, a period of 374 years. The whole chapter has to do (1) with the temporal and local circumstances connected with the vision, viii: 1, 2; (2) the vision itself, viii: 3-12; (3) the Angelic Dialogue, viii. 13-14; (4) the Unseen One hovering over the Ulai, and the prophet's physical condition under the power of the vision, viii: 15-18; (5) the Interpretation of the Vision concerning the "Little Horn," by Gabriel, viii: 19-25; (6) the certification of the Truth of the Vision, viii: 26; (7) the subsequent effect of the vision on Daniel and his companions, viii. 27.

I. As to the Date of the vision. It as in "the third year of the reign of the King Belshazzar," viii: 1. Assuming that Belshazzzar is the "Bel-sar-usur" of the monuments, and according to Oriental usage, a "King," the date of the vision is B. C. 538, the year of Babylon's fall and of his feast, v: 1-30, first year of Darius, the Mede, to whom Cyrus had given the rule over Babylon, the year when Daniel was thrown to the lions' "Den," the second year before the edict of Cyrus, B. C. 536, releasing the Jews, sixty-eight of the seventy years of the captivity having passed away.

II. As to the Place of the vision. The prophet, though bodily in Babylon, was transported in spirit to Susa, whose Assyrian name was "Shushan," the city of the lily and the lotus-flower, once the capital of the Elamite kings far back as the days of Abraham. Situated on the river Ulai, whose waters alone the Persian monarchs drank—the Eulaeus, or Choaspes, or modern Karun—it was conquered by Sardanapalus, B. C. 1650, afterwards by Cyrus, and became one of the capitals of the Medo-Persian empire, the chief city in the province of Elam. The province lay in the lower valley of the Euphrates, called by the ancients "Anzan," over which Cyrus reigned before his conquest of Media, Lydia and Babylon. On the south is the Persian Gulf. The city of Shushan is memorable in Scripture as, not only the scene of Daniel's vision, but as the home of Nehemiah, who was "Cup-bearer" to Artaxerxes, and as the scene of the whole book of Esther. Modern English and French explorers have excavated from its tumuli relics of its ancient "Apadana," or "palace," magnificent in Assyrian, Egyptian and Corinthian architecture, and brilliant with colors of crimson, and gold, silver and blue. At Shushan stands the tomb of Daniel, venerated by the Moslem, and sacredly guarded. The Holy Spirit chose the place as the locality of the vision here, because the vision itself foretells the overthrow of the empire of Cyrus, by Alexander, who occupied the city. The prophet's position in the vision is not *"in the palace"* (as our English version reads), but *"near the fortress,"* encircled as it was by the river.

III. The Vision itself. It is no less than that of the "*Eastern Question,*" a vision of conflicting civilizations, the Asiatic and European struggling for the mastery of the Old World. Daniel sees a "Ram," starting from the East, and pushing Westward, Northward and Southward, an effort of Asia to overrun Europe and Africa, the effort of the Medo-Persian empire. He sees, in turn, the counter-effort of Europe to overrun Asia and Africa, the effort of the "Goat," or Græco-Macedonian empire. It is Oriental and Occidental civilization in collision, contending for universal rule. On the one hand is an invading host crossing the Tigris and Euphrates and rolling like a tide westward to the Mediterranean; on the other a less numerous but more intelligent, active and efficient one crossing the Hellespont and darting eastward, conquering everything before it; in both cases tribulation for the Jewish people, and Gentile downtreading for Palestine, the union-point of three continents. These great world-movements, like those afterwards between the north and south, are mirrors of like collisions to occur in the last days, marking the "Time of the End"—the East seeking to control the West, the West the East, Palestine at last the scene of the hottest conflict; and furthermore, the same international struggles involving not only the North and the South, but all the semi-civilized nations and barbarous tribes outside the limits of the old Roman territory. It is the fixed law of history, ancient, mediæval and modern. There is something very impressive in the thought that the Holy Spirit, an angel from heaven, and inspired prophecy, should so splendidly anticipate the inductions of the ablest modern scientific study in the field of history, and forecast, two thousand years ago, the very laws of historical movement, whose recent mention has crowned with laurels the supposed discoverers of them. And the thought that Daniel wrote his book, not only in the face of his apostate countrymen, but in the face and front of Babylonian and Persian supremacy, anouncing the doom of both, and of all world-empires and kingdoms, adds grandeur to the heroism of the prophet, as it adds ten-fold interest to his predictions. The prophet, so glorious, has merited the title of both an "Anarchist" and "Pessimist" in our day. The disease of "modern progress" ill brooks any hint of its failure. But prophecy is a light and a lesson. The great world-movement of history is planetary motion. "It returneth again according to its circuit." The End-Time will renew the Old-Time, though under new conditions. "That which hath been is that which shall be, and what is done is that which shall be done, and there is no new thing under the sun!" Eccl. i: 6, 9. Empires and kingdoms must "go" that the Kingdom of Christ may "come."

Lifting his eyes, entranced, the prophet sees the two-horned Ram standing in front of the Ulai on its opposite side, the horns of unequal height, the higher nearest the stream, denoting the superiority of the Persian over the Median element in the Medo-Persian empire of Cyrus. The duality of the dynasties is merged in the unity of the empire. The Ram's motion indicates the conquest of the whole Medo-Persian succession, for two hundred years. Invincibly the Ram butts westward, toward Babylonia, Lydia, Asia Minor and Greece; northward toward Armenia, the Caspian, Bactria, Scythia; southward toward Egypt, Lybia and Ethiopia, viii: 14. A bounding goat with projecting horn, interocular, comes leaping from the West, and with unexampled speed skipping across the face of the earth, as if spurning the ground, rushes with irresistible and mad onset into the Ram, breaking his horns, casting him down, stamping upon him; no allies able to save him out of the goat's power. That "Notable Horn" is young Alexander, first king of the Græco-Macedonian empire, but twenty years of age, whose first leap at the Ram was across the Hellespont, B. C. 334, with 40,000 men, and whose rapidly-fought battles from the Granicus, 334, to Arbela, 331, thence to the banks of the Indus and the Nile, thence again to Shushan, 325, and dying at Babylon, 323, broke the horns of the Ram, cast him down, stamped on him, paid him in full for his invasion of Greece, and ended forever the Medo-Persian empire. "Notable Horn!" In the words of Napoleon, "Alexander deserved all the glory the world has given him." By such symbols the Holy Spirit foretold the fortunes of the Persian and Greek empires.

While the prophet is gazing he sees the notable horn "broken," reads therein the premature death of Alexander, and beholds the "four notable horns" rising in its place, toward the four points of the compass. They are the four kingdoms into which Alexander's empire was parted, Syria, Egypt, Macedonia and Asia Minor, viii: 8, all of which have been ruled and are now claimed by the Turk. "Out of one of them," Syria, he beholds an upstart waxing to greatness, a "Little Horn," pushing southward toward Egypt, eastward toward Persia, Media, Armenia and Babylon, and toward "the Beauty," *i. e.*, the Holy Land, viii: 9. That "Little Horn" sprung from one of the four kingdoms of Alexander's divided empire, is Antiochus Epiphanes, born B. C. 221, the eighth king of the Seleucid dynasty, usurping the Syrian throne, B. C. 175, and reigning eleven years, the Greek Antichrist, whose capital was Antioch; the brother of Cleopatra, the mother of all the Cleopatras, the tyrant and oppressor of the Jews, and called by the nickname "Epimanes," *i. e.*, "the Madman."

The vision presents to the eye of the prophet a scene of sacrilegious horror enacted in the temple-court and city of Jerusalem; an attempt to exterminate the holy people and the religion of Jehovah, and substitute for both a heathen colony and the Greek idolatry; the first attempt ever made in history to force a people to forswear their faith, or suffer death for disobedience. The God-defying insolence of the Horn was, till then, without a parallel. Other conquerors of the Jews had, at least, respected their religion. This one had no respect. Nebuchadnezzar, Cyrus and Alexander, paid homage to "God, Most High," and bowed before the holy oracles. This one pays none, and tramples the "Truth" to the ground.

With self-magnifying egotism he invades the Holy Land, and raging in hate against the Holy Covenant, takes the Holy City, assails the "Host of Heaven," *i. e.*, Israel, casts a part to the ground, "stamping" on them, among them the "Stars" of the host, the princes and priests of Israel. Even to the "Prince of the Host," *i. e.*, the High Priest, Onias III., he opposes himself, "doing great things," taking away the "Daily," the stated morning and evening service at the altar; polluting and degrading (not "destroying") the place of the sanctuary, erecting a pagan altar upon the Altar of Burnt-Offering, sacrificing a swine upon it, sprinkling with swine's broth the holy places, and setting up beside the altar a statue of Jupiter. Yet more, in his madness, he continues his work, introducing the youth of Jerusalem to the Greek gymnasia, customs and games established for their recreation, weaning them away from their religion, supplanting the practice of virtue by the lewd sports of Hercules, the Feast of Tabernacles by the festival of Bacchus, and teaching them to undo, by artificial means, the token of their national distinction. With those who "forsake the Holy Covenant," xi: 30, he enters into a new "covenant," 1 Macc. i: 11, 12, putting up the high-priesthood for sale to the highest bidder, farming out the mitre, breast-plate and robes of Aaron's office for 440 talents of gold as annual payment for the dignity; the apostate bidder selling the golden altar of incense, the golden candlestick, the table of shewbread and the sacred vessels, in the market of Tyre, for 1,800 talents, to pay Antiochus the annual sums demanded. To crown the infamy, he winks at the assassination of the lawful High Priest, Onias III., because protesting against the sacrilege, defaces, by obscene pictures, and casts to the ground, the Pentateuch and the Prophets, the authoritative law and sanction of the Hebrew worship, forbids Jewish rites, orders the erection of idol altars in every town and city, massacres 80,000 of God's saints in his first attack, 20,000 at the second, devastates the city, and with abominations surpassing those of Manasseh, and lust beyond that of a Sardanapalus, defiles the place, the holiest known on earth since the beginning of the creation of God. Thus does he " do." The full story of his deeds, here recited only in part, is found in the books of the Maccabees—a picture of horror symbolized in outline, in the vision here given to the prophet. Using the language of the Levitical law, in Num. iv: 23; viii: 24; in which the word " Host " is employed to denote the Hebrew sacrificial " Service," the prophet states that " a host was given " to the tyrant, *i. e.*, allowed to him by God's permission, because of Israel's transgression in forsaking God's covenant—a heathen "Service" ministered by heathen priests within the temple-court, in place of the daily offering, and that the Horn " practiced and prospered " in unhindered activity—the Jewish worship abolished, the sanctuary and Jewish Host trodden under foot; apostasy installed in the form of an abomination in the very precincts of the temple. To the soul of the prophet the vision was appalling, viii: 10-12.

IV. The Angelic Dialogue. While the prophet is gazing at the horror, suddenly he hears " One Holy One speaking, and another Holy One saying to that Certain Holy One," as yet unknown—" Palmoni," or " Peloni Almoni," that " Some One or Other," a " Wonderful Numberer "—" How long the vision of the Daily, and the transgression of the desolation, giving both the sanctuary and the Host to be trodden down?" viii. 13. We have here a glimpse into the angel world, which rationalists use to discredit the Book of Daniel as a spurious production, deriving its angelology from the Zoroastrian system with its "Amshaspands," or fairy beings, analogous to the Sylphs and Fauns of the Greeks! Nothing is more false. The Biblical angels are the " Holy Watchers," Dan. iv: 13, 17-23; vi: 22; whose vigils remain unbroken, the sleepless sentinels of heaven who take interest in all the affairs of the earth, among whom are Gabriel, vi: 22; viii: 16; ix: 21; x: 10, 14, 18, 21; xi: 1; and Michael, x: 13, 21; xii: 1; and over whom the Unslumbering Keeper of Israel presides, Ps. cxxi: 4. Daniel hears Gabriel asking Palmoni " how long " the horror shall be. Palmoni answering " Until 2,300 evening-morning; and the Sanctuary shall be justified," *i. e.*, **restored to its lawful use,** since so long as profaned it lay,

CHAPTER VIII.—EASTERN QUESTION.

under condemnation. The dialogue is evidently meant for the benefit of Daniel, to whom the vision was given. If the "2,300 evening-morning" are whole days, they are six years, four months, twenty days; if half days, the recurring times for morning and evening sacrifice, they are three years, two months, ten days, the time of the Maccabean tribulation, B. C. 168-165, at whose close the sanctuary was "cleansed" by Judas Maccabaeus, and the Jewish worship restored — the death-year of Antiochus being 164.

V. The Apparition of a Man. The holy prophet is still perplexed. He betrays his confusion and anxiety to understand the "meaning" of what he had seen. It was not enough that the duration of the horror should be determined. He would know the import of the scene itself. "I, even I, Daniel, would know the meaning." The Lord regards his distress and commands immmediate relief. "That Certain Saint," the "Holy Some One or Other," " Palmoni," as yet unseen, utters his voice. With a tone of superior authority and dignity, such as belongs only to One made higher than the angels, He bids the questioner in the dialogue make known the "meaning" to Daniel. If we really desire to know the "meaning" of God's revelation, God will grant our desire. From between the banks of the Ulai, where hovered the form mysterious above its waters, the order comes, "Gabriel, make this one to understand the vision." Holy angels are admitted to the secrets of God, and reveal to mortals His mind. The prophet, affected by his environment, and overborne by more than magnetic power, and weak as a child, passes into a "deep sleep." The angel "touches" him, imparting strength to stand erect and receive the revelation. Gabriel bespeaks his closest attention, since the vision relates to the "Time of the End" and God's "Last Indignation" against Israel, for their apostasy from His holy covenant. "Understand, O son of man, for at the Time of the End the Vision shall be." "Behold, I will make thee know what shall be in the Last End of the Indignation, for at the appointed time is the End," viii: 19. Solemn the thought, that nothing happens by chance, not merely by man's free will, but that all history eventuates at the "time appointed" of God. The angel proceeds to interpret.

VI. *The Interpretation of the Vision.* Much of this has already been anticipated. First of all, the "Ram" and the "Goat" represent the kingdoms and kings of the Medo-Persian and Graeco-Macedonian empires. These are the second and third, and correspond to the Silver and Brass of the Colossus in chap. ii., and to the Bear and Leopard (or Panther) in chap. vii.; viii: 20, 21. Here we have Divine authority against the rationalism that substitutes wrong empires in the sacred text. We know that the first empire in the Colossus is that of Babylon, ii: 38, and the second and third those of Medo-Persia and Graecia, or Javan, viii: 20, 21. The fourth, therefore can only be the Roman, since all history shows that it succeeded Alexander's broken empire, and the Revelation by John demonstrates the fact that the ten-horned Beast in John is the Roman Beast, identical with the ten-horned beast in Daniel. The Median empire was destroyed by Cyrus in B. C. 549, or eleven years before his capture of Babylon, and to the empire of Macedon, founded by Philip, Alexander added his conquest of Graecia. It is absolutely certain, therefore, that the fourth empire, in chap. ii. and vii., is the Roman. Of the four kingdoms of Alexander's parted empire, and the rise of Antiochus Epiphanes "out of one of them," sufficient has been said. The angel adds that none of them should equal in strength that of Alexander; "not in his power," viii: 22. Gabriel's interpretation of the rise and career of Antiochus is full of political significance, and might be applied, with perfect justice, in most respects, to the rise and career of the Moslem power, and in fact to the international politics of Europe. The Horn, as to his personal aspect, will be "a king of fierce countenance," viii: 23, a cruel-faced man, yet more, a master in diplomacy, quick to detect and skillful to frame and understand dark sentences," viii: 23, *i. e.*, a man of double-dealing, expert in obscure and ambiguous propositions, a political intriguer, intelligent as a Macchiavelli, a Talleyrand, a Sultan, a Vienna, London, or Berlin congress, dealing deceitfully, uttering lies while pretending to speak truth, entering into covenants and treaties—not purposing to keep them, promising but not performing. A power among "Powers," he will be "mighty," yet "not by his own power," viii: 24, but by the help of other powers, maintaining him, aiding him, and entering into compact with him—the mode by which Antiochus arose, acquired and kept his throne, xi: 21-23, 27. By such means, he should wax to greatness, and persecute God's saints, leagued with apostates from the true faith, men who should espouse his own in order to save their lives. "He shall destroy wonderfully," the world astonished at his cruelty—80,000 massacred during his first assault upon the Holy People at Jerusalem, B. C. 170; 22,000 during his second, B. C. 168—men and women "of whom the world was not worthy," Heb. xi: 35-40; 1 Macc. vii: 1-20. Practicing and prospering he should "destroy the mighty and the Holy People," viii: 24, by means of his policy, viii: 25. Affecting to favor peace, while preparing for war, he should "cause craft to prosper in his hand," *i. e.*, his own intrigues to be successful, viii: 25. "by peace destroy many," creating confidence in his promises, then betraying his victims, and thus possess and hold, as did Antiochus, Palestine, Egypt, Macedonia, Syria and Asia Minor, "for an appointed time," viii: 19. His self-exaltation and deification will be not a momentary passion but an abiding conviction "in his heart," viii: 25, leading him to stand up defiantly even against the "Prince of princes," viii: 25, the God of Israel. Nevertheless he "shall be broken," not as other horns are broken in the day of battle, but "without hand," viii: 25, by some mysterious judgment of God. So did it happen to the tyrant who, by the strange judgment of God, was struck with loathsome and mortal disease while returning from the plunder of an ancient temple, and died at Tabae in Persia, B. C. 164. The awful vision and its interpretation, Gabriel certifies to Daniel as "true," commanding him to "shut up the vision," because its time of fulfilment was yet "many days," *i. e.*, years, viii: 27.

Five different expressions are used to mark the time when

the vision would be accomplished. (1) The "Time of the End," viii: 17; (2) the "Last End of the Indignation" of God against Israel's apostasy, viii: 19; (3) the "Latter Time of their Kingdoms," *i. e.*, the time of the decline of the four kingdoms into which Alexander's empire was divided, viii: 23; (4) "when the transgressors are come to the full," *i. e.*, when Israel's apostates have filled up the measure of their sins; (5) "for many days," *i. e.*, many years after the date of the vision, viii: 26. By the "Time of the End" is not meant the end of time, nor the end of the world, but the closing days of a period of "many days," *i. e.*, years preceding; a long time elapsing between the giving of the vision and its fulfillment. Here is proof conclusive that the prophecy was not written in Maccabean times, by a Maccabean Jew, but long years previously. xii: 4; vii: 1; xi: 21. The phrase "Time of the End" is a technical expression in prophecy, indefinite and general in itself, including (1) a near horizon of fulfillment, and (2) a horizon more remote, as in all typical prophecy. Here, it denotes, first of all, the "2,300 evening-morning" at the close of the third empire in its four-parted state, "the latter times of the four kingdoms," when the Jewish apostasy would come to its height in pre-Christian times—"many days," *i. e.*, 370 years after the date of the vision. History has proved the truth of the prediction. On the other hand, the "Indignation" is a technical term in prophecy, denoting God's judicial wrath against Israel for their transgression of His covenant, and the "Last End of the Indignation" that final stroke of punishment on all apostates from the covenant immediately preceding the final deliverance of the Jews, Deut. xxxii: 35-43, and of which the previous strokes, Isa. x: 23; xxviii: 23; and the Roman destruction of Jerusalem, Rom. ix: 28, are types. It is the period of the "Great Tribulation," Dan. xii: 1; Matt. xxiv: 21; Rev. vii: 14; xiii: 5. It is clear, therefore, that not only was the period B. C. 168-165 not the "Last End of the Indignation," since the Jews "filled up the measure" of their fathers' sins by crucifying Christ, Matt. xxiii: 32, and the "Indignation" again fell upon their city and upon themselves, but that, once more, in the far "Time of the End," it will fall upon them in the last crisis of their history, vii: 26; ix: 27; x: 14; xi: 40-45; xii: 1, 7, 9. Therefore the "meaning" of the prophecy is not limited to the times of Antiochus, but looks to the close of the last 1,260 days of the Horn in chap. vii. In this sense, again, the vision is "for many days." Every child of Abraham knows the "meaning" of the great phrase "the Time of the End." It is the time of the cessation of Israel's last suffering and unbelief, and their enjoyment of the Kingdom when Messiah comes. To that the eyes of Daniel were directed, as were those of Moses and dying Jacob—a goal the desire of all the patriarchs, the transport of the prophets, and the expectation of all the ancient people of God.

Modern false criticism has labored hard to identify the two "Little Horns" of chap. vii. and viii. in order to arrest the scope of Daniel's predictions at B. C. 164, and so deny the Messianic character of the book, and its eschatological value. Vain effort has been made to equate the 1,150 days of Antiochus with the 1,260 days of the Antichrist, and to insert an independent "Median Kingdom" between the fall of Babylon and the alleged rise of the Persian under Darius Hystaspes. By this means the second empire becomes the "Median," the third the Persian, and the fourth that of Alexander and his successors! This is done because of the "Similarities" that exist between the two Horns. These are the invasion of the Holy Land by both, the persecution of the Jews, the profanation of the Temple, a defined career for both, an egotistic, self-magnifying and self-deifying character for both, and a tragic end. But the "Differences" between the Horns are so great, the identification becomes impossible. The Horn in chap. viii. rises out of one of four kingdoms into which the third empire was broken in pre-Christian times, persecutes during 2,300 evening-mornings, and dies at Tabae, in Persia, B. C. 164. The Horn in chap. vii. rises among ten kingdoms into which the fourth empire is divided, plucks up three, and persecutes during 1,260 days, next preceding its destruction at the Second Coming of Christ. One expires at the close of the forty-fifth of

Daniel's seventy weeks, ix: 24, the other expires at the close of the seventieth week, ix: 27; vii: 26; xii: 7. Other points of similarity and difference it is needless to mention. The "Similarities" are as undeniable as are the "Differences," and as necessary, too. For this reason, Paul gives the title "Man of Sin"—"Aner Hamartolos" (Sept.)—which the martyrs of the law gave to Antiochus, to the future Antichrist himself, and paints the last in the colors of the first, but with features also different from the first. The Horns are morally one, historically two. One is past, the other is to come.

The deep ground of the "Similarities" lies in the fact that the Ages and Ends are all prearrranged in the counsel of God, each a mirror in which the other is seen, and that the World-Power is an organic growth of essentially the same nature in every age, and producing essentially the same characters at the end of each age, only in higher development. It lies in the fact that a law of degeneration runs parallel with a law of improvement, evil ever waxing to its height, coming into closer and deadlier antagonism with the good that seeks to restrain and hem it in. The more energetic the forces of good, the more powerful and persistent the aroused and excited forces of evil, and but for the intervention of God, the evil overcoming finally the good. Sharper, and deeper, and wider becomes the conflict. Wholly by the supernatural power of God is the life of His Kingdom maintained. Its supremacy is not due to human agencies. Civilization is not grace. Ethics, better laws, science, sociology, never eradicate sin, bind Satan, or remove the material objects that tempt men and nations to aim at self-aggrandizement regardless of justice, truth, humanity and liberty, and the equal rights of the weak and oppressed. The moral wickedness of the World-Power in its social, civil, political and international relations, its lust after wealth and supremacy, its opposition to the spirit and the truth of God, and its alienation from righteousness, precipitate the last struggle between evil and good, and make the dissolution and the "End of the Age" a necessity, in order to save the Kingdom of God. And with the "Time of the End," the old personalities reappear, according to an ever unerring law of history and of nature, like producing like, deepening opposition to God and His Kingdom here, intenser devotion there, the world-kingdoms ever more deaf to the appeal of the people of God. And the nearer the "End" of any dispensation, age, or period, to the "Last End," the more "Similar" to the last Antichrist appears the one that preceded him—Belshazzar pointing to Haman, Haman to Antiochus, Antiochus to Antichrist. Such is the law of development along the ages, and such the grounds of the "Similarities" between the two Horns. Only with the ruin of the last, and of all Gentile politics and powers, come Israel's redemption and the Kingdom of Christ in victory "underneath all heavens."

This vision was given to unveil the future of the Jewish people subsequent to their return from Babylonish exile, to warn apostates and prepare and comfort the faithful in view of the tribulation to come upon them. It is a signal proof of the fidelity, care and compassion of God. Though severe, yet the tribulation should be short, and the outcome as glorious as the conflict was painful. In any case, "the righteous are in the hands of God," and "their blood is precious in His sight." The vision is elaborated in chap. xi., where the several campaigns of the Syrian tyrant are exhibited and the grand resistance of the Maccabean heroes is immortalized: a resistance in behalf of the "Truth" and "Covenant" of God, which, with a perfect knowledge of their history, fired the soul of Paul to re-immortalize their deeds, and celebrate their faith as worthy to stand beside the faith of an Abel, Enoch, and Noah, an Abraham and all the patriarchs, a Moses, Joshua and all the Judges, supported alone by the promises of God, and cheered by the hope of the resurrection from the dead. But for this prophecy, the history might have been otherwise. It shows what a power the hope of Messiah's Second Coming had even with Old Testament saints. And how the example of the Maccabees inspired New Testament believers to witness a good confession, "looking unto Jesus," the words of Paul suffice to show. They are set forth as an example for us. "They, without us, are not made perfect."

"The earliest attempt to interpret the seventy weeks was in Maccabean times. Ignorantly, the Two Little Horns and the prince that shall come were identified, and a perverted reckoning was accepted by the Alexandrian amenders of the Septuagint. Both the reckoning and the Septuagint were repelled by the post-Maccabean Palestinian Jews and by the Christian Church which adopted the text of Theodotion. Our Lord's use of the expression, 'abomination of desolation,' Matt. xxiv: 15, applying it to future times beyond His own day, proves that He interpreted Dan. ix: 26, 27, as a double prophecy, pointing first to the destruction of Jerusalem, and next to the 70th week that closes the Times of the Gentiles. His own prophecy thereby became a double one, and for this reason the admonition is given, 'Let him that readeth understand.' Clearly, His mind was resting on all the places in Daniel where the expression, 'abomination of desolation,' is used, or the idea is given, viz., Dan. ix: 27; xi: 31; xii: 11; the times of Antiochus being regarded as typical of the last times. Here is seen that law of delay in prophecy and history by which the end of one age becomes the type of another."—Fraidi.

Chapter VI.

DANIEL, CHAPTER IX.—THE SEVENTY WEEKS.

Chapter IX. affords a fourth and signal confirmation of our thesis, viz., that the Kingdom of Christ can never come to victory over all the earth, till the Coming of the Son of Man in the clouds of heaven. The great prediction, here, is the answer to a prayer of the prophet, and is found in the last four verses of the chapter, ix: 24-27. The angel speaks in plain and obvious language, although sometimes of difficult construction, owing to its brief and lapidary style, piling clause upon clause, and even of various interpretation. The first necessity is that of a good translation, King James' version being both obscure and defective, the Revised Version itself not without fault. Twenty different events are here foretold, in four verses, extending over the Times of the Gentiles, and relating entirely to Jewish affairs. Among these are the Return of the Jews from exile under the edict of Cyrus, the Building of the Second Temple and the City in times of distress; the First Coming of Christ, His Crucifixion, the Destruction of the Rebuilt Temple and City, and subjection of the land and people to war and desolations down to the end of Gentile times. Still further, the coming of the Antichrist is again predicted as that of "a prince, *the one* that shall come," (alluding to chap. vii: 8,) a Desolator, on wing of abomination, invading the Holy Land, having previously enacted a covenant, for a Week of Seven Years, with the masses of the Jewish people while in their unbelief, granting the practice of their ancient worship for financial consideration, as did Antiochus, and as matter of political necessity; then, in the middle of the "Week," breaking his covenant by causing "oblation and sacrifice" to cease, and inaugurating the

Great Tribulation. Finally, his end is announced as "in the flood," i. e., in the military overflowing of the Holy City, and under the outpoured vials of the wrath of God. Everywhere in the Scriptures a military invasion is compared to the rising of a flood advancing on the land. Still, again, the angel predicts that, so far from the withdrawal of the divine mercy from the seed of Abraham, the Lord will crown their last struggle with a sixfold blessing, the sum to them of all salvation. Six great events shall occur, viz., (1) the finishing of Israel's national apostasy, called "*the* transgression, or breach of God's covenant; (2) the cessation or end of their "sins;" (3) the covering of their "iniquity;" (4) the introduction of enduring "righteousness;" (5) the sealing or verification of "prophecy and vision" concerning them, and (6) the consecration of a new "Holy of Holies," or Sanctuary, unto God. In short, Israel will never more be apostate from God, but pardoned, renewed and restored, will serve Him in "newness of the spirit and not in the oldness of the letter," nor even wander from His commandments. Reconciled to God by atoning blood and sanctified by the Holy Spirit, they shall be His people, He their God. The whole prediction is given under the terms of a definite chronological scheme of definite periods of time, with their included intervals, stretching from Daniel's day to the Second Coming of Christ.

I. As to the Date of the Prophecy. It was "in the first year of Darius, the son of Ahashuerus of the seed of the Medes, ix: 1, who was "made king," by Cyrus, "over the realm of the Chaldeans," ix: 1, 2, and from whom he "received (not "took") the kingdom" when Babylon fell. No exegete denies the difficulties of the problem here presented, and the Higher Criticism has made the most of them, in disparagement of Daniel's book. Even Professor Sayce, imagining that the monuments have told us all they have to tell upon the question, has concluded that a stupendous error is here, and that the supposed Maccabean writer of the book has "reflected" the times of Darius Hystaspes into the times of Cyrus, and Farrar with a keen zest for anything that tends to make Daniel a myth, and his book a nursery-tale, leaps at the unguarded concession. Scholars and archaeologists, of equal authority with Sayce, earnestly dispute his conclusions. It is refreshing to hear a life-long student of such problems as the one here presented, Professor Hommel, say this present year, "I see signs of the approach of a new era in which men will be able to brush aside the cobweb theories of the so-called "Higher Critics," and leaving such now old-fashioned errors behind them, attain to a clearer perception of the real facts." What we need is more "Fresh Light from the Monuments," and a better knowledge of ancient history. This much is certain, that it was the custom of Oriental kings, Egyptian, Assyrian, Babylonian and Persian, to associate with themselves a co-regent, and of history to date the reign of the associate, not from the date of his *sole* reign, but from that of his *co-regency*, and to honor the associate with the title of "king." In the words of Beswick, "The reigns of the kings were counted from the date of co-regency, so that the total length of a dynasty is greater than the actual length would be by counting the sole reign of each. The associate became the heir apparent, and was henceforth regarded as king and successor to the throne." Thus Daniel calls Nebu hadnezzar "king" before his father's death, and Belshazzar "king" before the death of Nabonnaid. What he teaches as to Darius the Mede is that Cyrus, having captured Babylon, and being king of Babylon as well as of Persia, delegated the rule of Babylon to Darius the Mede, he Cyrus remaining in the field to pursue his conquests. Thus B. C. 538 was the "first year of Darius, the son of Ahashuerus, of the seed of the Medes." With a masterly hand, Lenormant, Düsterwald, Unger, and many others have defended the verity of Daniels statements. The objection that "Darius the Mede" is, by this name, unknown to history and to the monuments, is absolutely worthless, since ancient history omits, in various authors, the names of many kings whose reigns were brief, and the names of Abraham, Pul, and Sargon, were unknown to the monuments till recent excavations. Equally vain is the objection that Darius and Ahashuerus are not Median, but Persian names. It is set aside completely by the facts (1) of the common origin and affinities of the Medes and Persians, and of their languages, their contiguity and intercourse, the use of the same words and names under different forms, and the plurality of royal titles used as proper names and applied to different persons; (2) the fact that both Cyrus and Xerxes were called Ahashuerus, a name derived from the old Persian "Kshayarsha," which is the Median "Uvakshatra," Persianized in form into "Kshayarsha," Hebraized into "Ahashverosh," Graecized into "Kyaxares," and Latinized into "Assuerus;" (3) the fact that Darius, both a title and proper name, is the Median "Dareh," a "holder" or "actual ruler," its old Persian equivalent "Daravesh," its Hebrew form "Darjavesh," or Darius, its Greek "Dareios." Again, in the words of Rawlinson, "The language of the Persians was almost identical with that of the Medes. The remnant left us, of Median speech, bears out the statement that substantially one and the same tongue was spoken by both people. Many Median names are absolutely identical with Persian. Others are merely variants. Kyaxares (Cyaxares) is the Grecian form of the Median Uvakshatara." (4) The fact that notwithstanding all criticism, Xenophon's account is still trustworthy, and that Astyages the Mede was the Ahashuerus in Dan. ix: 1, his son Cyaxares II., no other than the Median Daravesh, to whom Cyrus, as a stroke of policy, committed the rule over Babylon, in lieu of the overthrow of the Median empire, the Median and Persian dynasties now united in one; (5) that the temporary appointment of Gobryas, the general of Cyrus who entered Babylon, as governor of the city, in no way conflicts with this; (6) that the intermarriage of the royal houses confirms it, and (7) that the statements of Daniel, so long familiar with all the details of Median, Persian and Babylonian history, are not to be discredited by any haste, rashness, ignorance or speculations of modern critics, at whose blunders in deciphering many inscriptions, and at whose conclusions, Daniel, were he alive, could only smile. "Darius the Mede" is as historical as Daniel himself, and the date of the prophecy is 538 B.C. Time will solve whatever difficulties attach to the discussion of the question.

II. As to the Place of the Prophecy. That it was Babylon is clear from the fact that the exiles had not yet been released from captivity, that in this year, under Darius, Daniel was thrown into the Lion's Den, and that the whole prayer of the prophet assumes his presence in the heathen capital on the banks of the Euphrates, pleading for the restoration.

III. As to the Occasion of the Prophecy. It was the fact (1) that Babylon had fallen, (2) that 68 of the 70 years of the captivity had expired, (3) that Daniel had betaken himself " by prayer and supplications with fasting and sackcloth," ix: 3, to plead with God, if so be that he might *advance* the hour of Israel's deliverance, and not delay their release, and (4) that, although he "understood," from Jeremiah and the sacred books, "the number of the years the Lord would accomplish," even 70, "in the desolations of Jerusalem," ix: 2, yet, peradventure, the time might be conditional in God's purpose, and the Lord, full of mercy, might shorten it just a little, and now, even now, end the captivity; all the more since Babylon had already fallen! He knew well the enormity of Israel's transgression, for he had the Pentateuch before him, and had read "the curse, and the oath written in the Law of Moses," ix: 11, 13. He had the prophets before him, the whole extant canon of the Old Testament, "Hassepharim," the "Biblia," or "Books," and saw the mighty promises of mercy and love even to a sinful people not forsaken, ix: 2. He was himself a writer of Holy Scripture, vii: 1; viii: 26; x: 21; xii: 4, 9; Matth. xxiv: 15; a deep "searcher" of the Word of God, 1 Pet. i: 10-12; 2 Pet. i: 19-24; and if any had a claim on the ear of God, it was he. Therefore did he plead. In pressing his suit he confesses the crimes of the whole nation of Israel from the day of its birth, and pleads with his mouth in the dust—the crimes of "Judah," "Jerusalem," "all Israel near and far," their "kings, princes, judges, and fathers," the nation God had delivered "out of the land of Egypt," and implores "forgiveness and mercy" for the sanctuary, city and people, even "the People of the Saints of the Most High," " Thy City Jerusalem," " Thy Sanctuary," " Thy People," the whole organized nationality of Israel, as one body, now broken and scattered, and made a "reproach." And the burden of his prayer is this, that God will end Israel's apostasy, i. e., the great "transgression," pardon their "sins," and cover their "iniquity," closing their "rebellion" against Him, and make haste to restore them, and rebuild Jerusalem, and "do," and "defer not" for His own name's sake, ix: 3, 19. He pleads with a "covenant-keeping God," for those who had broken the covenant, ix: 4, 11, 13.

IV. The Answer to the Prayer, the Prophecy Itself. It is in the last four verses of the chapter. It came at 3 o'clock in the afternoon, or "about the time of the evening oblation," ix: 20, 21. At such a time "Gabriel," whom he "had seen in the vision," in chap. viii., "being caused to fly swiftly," sped his way through the constellations, entered the earth's atmosphere, and alighted near Daniel, with a message from the throne of God, and "touched" him. He accosts him: "O Daniel, greatly beloved!"—man filled with holy desires after the kingdom of God—" I am now come to give thee skill and understanding." " The order came to me, at the beginning of thy supplication, and I am come to show thee, for thou art greatly beloved. Therefore understand the matter," i. e., the import of my appearing here, "and consider the vision," ix: 23.

V. 24, "Seventy sevens (of years) are decreed upon thy people (the Jews) and upon thy holy city (Jerusalem) to finish the transgression, and to make an end of sins, and to cover over iniquity, and to cause everlasting righteousness to come, and to seal (verify) vision and prophet, and to anoint a holy of holies."

V. 25, " Know, therefore, and discriminate; from the issuing of a word to restore, and to build Jerusalem, unto Prince Messiah, shall be Seven Sevens (of years), and Sixty and Two Sevens; she shall be restored and built as to street and rampart (street and wall), and in distress shall be the times."

V. 26, "And after those Sixty-two Sevens, Messiah shall be cut off, and there is not to Him (no guilt and no just judgment); and the city and the sanctuary shall they destroy, viz., the people of a prince, the one that is to come, and his end shall be in the overflowing; and unto that end shall be war, a decreed (measure or limit) of desolations."

V. 27, "And he (the prince to come) shall cause to prevail a covenant for the many, One Seven; and he shall cause sacrifice and offering to cease, Half of that Seven; and upon wing of abominations (he shall come) a desolator, even until the consummation and (until) that which is decreed (God's wrath) is poured upon the one desolating."

This marvelous prophecy and answer to the prayer covers every point made in the prayer itself, as to the Jew, Jerusalem, the Sanctuary, unveiling the whole future of Israel down to the Destruction of the last Antichrist. The restoration of the Jews pursuant to "a word" or order, issued by Cyrus, B.C. 536, the Building of the Second Temple, and the City, the First Advent of Messiah, His Rejection by the Jewish Nation, and because of it, the Destruction of Jerusalem and the Temple by Titus, and the Times of the Gentiles following, full of war and desolations; all these, with the conversion of the Jews to Christ, a pardoned and righteous nation, apostate no more, but serving God in their own land, in a new sanctuary, all are here predicted in the clearest manner. That all this mercy to Israel is grounded in the atoning work of the Messiah at His first advent, and that in Him personally—that "Holy Thing" born of the virgin, Himself a "Temple," "Altar," and "Sacrifice" anointed by the Spirit—and that in each believer "a temple of the Holy Ghost," and in the whole church collectively, a "spiritual house," the prophecy has been fulfilled, is beyond all question. As little to be questioned is the fact that the six-fold blessings promised to Israel, in verse 24, as the outcome of the 70 weeks with their intervals, are applied, in the New Testament, to the literal seed of Abraham according to the flesh—Israel in the Old Testament sense—and eminently so in Paul's epistles and in John's Apocalypse. There is, therefore, a glorious future for the ancient people of God. That the Jews will be gathered again to their own land, be born of the Spirit, converted to Christ, and established as a holy nation, at the second coming of Christ, and be as "life from the dead" to the nations, is as certain as the word of God is true. The wealth of the proof is amazing. We read it in Isa. lix: 21, 22; Rom. xi: 25; Acts iii: 19-21 (R. V.) Isa. lxvi: 5-16; xi: 4; 2 Thess. ii: 2, 8; Dan. vii: 21-27; xi: 40-45; xii: 1-3, 7; Mic. iv: 8; Ezek. xxxvi: 24-28; xxxvii: 1-28; Jer. xxxi: 33-40; Zeph. iii: 8-20; Zech. xii: 2-14; xiii: 1; xiv: 2-11; 16-21; Matth. xxiii: 39; xxiv: 25-28, 29-31; Rev. vii: 4-8; xiv: 1-5; xx: 9; and scores of other texts too numerous to enumerate. And "the strength of Israel will not lie," Deut. xxxii: 36-43; xxxiii: 26-29. The six-fold blessing foretold in Dan. ix: 24, is simply the sum of the whole Messianic hope of Israel, to be fulfilled in them, literally in the Time of the End. The Israel, Jacob, Judah, Jerusalem, Zion, of Old Testament prophesy, are not the "Church," but the literal Israel, Jacob, Judah, Jerusalem, Zion, of Old Testament history and of the Four Gospels, the Acts, the Epistles, and the Apocalypse.

V. The Interpretation of the "Seventy Weeks." The understanding of the weeks is indispensable to every student of prophecy. Neither our Lord's Olivet Discourse concerning the End, nor Paul's Thessalonian letters concerning the Tribulation and the Antichrist, nor John's Apocalypse can be understood without them. It is no objection that men have failed, so long, to understand them. They were given to be understood; "Know, therefore, and understand," ix: 25. The angel declares that in the "Time of the End" they shall be understood, xii: 4. From the bosom of the prophecy a sun-burst of surpassing brilliancy will break forth, as Israel's deliverance draws nigh. The book is not an undecipherable hieroglyph, a Sphinx whose riddle is insoluble, least of all an apocalypse whose apocalypse is unapocalypsed, but an effulgent unveiling of the future, whose light is obscured only by our ignorance.

The "Seventy Sevens," or "Weeks," selected from the whole course of time, as weeks relating entirely to Jewish affairs, are Weeks of Years, each seventh part being literally one year. As seven days constitute a week, so seven years constitute the prophetic week. All the weeks are of equal chronological measurement, each week consisting of seven literal years, or

2,520 literal days. The sum is, therefore, 490 years. These weeks are distributed into three divisions of 7,62,1, that is, into 49,434,7, years respectively, and, excepting Babylon, span the whole height of the Colossus in ch. ii., and the lives of the Four Beasts in ch. vii., i. e., from B. C. 536, to the second coming of Christ. They cover the whole subsequent period of Israel's national prostration under the Gentiles. They are said to be " Nihtak," ix: 24, "severed off," "decided," "determined," along the course of Gentile time, and given entirely to Jewish affairs. Two *Intervals* come in between them, one unseen and undefined between the third and fourth weeks, the other stated as between the 69th and 70th weeks. They are, therefore, not to be counted unbrokenly. The first group of seven falls into two groups of three and four, i. e., of twenty-one years and twenty-eight years, as the history of the time shows. The true starting-point of the 70 weeks is the Edict of Cyrus, B. C. 536, or "going forth of a word to restore and build Jerusalem," Dan. ix: 25; Ezra i: 1, 4; 2 Chron. xxxvi: 22, 23; Isa. xliv: 26-28; xlv: 1-6. The beginning of the 21 years was that Edict, their end the completion of the Second Temple, in 6th Darius Hystaspes, B. C. 515. Then came the first Interval of 57 years. The beginning of the 28 years, following this Interval, was the commission of Ezra, in 7th Artaxerxes, B. C. 458, their end the close of Nehemiah's activity or end of the Restoration-period, B. C. 430, in 34th Artaxerxes, Ezra vi: 15; vii: 1-7; Neh. xiii: 6, 7; v: 14. The Interval of 57 years consists, therefore, of the following periods, (1) from 6th Darius to the end of his reign, 515-485, a period of thirty years. (2) The entire reign of Xerxes the Great, 485-464, a period of 21 years. (3) Six years of the reign of Artaxerxes, 464-458, a period of six years ending with 7th Artaxerxes, Ezra vii: 1-7.*

*That the *Jews* will build their Temple again is certain. Also revive their bloody sacrifices. (1) Isaiah predicts it. Isa. lxvi: 1-4. (2) Gabriel says it will be the result of a covenant. (3) Jesus Christ predicts the "abomination," Matt. xxiv: 15, "of which that in Dan. viii: 13, 14; xi: 31, was the type. (4) Paul says the "Man of Sin"

The sum of this Interval, 30+21+6 is 57 years. The Restoration-period was a Double-period, the total secular time being 106 years (21·57+28=106) of which the 21 and 28 were the first "Seven Weeks," or 49 years, assigned of God for Restoration-work, the uncounted Interval being one of open apostasy from His covenant. The diagram of the time stands thus:

THE RESTORATION PERIOD.

$$\frac{B.C.}{536} \quad \frac{3}{21} \quad \frac{B.C.}{515} \quad \left(\frac{\text{Interval}}{57 \text{ yrs.}}\right) \quad \frac{B.C.}{458} \quad \frac{4}{28} \quad \frac{B.C.}{430}$$

the first section, that of the "Days of Zerubbabel," Neh. v: 49: the last that of the "Days of Ezra the Scribe and Nehemiah," Neh. v: 26, 47.*

The rest of the interpretation is not difficult. The 62 weeks reach from the close of the Restoration to the birth of Christ A. D. 1. These united to the seven preceding are 69 weeks, or 483 years, to which adding the 57, the result is 540, the excess of four years due to the error in our common Dionysian reckoning, the true date being B. C. 536. Thus, by the discovery that the Interval of 57 years was really concealed in the

shall sit in the "temple of God," in the time just preceding the Second Advent, the rebuilt temple at Jerusalem. 2 Thess. ii: 4. (5) John exhibits the Anti-Christ's Week, the 70th, and the building of the temple, Rev. xi: 1-3, 7, the very time given in Isa. lxvi: 1-5. (6) Daniel foretells the period of the reconstruction of converted Israel's worship, after the revived time of Israel's national repentance, faith, and Pentecostal baptism by the Spirit, Zech. xii: 10-14; xiii: 1. The true title of Isaiah, chapter lxvi., and Revelation, chapter xi., is *Scenes in Jerusalem under the Anti-Christ*. As to Ezekiel's Temple and its sacrifices, see "*The Thousand Years in Both Testaments, by Rev. Nathaniel West, pp. 424-434*. F. H. Revell, Chicago and New York."

Note. "Silently the book of Ezra passes over the time following the dedication of the second Temple, and a *gap* of more than fifty years yawns unbridged before us." Rabbi Rosenzweig, "Das Jahrhundert nach d. Bab. Exile," p. 50.

"The times of Zerubbabel are not connected with the times of Ezra, in the book of Ezra, except by the phrase "after these things,"

DANIEL'S SEVENTY WEEKS.
Dan. ix: 24-27.

The Kingdom.
The Deliverance.
— End of 70th Week.
The Resurrection.
The Second Advent. After the Sixth Vial.

70th Week End. | 3½ / 1260
— Middle of 70th Week.
3½ / 1260
— Beginning of 70th Week.

The Antichrist.

Great Interval. "And Unto the End, War." | Dan. ix: 26; Luke xxi: 24. | A.D. 1898?
Church-Period. Israel in Unbelief. Missions. War.

Destruction of City and Sanctuary. A. D. 70.
The Crucifixion. After the 62 Weeks. A. D. 33.
The First Advent. Birth of Christ. A. D. 1.
The Maccabees. 168-165.
Antiochus. 175-164.

62 Weeks. | 434 years.

Course of Empire from B. C. 536 to Second Advent.

End of the Four Weeks. End of Restoration. 430.
4 / 28
End of Interval. Beginning of the Four Weeks. 458.
57 | 57 Years' Interval.
End of First Three Weeks. Temple Finished. 515.
3 / 21
Edict of Cyrus. The Liberation. B. C. 536.

THE SEVENTIETH WEEK.
Dan. ix: 27.

Covenant with Antichrist.	3½, 1260. This first Half-Week is Unfilled, in Daniel ix: 27. Filled, in Revelation xi: 2.	The Abomination.	3½, 1260. The Great Tribulation. Filled, partly in Dan. ix: 27; vii: 25; xii: 7; and further, in Revelation xii: 6, 14; xiii: 5; xi: 3. 7.	Destruction of Antichrist.

The Antichrist's Week.
The End.

breast of the "Seven Weeks," the perplexing problem, unsolved for 2,200 years is satisfied at last, and Biblical and secular chronology brought into perfect harmony.

The second Interval lies between the 69th and 70th weeks, with two great events at its head, the Crucifixion of Christ, A. D. 30, and the Destruction of Jerusalem, A. D. 70. It is called *"Unto the End,"* Dan. ix: 26; interpreted by our Lord as meaning, "Until the Times of the Gentiles be fulfilled," Luke xxi: 24. During this period, 1,826 years of which have passed away since the legions of Titus camped on Mount Olivet, Jerusalem has been "trodden down of the Gentiles," unable to rise to her glory because of the unbelief of her sons, and the occupation of the Holy Land by a "European Concert" that gives to the Turk his power. Upon the Holy City "war and desolations" are decreed and upon the people "dispersion" till the "End" of their weary way, when, under the providence of God, yet after severe conflict, Palestine will become the asylum of the Hebrew race, reclaimed from Gentile hoofs, a land "married to the Lord," her city a "city sought out, not forsaken," her people "the redeemed of the Lord," a holy nation of which it is said, "In righteousness shalt thou be established; thou shalt be far from oppression, for thou shalt not fear; and from terror, for it shall not come nigh thee." Isa. lx: 1-22; lxi: 1-11; lxii: 1-12; liv: 1-17.

But prior to this glorious outcome, lies the "70th week." It coincides with and closes the "Times of the Gentiles." It

Ezra vii: 1, i. e., after the dedication of the Second Temple, Ezra vi: 15. But it would be ridiculous to conclude that no Interval separated these two great epochs. We know that more than 50 years flowed between them."—D'Envieu, Le Livre du Prophète Daniel, Tome II., B., p. 1454.

After patient study, I have been led to this solution of this age-long problem, and have given it in full discussion in a previous work. Reviewed widely, and accepted by all who have tested the proofs, it remains unassailed from any side. See "The Thousand Years in Both Testaments," by Rev. Nathaniel West, Pref. VII., pp. 152-161, 175-197. F. H. Revell, Chicago and New York. It has remained a secret, till now, that the Interval, here mentioned, lay concealed by the angel in the bosom of the first seven weeks.—N.W.

is the last "7 years," or "One week," in Dan. ix: 27, the Antichrist's week, the week of the " Little Horn" in ch. vii., the week of "the prince that shall come on wing of abomination," ix: 27, invading the Holy Land, and swooping like a vulture on its prey. His last campaign is given in Dan. xi: 40-45, and elaborated in Zech. xii: 2-8; xiv: 1-4, 12-15, and in Joel iii: 9-17. The week is opened by the advent of the Antichrist and his "covenant" with the Jewish masses, Dan. ix: 27, a treaty whereby the power holding Palestine will concede a peaceful *modus vivendi* with the Jews, tolerating their ancient worship, and obtaining from their magnates financial help as in the days of Antiochus. The week is divided into two equal parts, each "Half" a period of 1,260 days, or 42 months. The first "Half," unfilled in Daniel, is filled in John, Rev. xi: 3, with the preaching of the "Two Witnesses" sent to form the Jewish Christian Church of the "Time of the End" and prepare the Jews for the Second Coming of Christ. The "covenant" with the Jewish masses is broken in the middle of the week, the revived "oblation and sacrifice" being caused to cease, ix: 27, an event contemporating with the slaughter of the "Two Witnesses," Rev. xi: 2, 7. This violation is, doubtless, due to some signal event in the history of the Jews, at that time, to all appearance their conversion, and which leads the Antichrist to vent his rage against *all* Jews, believing or unbelieving, and all Christians. The second " Half " of the week is the " Great Tribulation," when the Desolator, on wing of abomination, shall devastate everything before him, occupy Jerusalem, sit in the temple, then in process of completion, Rev. ix: 1, Isa. lxvi: 1-6, claiming divine honors for himself, 2 Thess. ii: 4, persecuting "the people of the saints of the Most High" and all God's saints everywhere, vii: 25; xii: 7; Matth. xxiv: 15-28; Rev. ix: 2; xii: 6, 14, 17; xiii.*

It is the final testing for both Jews and Gentiles who believe

Note.—No "*Year-Day*" theory exists any where in Daniel. The word to Ezekiel, "Son of Man, I have given thee each day for a year," was not spoken to Daniel. His " Sevens" are not seven days put for *years*, but seven *years* of 360 days each, prophetic time—a year

in Christ, the "Great Tribulation" spoken of in Jer. xxx: 7, as that of "Jacob's trouble," in Matth. xxiv: 15-28, as that of "Christ's Elect," in Rev. vii: 14, as that out of which the election of Israel, vii: 4-8, and the election of the Gentiles, vii: 9, shall come; and in Dan. xii: 1, as that which is followed by Israel's deliverance and the resurrection of the holy dead. The close of the last 1,260 days of this week is the close of the "time, times, and dividing of a time," i. e., 3½ years, in Dan. vii: 25; xii: 7, which is signalized by the overthrow of the Antichrist at the Second Coming of the Son of Man. The same scene of the Lord's intervention is pictured in Joel iii: 16, 17; Isa. lix: 19-21; lxiii: 1-6; lxvi: 14-16; Zeph. iii: 14-20; Zech. xiv: 1-5. With these mighty events the "70th week" terminates, viz., with New-born Israel, the Second Advent, the Resurrection of the Holy Dead, the Destruction of the Antichrist, the Downfall of the Colossus and the setting up of the Kingdom of Christ in victory over all the earth. Then are fulfilled to Israel the six-fold blessings predicted in chap. ix: 24, viz., the termination of Israel's apostasy, the pardon of Israel's sins, the reconciliation of Israel to God, the introduction of enduring righteousness, the verification of all prophecy, and the consecration of a new Holy of Holies. This is the glorious goal at the " End " of Israel's long and painful way.

Here, then, in ch. ix., we have attained a view of the world framed in a chronology of the world, in connection with the Jewish race, and their relation to the empires and kingdoms of the world, which entitles Daniel to the proud distinction of being the founder of the true philosophy of history, the first writer on universal history itself. The four great conceptions of " Welt-Anschauung," " Welt-Geschichte," " Welt-Gericht," and "Welt-Chronologie," are here represented. The second, third and fourth empires, Israel's pathway full of sorrow, and Israel's end full of joy, the doom of Gentile politics and power,

for a year, and in each year a *day* for a *day*, and not a day for 360 years. The 70th Week in Daniel ix: 27 is not 2,500 *years*, but twice 1,260, or 2,520 *days*. The 1,260, or " time two times, and a half," are not 1,260 years, but 3½ years. Otherwise, the 69 Weeks would be 173,880 years! All the Weeks are commensurate.

and the kingdom of God in victory, all are here. In the most solemn manner Gabriel informs the prophet that the history of God's people courses its way through different periods of time, all determined by the immutable measurements of God; that as the road-surveyor determines his track with culvert, tunnel, curve and grade, or a landscape painter sketches his plan on the canvass, draws its lines, fixes its measurements, projects the long perspective, the gloomed defiles and shining end, so God has constructed here the way for Israel's feet to walk and reach their rest. For wisest reasons, one point, alone, is undefined, impossible by us to be determined, until we come to it, the point when the "what withholdeth" is "taken out of the way," and the 70th week begins. 2 Thess. ii: 6, 7. Still, all is "Nihtak," decreed, determined, decided of God; the 70 weeks, the 7,62, and 1, the 2,300 evening-morning, the twice 1,260 days, and, as we shall see, the 1,290 and 1,335 days, xii: 11, 12, all measured by Palmoni, the Wonderful Numberer, that Certain Holy One, whose voice came from between the banks of the Ulai, viii: 13. To "know" and "understand" the true interpretation of the 70 weeks is the first necessity of the student of Old and New Testament prophecy, and apart from which, ignorant of God's plan, he will flounder and wander in darkness, the victim of a hundred false time-reckonings, and of expectations born of enthusiasm worse than these.

With perfect confidence we may rest in this interpretation. Great diversity of opinion has existed during the last 2,200 years as to the proper reckoning, owing (1) to defective chronology and history, and (2) to the unseen gap between the third and fourth weeks. Le Long enumerates 56 different views, Graetz 107, as far as to the 15th century, and Reusch, Fraidi, and D'Envieu, have tabulated all the views of the church fathers, the middle age, and of modern times. Three different hypotheses exist as to the scope of the 70 weeks, (1) that they end with the times of Antiochus, B. C. 164, (2) with the times of Titus, A. D. 70, (3) with the Second Coming of Christ to destroy the Antichrist. The first is impossible, since our Lord declares that Daniel predicts the Roman fall of Jerusalem. The second is deficient since our Lord declares that the "abomination" will stand "in a holy place" in the time immediately preceding His Second Advent. He thereby makes Dan. ix: 26, 27, a double prophecy, looking first to the end of the Jewish age, A. D. 70, and next to the end of the Christian age, at the Advent. The third is, therefore, the only correct one. The inverted Hebrew text and construction of ix: 26, viz., "and the city and the sanctuary shall destroy the people of a prince, the one that is to come," an inversion intended to connect as closely as possible the future "prince" with the subject of the verb "confirm" in the next verse, and to show that neither Antiochus, Titus, nor Christ can be that prince, finding "his end" in the military overflowing, establishes this beyond all doubt.* The 70th week is the last Antilishes this beyond all doubt. The 70th week is the last Antichrist's week, both by prophecy itself and our Lord's own

*" After the most thorough investigation, all modern scholars are agreed that the suffix 'o' in the Hebrew 'qetstso,' Dan. ix: 26, is masculine and refers to the 'prince that shall come,' and who is the subject of the verb 'confirm,' and that '*his* end' is the correct rendering." "It refers neither to Antiochus, Christ, or Titus." *Fraidi, Die Exegese der siebzig Wochen, p. 68.* " The suffix and its noun can only be rendered '*his* end,' viz., that of the hostile prince, and at Jerusalem. The prophecy here does not refer to Antiochus, nor his times, but to the times immediately before the second advent." *Wolf, Die siebzig Wochen, p. 50.* "The suffix refers directly to its nearest antecedent in gender and number, viz., the prince to come. It does not refer to the people of the prince, nor to the city, or the sanctuary, nor to Antiochus, Christ, or Titus, but to the last Antichrist." Klieforth, *Das Buch Daniels, p. 367.* Grandly, Prof. Tiefenthal, of the College of St. Anselm, Rome, says, "Nowhere, in the New Testament, does Christ confirm a covenant only for a week. The covenant here is that of the Antichrist with the Jews. It is the common opinion that in Matth. xxiv: 15, and parallels, the Lord refers the 'abomination of desolation spoken of by Daniel the prophet, solely to the destruction of Jerusalem, by Titus. On the contrary, Daniel speaks of the 'abomination' in Dan. xi: 31, and in xii: 11, the first of these texts containing the type of the second, the time of the second that immediately before the Advent. The suffix and noun are correctly rendered '*his* end,' viz., that of the prince that shall come." *Daniel Explicatus, p. 304-5.*

teaching. The use of the definite article "*the*" in the phrase "*the* one that is to come," i. e., after the destruction of the city by Titus, points back to the " Little Horn," in ch. vii., as to a character already well-known to Daniel, and which was the object of his interest in a previous vision. The translation "his end," instead of "the end thereof," and "unto the end, war," instead of "unto the end of the war," in ix: 26, rest upon an absolutely correct text, and are now conceded by all exegetes. The sudden spring from Jerusalem's destruction to the time of the last Antichrist, by means of the inverted Hebrew construction in ch. ix: 26, is in perfect harmony with the manner of Daniel's predictions. The English rendering, "and for the overspreading of abominations he shall make it desolate," ix: 27, must at once be discarded and the correct rendering, "and upon wing of abominations he shall come, a Desolator," put in its place. The idea that by the word "wing" (kenaph) is meant the "top of the altar," or "top or extremity of the Temple," rests upon the false Septuagint rendering of the Hebrew word (kenaph) by the word "temple" (hieron) and must be rejected. What the Hebrew text foretells is that "the prince to come" shall invade the Holy Land, coming on the "wings" of his army like a vulture swooping down on his prey, himself, his army, and its military ensigns an "abomination," xi: 40-45. These corrections are vital to the understanding of the text.

While it is true that, for 2,200 years, none have seen the gap between the third and fourth weeks, yet nearly all the early church fathers saw the gap between the 69th and 70th weeks. Of this the vast majority were certain, viz., that the 70th week is the last Antichrist's week, at the "End" of Gentile times, and that the starting-point of the 70 weeks is either the "first Darius the Mede," or "first Cyrus as sole king of Babylon." So Justin, Irenaeus, Clement of Alexandria, Tertullian, Eusebius in one of his calculations, Origen, Hippolytus, Hilary, later on Polychronius, and Bruno of Asti; still later, Calvin, Oecolampadius, Bullinger, L'Empereur, Cocceius, Bervaldus, Dathe, Blayney, Uri; later still, Jungman, Koch, J. D. Michaelis, Pringle, Hauenkamp, Velthusen; yet later, Kliefoth, Keil, Koch,

Christiani, Fraidl, D'Envieu, Tiefenthal, Dornstetter, Düsterwald and many others, Briggs holding also to the Cyrus date. Farrar's distortions of the evidence, and his special pleading, only repeat, second-hand, the efforts of the Higher Criticism to limit the prophecy to the times of Antiochus. It was not till the fourth century that the Artaxerxes date, invented previously by Africanus, was fastened upon the church, viz., 20th Artaxerxes as the beginning of the 70 weeks, and a "lunar" reckoning adopted, supported by the mistranslation of the word "decreed," "determined," in ch. ix: 24, as if it meant "abbreviated," a retrogade mode of reckoning from the crucifixion of Christ, working backward on the theory that the "middle of the 70th week" means the death of Christ!! It was meant also to close the Gap between the 69th and the 70th weeks, unmindful of the fact that our Lord had opened it out so luminously in Luke xxi: 24, when interpreting the words, "and unto the end, war," in Dan. ix: 26 (R. V.), and thus to smite "Chiliasm" by removing from the Church the idea of a Great Tribulation at the end of the Gentile Times, followed by Israel's restoration in the kingdom of God "underneath all heavens" at the second coming of Christ. The idea that time, history and the planet ended with the advent, and that the promises of God related to nothing earthly, began to prevail. A crass Chiliasm, held by some Judaizing sects, abusing the true doctrine, assisted the anti-chiliastic movement. The spiritualizing method of interpreting Old Testament prophecy, applying all the "curses" to the Jew, and all the "blessings" to the Church, came into vogue. A Pope of Rome headed the movement—Pope Damasus. The subject and the contents of the prophecy were changed to mean the "Church," whenever Israel, Zion, Jerusalem, Jacob, the land, were spoken of as destined to latter-day glory, and God's covenant with the literal believing seed of Abraham, and Israel's whole future, were wiped out from the faith of the Church. Such was the origin of Post-Millennialism—a fact which nearly every modern Church historian, outside of Rome, has emphasized. It placed the 70th week at the beginning, instead of at the end of our age. It was part of that tremendous revolution in the interpretation of prophecy, during the fourth century, when the Church emerged from the martyr-flame, and, united to the State, prosperous in temporal affairs, began to dance around the tranquility of the empire, supported by the State, and turned to politics and ethics, philosophy and science, and the reform of the world. It bred the fearful condition of affairs that gave to Mohammed his opportunity, to the popes of the Middle Age their pretentions and career. So much, in brief, for the Artaxerxes date and its environment. It involved the Church for fifteen centuries in hopeless confusion.*

If ever any people on earth kept time, they were the Jews. From Daniel's death to Maccabean times there was *no possibility of ignorance* as to the number of years elapsing. The date of the completion of the second temple was imperishable. The long-aged High-Priests made daily, monthly, and annual observations, and registered the years, as part of their official duty. Still more, the Seleucid Era, B. C. 312, they knew occurred in the 25th of the 70 weeks of Daniel, reckoned from the Edict of Cyrus, B. C. 536. That Era was accepted by them. It is the only Era from which the reckonings are made in the

---

*The following speaks for itself as a specimen of American imitation of the foreign Higher Criticism "There is one particular term of Seventy Weeks at the end of which *something is to happen*; and it is explained that these are weeks of years. * * * There is nothing in the world to hinder anybody from putting the *terminus a quo* at the time of the Battle of Waterloo, or the landing of the Pilgrims, and then looking for *something very important to happen* at the end, four hundred and ninety years from this time. And Farrar — always Farrar — is quoted, saying in his way, that the Christian Fathers leave us "*Weltering* in a chaos of uncertainties and contradictions." *Washington Gladden, Puzzling Bible Books, pp. 178, 179.* The "weltering" of the Critics in their own "chaos" as to this and other "particular terms,"— the "2,300 evening morning," the "1,290 and 1,335 days,"—besides the "Chaos" of the Seleucids and Ptolemies, the Second and Fourth Empires, the Date of the Book, and in fact the whole Book, is, of course unintentionally, omitted! Even Hitzig could call the Higher Criticism "*An abomination of desolation, standing in a holy place, the Scriptures!*"

Maccabean books. Still more, the assassination of the High Priest, Onias III., impressed the whole nation profoundly, and its date was never forgotten, B. C. 170. It was in the 45th of the 70 weeks. The continuity of the priesthood was unbroken, and its official relation to the calendar and to history made its entries authoritative and conclusive. The chain of tradition was complete. Nehemiah, when young, knew Daniel, and lived to a "high old age." The high priest Alexander, when young, knew Nehemiah, and also lived to be "very old." Simeon, who held the infant Jesus, had known many men whose fathers had seen Judas Maccabaeus. The same was true of Zacharias to whom Gabriel came. It was also true of the teachers of Gamaliel, the teacher of Paul. All knew, perfectly, that the 69th week did not end in the times of Antiochus, much less the 70th. None of the blessings in Dan. ix: 24, had been realized. Messiah Himself had not come; how could they be? They knew perfectly that the awful vision concerning Antiochus, in Dan. viii: 9-14, and xi: 21-35, had been fulfilled, and as certainly they knew that the prophecy in ix: 26, 27, had not been fulfilled. They knew that no such campaign as that described in Dan. xi: 40-45, ever occurred in their history. When Caesar was assassinated, in B. C. 44, they knew it was in the 62d of the 70 weeks, reckoning from B. C. 536. When Augustus was made emperor, they knew it was in the 66th week, B. C. 28, and but three more weeks had to run "unto Messiah the Prince." Carnal Judaism was in revolt shouting for a Maccabean Caesar. The few who were godly, like a Simeon and Anna, waited in hope for "Israel's Consolation." The counting of the years was daily. As the time wore away, the excitement grew, and false Messiahs appeared. The perverted reckoning in the Septuagint, of the 70 weeks, the Palestinian Jews rejected. They had common sense enough to know that the 70th week had no more to do with the 2,300 evening-mornings, B. C. 168-165, than Julius Caesar had to do with David, and that the 69th week was even then impending.

That the 69 weeks ended with the birth of Christ, is confirmed by the world-wide expectation of *.is coming—an expectation held by Jews and Gentiles alike. It pervaded pagan literature as well as Jewish. It found an echo in the Sibylline books, and was sung in the "Secular Song" of Horace, and in the 4th Eclogue of Virgil—a Christmas carol before the time. It was discussed in the Senate House of Rome by Lucius Cotta and the friends of Cæsar, insisting that the "King" predicted in the oracles was Cæsar himself, and resisted by Cicero and Brutus to the last extremity. By order of the Senate, the Sibyl was remanded to her chest, under lock and key, the question left undecided, till the Star shone over Bethlehem. On no other ground can this universal expectation be accounted for. Only the knowledge of Daniel's predictions by the Magi, at the head of whose order Daniel stood for 70 years, and the currency of Balaam's prophecy among the Gentiles, concerning the "Star out of Jacob," brought the "Wise Men" from Babylon and Persia, with the question on their lips, "Where is He that is *born* King of the Jews, for we in the East have seen His star and are come to worship Him?" Matt. ii: 2. They reckoned well! Significant for faith in prophecy, is the fact that the heathen were the first to bring to the Jews in their capital, the announcement of the birth of their own Messiah! It is the strongest confirmation that B. C. 536, is the true starting-point of the 70 weeks. Gabriel moreover, who gave the prophecy, had already come to Zacharias and to Mary, Luke i: 11, 26, 27. It was the "fulness of *the* time when God sent forth His Son," Gal. iv: 4. The events that follow the birth of Christ, viz., (1) His Crucifixion, and (2) the Destruction of Jerusalem, Daniel has predicted with the same unerring clearness. The Roman Times of the Gentiles succeeding that catastrophe, even "unto the end, war," have been literally fulfilled as far as to A. D. 1898. What remains of these times is known only to God. At their close comes the 70th Week, the Antichrist, the Second Coming of Christ, Israel's Deliverance, the Resurrection of the holy dead, and then the " Kingdom." Our thesis is the one thesis underlying the whole book of Daniel and is invulnerable. To know this and see it, is a blessing.

To teach and to preach it, is to teach and preach the Word of God.

Finally, the jurisdiction of the doctrine of the seventy weeks is absolute over both Testaments, New and Old, and determines for us the time-point of both Advents with unerring certainty. For this purpose it was given. The angel reveals the Parousia in Humiliation, Dan. ix: 26, the Parousia in Glory, Dan. vii: 13, and assigns to each its own time-point in the calendar of history. The first occurs at the close of the 69th, the second (after the Interval "unto the End") at the close of the 70th week. As to the close of the 69th week all the prophets looked, even though to Daniel it was reserved to furnish chronology, so to the close of the 70th week they all looked from Moses (Deut. xxxii: 36-43) to Malachi (iv: 1-6), as did the evangelists and apostles from Matthew (Matth. xxiv: 15-31) to John (Rev. xix: 11-21). Here, as everywhere in prophesy, the way of simplicity is the way of truth. Nowhere in all the Word of God is there any First Advent for any purpose, prior to the close of the 69th week. Nowhere, in all God's Word, is there any Second Advent, for any purpose, prior to the close of the 70th week. In every representation, in both Testaments, the Parousia in Glory follows the Parousia of the Antichrist, and occurs in order to terminate the Great Tribulation (1) by the Resurrection of the holy dead and Rapture of the Church, and (2) by the Destruction of the Antichrist and the Judgment of the living nations, 2 Thess. i: 6-10. Clear, simple, uniform and persistent is this divine revelation of the time—a rock of truth against which all the wild theories of men dash themselves into foam. By no vain dream of an imagined "special revelation" to Paul, in 1 Thess. iv: 14-18; by no perverted exegesis of Matth. xxiv: 29-31, or of 1 Thess. iv: 14-18; 2 Thess. i: 6-10; 2 Thess. ii: 1-8, or of any other texts, can this remarkable decree of God be set aside. In the Old Testament this Parousia in Glory, at the time-point stated, as a Parousia to raise the holy dead, destroy the Antichrist, deliver Israel and judge the nations, is everywhere exhibited as one that is a "Shining," an "Appearing" of Jehovah, *for* His saints, *with* His saints the holy angels. It is enough to cite Ps. l: 1-6; Isa. lxvi: 5; Dan. vii: 13; xii: 1-3; Zech. xiv: 1-6. In the New Testament that great and definite event is exhibited under three different terms, all of equivalent signification. viz., *Parousia, Epiphancia, Apokalypsis, i.e.,* "Arrived Presence," "Appearing," " Revelation." All are one and inseparable, one conception in three relations —the first relating to Time, the second to Space, the third to Circumstance or Condition, the close of the 70th week dominating all. The first marks the timepoint of the personal arrival of the Son of Man in the clouds of heaven, viz. at the close of the " time, times, and dividing of a time." The second denotes the outbursting splendor of His presence, the glory radiating into space. The whole expresses the fact that He who so long has been concealed is now no longer so, but openly revealed. It is the same everywhere in the New Testament. The hope of His "appearing" is the one hope to which the faith of all believers is directed, and not to any invented secret unseen advent prior to the close of the Tribulation. Had our Lord or His apostles taught otherwise, they had arrayed against themselves the whole body of Old Testament prophecy, put the New Testament in opposition, and involved both it and themselves in irreconcilable contradiction. But " the Scripture cannot be broken." On the doctrine of the 70th week, the Interval between the 69th and 70th, and the 70th week itself, all the devices of interpretation which torture the word of God to support a vain theory of exemption of the Church from the Tribulation, are forever shattered. The Lord identifies His Second Coming for the Resurrection of the holy dead and the Rapture of the Church, Matt. xxiv: 29-31, 40, 41, 42; xxv: 1, with the timepoint at the close of the 70th week in Daniel, for the Resurrection of Israel's holy dead and the destruction of the Antichrist. The Parousia in Dan. vii:13; xii:1-3 is the same Parousia and at the same time-point as in Matt. xxiv: 29-31. The resurrection of Israel's holy dead and our resurrection, our "gathering together unto Christ," and "in the air," 2 Thess. ii: 1; 1

Thess. iv: 17, are coincident. It is one and the same event. "They without us are not made perfect," Heb. xi: 35-40; x: 35-37.

It is remarkable how plainly the 70th week dominates the structure of our Lord's Olivet-Discourse from Matt. xxiv: 15 to Matt. xxv: 40. Warning against three snares, (1) that His Advent might be any moment, xxiv: 4; (2) that it might be a secret one, xxiv: 27; (3) that it might precede the close of the Tribulation, xxiv: 29-31, He addresses the four apostles Mark xiii: 3, as representatives of "the Twelve," and of the whole Church as a corporate unit surviving till He comes— the "Ye" and the "You" of the great commission—and answers the questions as to the "When" and the "What," the Time and the Sign of His Second Coming and of the End of the Age. He first of all describes the painful and chequered "Times of the Gentiles," down to the "End", the Interval between the 69th and 70th weeks, yet covering silently the 70th week itself, even to the "End," xxiv: 4-14. He then reverts to the middle of the 70th week, when the "Abomination" will "stand in a holy place," xxiv: 15, and proceeds to describe the great Tribulation, or last 1260 days of the Antichrist, xxv: 15-29. At the close comes His Parousia for His saints, precisely as Daniel had pictured it, Dan. vii: 13, 25-27; xii: 1-3. He calls it the *"thief-time,"* xxiv: 44, as John also does, placing the *"thief-time"* after the 6th Vial, Rev. xvi: 15, which with the 7th closes the Tribulation at the last loud sound of the 7th Trumpet, Rev. xi: 15-18. He makes the Resurrection and the Rapture the first acts at His coming, the gathering of His elect by His angelic ministry, xxiv: 30, 31, 40, 41, 44; xxv: 1. He next pictures the judgment of the living nations, xxv: 31-46, gathered, as they will be, at Jerusalem, in their last conflict with Israel, His throne of glory overhanging Olivet in front of the city, the nations separated right and left, converted Israel holding the city delivered by His hand. In that Judgment the Antichrist is destroyed. He points to New-Born Israel, the nearest His throne, and calls them "these my brethren," xxv: 40—Daniel's "people of the saints," Dan. vii: 27. He makes their deliverance immediately subsequent to the rapture of the church, this occurring at xxiv: 30, 31, 40, 41; xxv: 1; that at xxv: 40; and, like Daniel, crowns the whole scene with the destruction of the wicked, the salvation of the righteous, the "Kingdom" and the "Life everlasting," Matth. xxv: 34, 46; Dan. xii: 1-3, 13. From first to last the book of Daniel is his guide. He simply puts together the events in the Ends of Daniel's book, chapters ii., vii., ix., xi., and all of xii., the events of the 70th Week, and assigning the church to her place, "ye" and "you," in the same perspective, adding parables and admonitions, concludes His answer to the questions proposed. He separates Jerusalem's destruction, Dan. ix: 26, from His Parousia, Dan. vii: 13, by the interval of the "Unto the End," Dan. ix: 26, or "Times of the Gentiles," Luke xxi: 24. He identifies His second coming with the "End of the Age," the end of Gentile times, the end of the 70th Week. In Heb. xi: 35, 39, 40, Paul declares that Israel's resurrection and ours occur at the same point of time, and are one.

It is needless to say that the apostles followed their Master's teaching, and took His Olivet discourse as the text-book of their eschatology. It ruled the whole faith of the early church. It settled every heresy as to the time of the advent. It corrected the Thessalonian error as to the "any moment view." Paul appeals to it to decide the question. He calls it the "Word of the Lord." He had it on his table when he wrote both letters to the Thessalonians. He uses its very language. The 70th Week covers his own words in 2 Thess. ii: 1-8. John reproduces it in full, in its two halves of twice 1,260, and gives its middle point as that of the slaughter of the "Two Witnesses" in Jerusalem, by the Antichrist, during the time of the building of their temple in unbelief, Rev. xi: 2, 3, 7. See Isa. lxvi: 1-6. He repeats the last 1,260 days again, in Rev. xii: 6, 14; xiii: 5; and gives their end-point in xi: 15-19; xiv: 13-20; xix: 11-21. Every prophecy of the New Testament, and every representation of the time-point of the second coming of Christ for His saints, is dominated and determined by the jurisdiction of the Interval and the 70th Week. This is absolutely conclusive against all the vain time-reckonings and the groundless inventions of men of modern times unskilled in the "sure word of prophecy."

The doctrine of the Seventy Weeks provides for us the only data in connection with the "signs of the times," as foretold by our Lord, for any approximate determination of the nearness of the advent. How much of the interval between the 69th and 70th weeks remains to run is known only to God. When the Antichrist and the Jews are in "covenant," at the beginning of the 70th week, and clearer still, when the breach occurs between them at the "middle of the week," then the determination of the year, perhaps the month, but never of the "day or hour," will be certain, i. e., to all believers. To watch always and wait patiently is the believer's privilege. Prophetic nearness is one thing, chronological nearness another, and yet faith and hope overleap all intervening events. The relatively brief remainder of the interval, and the Antichrist, are what is immediately before us, and with all sobriety we can say that it is this that lends an interest, so solemn and absorbing, to the attitude of the nations, the extension of missions, the Jewish movements, the Eastern Question, the crimes of Christendom, and the current events in both hemispheres of the world.

"Here we have a true Apocalypse. The Glorious One who sways over the Hiddekel is the 'Alpha and Omega' who appeared to John upon the island of Patmos in the Aegean sea, not far from Ephesus, and is the 'Son of Man' whom Daniel had already seen in the vision of Chapter VII.;—there, in a night-dream; here, in open day;—there, in one form; here, in another. He is the same whose back part Moses saw from the cleft of Horeb, and Isaiah saw high and lifted up, and Ezekial saw above the firmament, and whose fear fell upon them. Unable to endure the sight or the voice, Gabriel interposes to strengthen and compose the shattered frame and mind of the prophet, and restore him to his strength."—Fehrmann.

Chapter VII.

DANIEL, CHAPTERS X-XII.—VISION OF THE "TIME OF THE END."

These chapters form one continuous prophecy, the longest in the book, and furnish the last and crowning proof of the truth of our thesis, viz, that the Kingdom of Christ can never come to victory on this present earth until His Second Advent in the clouds of heaven. The time covered by them is the entire future, from the date of the vision to the Advent, i. e., the whole time of the Colossus, save the Head of Gold, and of the Four Beasts, save the Lion, therefore including the time of the Ram and the Rough Goat, the Four Horns and Little Horn of the Third Empire; also the Little Horn of the Fourth Empire, both Horns; in short, the period of the seventy weeks together with their Intervals. The Two Tribulations are here, that under Antiochus, xi: 28-35, and that under the Last Antichrist, xi: 40-45; xii: 1, the great prophecy ending with the final Deliverance of the Jews, the Resurrection of the holy dead, and the blessed time in the victorious Kingdom of God on earth, xii: 1-13.

Chapter x., which gives us the Christophany and a wider glimpse than before into the unseen world, is the Prologue, or introduction to xi. and xii., which contain the proper "Revelation" made to the prophet concerning the "Time of the End," including the near and far horizons of the third and fourth empires. The Epilogue is xii: 5-13. The theme of the prophecy is the "Warfare Great," the Eastern Question and its solution. Each of the chapters, x., xi., xii., forms a general separate section of the whole prediction, the first verse of xi. properly belonging to the close of x. All the way from x: 4 to xii: 13, we stand on the banks of the Hiddekel, see the vision, watch the actions of the prophet, hear the Lord, the Angels, and Daniel talk, and listen to the revelation given. At xii: 4, the scene changes, final explanations are made, and the prophet is dismissed to his rest.

I. As to the nature of the Revelation itself. The prophet says, a "Thing," literally a "Word," was revealed to him by means of a "Vision," and that the word was true, and related to great and long-continued military struggle. The translation of the clause in King James' Version, "and the time appointed was long," is simply a defective paraphrase of the Hebrew text. The correct rendering is, "and Truth is the Word, even Warfare Great," i. e., the Revelation he records is that of Israel's long struggle with the World-Power in its successive empires and kingdoms, from the third year of Cyrus down to the final deliverance of the Jews from Gentile hands, and the consummation of the Kingdom of Christ at His Second Coming. In a somewhat similar manner Virgil and Homer began their great epics with "Arms and the Man I sing," and Thiers and Macauley their histories with "I propose to write" so and so. If, imitating the title to John's Apocalypse, we might affix one to this section of Daniel's book, it would be this: "The Revelation of the Angel of Jehovah which God gave to Him to show unto His servants the things which must come to pass in the latter days, concerning the destiny of Israel and the World-Powers; and He told this word by His angel Gabriel, whom He sent to His servant Daniel, commanding him to shut up and seal the book unto the Time ꝶ End. Blessed is he who waits and comes to the end of the days."

II. As to the Date of the Prophecy. According to Babylonian reckoning, the "first year of Cyrus" was that of the overthrow of Babylon, B. C. 538. For this reason, it is said that Daniel "continued to live" in his official activity under the king of Babylon, i. e., under all the Chaldean kings, "to the first year of Cyrus," when their empire expired, Dan. i: 21. He also "prospered in the reign of Darius" (the Mede), vi: 28, who "received" the kingdom or rule over Babylon from

Cyrus himself, verse 31, and "was made king" over the Chaldeans at that time, B. C. 538. Upon the death of Darius, B. C. 536, Cyrus assumed the sole reign over Babylon, issuing his edict for the emancipation of the Jews. According to Jewish reckoning, as seen in II. Chron. xxxvi: 22, Ezra i: 1, "the first year of Cyrus" was regarded as the first of his sole reign, the year of Jewish liberation. The "third year of Cyrus," therefore, according to this first post-exilic prophecy, Dan. x: 1, was B. C. 534, or the fourth year after Babylon's fall, or two years after the Edict of Cyrus. Cyrus is called the "King of Persia," first, because he was "King of Persia" first of all, and as such conquered both Media and Babylon; and, second, because in 536 Darius, the Mede, having passed away, the Persian dynasty, the higher of the two horns of the Medo-Persian empire, was now in the ascendant. Dan. viii: 3-20. If, as the best tradition reports, Daniel was seventeen years old when carried captive, B. C. 606, his age was eighty-nine when this last revelation was made, B. C. 534.

III. As to the Place and Time of the Vision. The place was by the banks of the river Tigris, whose Accadian name was "Iddiklat," called biblically "Hiddekel," the third of the four great rivers into which the river of Eden parted, "that which goeth toward the east of Assyria," Gen. ii: 14. Daniel's definite statement, "I was by the side of the great river Hiddekel," taken in connection with his description of the conduct of his companions, "the men that were with me," makes it certain that the prophet was not visionally transported there, but was bodily present, x: 4, 7. The Euphrates and Tigris, Nineveh and Babylon, were now the possessions of Cyrus, and Daniel's official duties doubtless required his presence in this part of the augmented empire. The special time of the vision is given as the "four and twentieth day of the first month," i. e., the 24th Abib, called Nisan by the post-exilic Jews, our March-April, the Passover month whose feast commemorates Israel's deliverance out of Egypt. Yet, further, the vision was given at the close of "three full weeks" of fasting, the fast commencing on the 3d and ending on the 24th of Nisan. Some deep significance lies here, in the association of this vision of Israel's deliverance from their last oppressor, with the Passover month that commemorates their deliverance from their first oppressor, the Egyptian. Already, one seems to hear the " Song of Moses and the Lamb " united. All the more impressive is this association since in xii: 5, in the Hebrew text, "the River " is called by the name of the Nile—" Yeor "—one of those quick-glinting intimations we often meet in prophecy when least suspecting it, to tell us that, hereafter, in the End-Time it will be with Israel " as it was in the day that he came up out of Egypt " Isa. xi: 16, Rev. xv: 2-4. The Holy Spirit's prophetic glances, fore and aft, are wonderful!*

IV. As to the Occasion of the Vision. It was the sad intelligence received concerning the state of affairs at Jerusalem. Babylon indeed had fallen, and 45,000 exiles had returned, pursuant to the order of Cyrus, to build the temple and the city. The "foundations " had indeed been laid, but the old men had " wept with a loud voice " as they contrasted the present poverty of structure with the grandeur of the ancient house, Ezra iii: 11, 12. Worse than all, the temple-work had been suspended, through the machinations and accusations of Samaritans against the Jews, and Persian sympathy had been withdrawn, Ezra iv: 4-16, 23, 24. Moreover, a scheme was contrived to build a counter temple on Gerizzim, in Samaria. De-

---

*As the waters were divided, so will it be again, Isa., xi: 15; Rev. xvi: 12. As the walls of Jericho fell, so shall it be again, Isa., ii: 15; Rev. xv: 19. As the mountains were rent and skipped, so shall it be again, Ps. cxiv: 4, 10; Rev. xvi: 19. As hailstones fell at Bethoron, so, with mightier force shall it be again, Rev. xvi: 21. **As the** transjordanic regions, Ammon, Moab, Edom, were held **by Israel**, so shall it be again, Isa. xi. 14; Dan. xi: 40-45. As plagues of sores and darkness and of water turned to blood, marked the coming out of Egypt, so shall Israel's final deliverance be marked, Rev. xvi: 2, 3, 10. As the dividing of the sea for Israel's escape, so for the same purpose the Mount of Olives shall be divided; and as Sun and Moon stood still during Joshua's long day, so Zechariah's nocturnal day and solar night, a day unique, "not day, nor night," points to yet corresponding phenomena. " It shall be as it was," in multiplied ways. Zech. xiv: 4, 6. 7.

jected in sorrow, the prophet gives himself to "mourning, fasting and prayer for three full weeks," even in joyous passover-time, during which he "ate no pleasant bread, neither came flesh nor wine into his mouth, nor did he anoint himself," x: 3. At the close of this period, the venerable saint, burdened with the weight of years, and enfeebled by this long fast, received the Vision and the Revelation, 24th Nisan, B. C. 534.

V. The Vision itself. It is a Christophany, or appearing of the Angel of Jehovah in human form. The prophet lifts his eyes and sees in open day a "Certain Man" of supernatural presence hovering over the waters of the Hiddekel, a man wearing not the "Talar," but the shining byssus garment of a Jewish High-Priest, his loins cinctured with "gold of Uphaz," his body in color like a "Tarshish," or brilliant Chrysolite such as sparkled in the pectoral of Aaron, his face "flashing like the lightning," his eyes like "torches blazing," his arms and feet like "polished brass," and his voice as "the voice of a multitude," x: 5, 6; or, as the word imports, like surges breaking on the shore, or the noise of shouting armies in the distance, or as of deep, low, bursting thunder. Omnipotence and sublimity are here. It is a vision of Jesus Christ before His incarnation, yet symbolized in the dignity of His royal, priestly and prophetic offices, in the terror of His judicial majesty, the forecast splendor of His exalted humanity, and the glory of His deity; a "Man," both Man and God, incomparable in the mystery of His person and His natures—a face above the brightness of the sun, a voice vocal as the thunder. His transparent body means His sanctity and glory. His white robe means that He is a priest, His golden girdle that He is a King, His uttering voice that He is a prophet. His eyes like searching fire mean omniscience. His arms and feet, like burning brass, mean judgment for His enemies. His face effulgent means that God is there! Elsewhere in the book of Daniel this same glorious person, who is the central figure of it all, is presented as the "Stone" detached from the mountain, ii: 34, 45; "One like a Son of God," iii: 25; a "Watcher and Holy One," who cares for Israel, iv: 13; "One like a Son of Man," coming in the clouds, vii: 13; a "Certain Holy One, Palmoni, Wonderful Numberer," whose voice Daniel heard coming from between the banks of the Ulai, viii: 15, 16; "Messiah" born and crucified, ix: 26, and now the "Linen Clothed Man" hovering sublime above the Hiddekel. In all these forms and relations He appears as the Crusher of the Colossus of earthly politics and power, the Companion of His suffering saints in the furnace and the den, the Judge of all the earth, the Measurer of the Ages and the Ends, the Seasons and the Times, the Revealer of the truth and Unveiler of Israel's pathway and goal, the atoning Redeemer of His people, the Destroyer of the Antichrist, the Deliverer of the Jews, the immortal Monarch of the Fifth Empire, and Bringer of the Kingdom of God to victory over all the earth. Here, in the present vision, x: 5, 6, He appears in His greatest splendor and is that Glorious One John saw "in the isle that is called Patmos," 630 years later; the Walker in the midst of the golden candlesticks, the Lamb on the Throne, the many-crowned Warrior on the white horse, and, as in Moses and John, so here, the Oath-Swearing Angel with uplifted hand to heaven, Deut. xxxii: 40; Rev. x: 5, 6; Dan. xii: 7. He is the "Angel of the Covenant," Israel's "Savior" and "Hope in time of trouble." He ate in Abraham's tent, saved Isaac from the altar, was the Mystic Ladder Jacob saw. He spoke to Moses at the Bush, and from the Pillar of Cloud by day and Fire by night. Ezekiel, Daniel's contemporary, calls Him the "Glory of the Lord," Ezek. i: 26-28, and saw Him lingering, then departing from Jerusalem, yet returning to the eastern gate. Zechariah, alluding to the very time the present vision closes, says of Him, "The Lord my God shall come, all the holy ones with Thee! and His feet shall stand, in that day, on the Mount of Olives," Zech. xiv: 1-5.

VI. The Persons in the Scene. They are (1) the Linen-Clothed Man, (2) Daniel and his companions, (3) Gabriel, (4) Michael, and (5) "Two Others," referred to in chap. xii: 5, 6. Whether the companions of Daniel were Zechariah, Haggai and Malachi, or Shadrach, Meshach and Abednego, or some servants of the prophet, is indeterminable. Conjectural is every view as to who the "Two Others" are. Michael is expressly named, x: 13, 21. Gabriel is not named, but the characteristic mode of addressing the prophet as a "man greatly beloved," and of "touching" him to strengthen him, and the fact that he who addresses and touches is the revealing angel, leaves no doubt that the "hand" in contact with the prostrate prophet, x: 10, 16, 18, is not that of the Linen-Clothed Man, x: 5, 6, but is the "hand" of Gabriel. Compare chapter x: 21-23, with viii: 15, 16. There is nothing in the expression, "one like the similitude of the sons of Adam touched my lips," x: 16, to indicate otherwise. The expression is not the same as that in chapter vii: 13, "One like a Son of Enash," coming in the clouds of heaven. The action and speech of the angel in chapters viii. and ix., and here in chapter x., in connection with all these prophecies, prove that Gabriel is the Toucher, the Speaker and the Revealing Angel, all the way from Dan. x: 10 to xii: 4, and—save chapter xii: 7, where the Linen-Clothed Man answers a question—is the Speaker and Revealer of the whole prophecy. The prophet does not say that the Linen-Clothed Man laid "*His* hand" upon him, as John says of Christ in Rev. i: 17, but simply "*a* hand" touched me, Dan. x: 10, viz., the hand of Gabriel.

VII. The Effect of the Vision on the Prophet and his Companions and the Circumstances of his Recovery. (1) On his companions. Like those of Saul, when the Lord appeared to him on the way to Damascus, they "saw not the vision of the man." They heard "a voice," but not articulate. To both, a flash and a sound were the whole phenomena. To those who have no eyes to see, the glory of God is but as natural lightning. To those who have no ears to hear, the voice of Christ is only as rolling thunder. Unbelieving science neither sees nor hears anything supernatural. Unlike Saul's companions, who "fell to the ground," Daniel's ran away "quaking," and "fled affrighted to hide themselves," x: 7, Acts ix: 7, xxii: 9, xxvi: 14. (2) On the prophet himself, left "alone," the effect was utter physical and mental prostration. The supernatural shock suspended all normal functional activities of mind and body, destroying not only the power of locomotion, but of erect position, producing nervous and muscular paralysis and semi-consciousness and threatening dissolution. At the age of eighty-nine years, and after three weeks' fast, it seemed to be apparent death. So John, of nearly the same age, when narrating the effect of the Christophany in Patmos, says, " When I saw Him I fell at His feet as dead!" Rev. i: 17. Into the mystery of the necessity of such phenomena, when protracted, minute, and mighty revelations are about to be given, we may not pry. Doubtless the purpose was to strip the prophet of all human strength and cause him, in the strength of God alone, to receive and record the great communication.

He describes his condition. Pathetically he narrates that his " strength " had departed, his " comeliness " been turned to " corruption," and that, as soon as he heard the " voice of the words " of the Linen-Clothed Man he was thrown into a " deep sleep," prostrate, his " face toward the ground " x: 8,9. Haggard, withered, disfigured, the freshness of his countenance gone, stupefied, overpowered by the Divine presence, he fell comatose and heavy to the earth. The awful splendor and voice of Jehovah had shattered him. Once before, under a vision less powerful, he says he was "astounded," "fainted," and was " sick for many days," viii: 27. Nevertheless, the power that prostrated him re-invigorated and recovered him. The mysterious Form that hovered over the Hiddekel withheld himself now from the eyes and ears of the prophet unable to endure more, and sent an angel to succor and support him. Thrice the prophet is " touched " and addressed by Gabriel x: 10-20. At the first touch, x: 10, he is raised from the ground, resting on his " knees " and the " palms of his hands." Like a quadruped, he stands on all fours. His crouching position is that of one endeavoring to rise but too feeble to succeed. The angel comforts and instructs him. " O, Daniel, man greatly beloved!" tells him he has a message for him, desires him to understand it and bids him " stand upright."

Weak, yet obedient, the prophet rises. " When he had spoken this word to me, I stood, trembling " x: 11. The angel assures him that, from the first day he had " set his heart to understand and chastened himself before God," his prayer had been heard, and that now, in answer to prayer for his sake, he, Gabriel, had come to him, x: 12. He explains the delay and gives the prophet a glimpse into the conflicts of the unseen world, showing what interest the angels, good and evil, take in the affairs of human governments. He says that for twenty-one days following the beginning of Daniel's prayer, he had stood at his post counteracting the influence of the evil angel-prince of Persia, who was responsible for all the mischief and machinations at Jerusalem, and for the cunning schemes to change the Persian policy adversely to the Jews; that Michael, the guardian prince of Israel and commander of the heavenly hosts, had come to his help, that both had won a victory over the evil influence at the Persian court, and that thus relieved from his watch he, Gabriel, had hastened as rapidly as possible to cause the prophet to understand not only this but future things, x: 13, 14. Herein the prophet is assured, first of all, that, in spite of all opposition, the Temple should be built, although in troublous times, and, so far, the prophecy in chapter ix: 25 be fulfilled; that the lost edict of Cyrus would yet be discovered and reenforced by a new decree of Darius, the son of Hystaspes, and the court-demon, whether at Babylon, Shushan, or Achmetha, be foiled, Ezra v: 13, 17; vi: 1-7, 8-12, 15-22. Here was comfort, indeed. But, as the prophecy in both chapters viii. and ix. looked into future times beyond the Persian rule, even into Greek and Roman times, and on to the end of Israel's long pathway, even to the 70th week in chapter ix, so had he hurried specially to tell the prophet what should " befall his people in the latter days, x: 14. He uses an expression—" *acharith hayyamim,*" " the afterness of the days "—well known to Daniel, a technical expression including all near and far horizons, but eminently the remote, Dan. viii: 17, 19, 23; ii: 28. He tells him, in sum, that the message he brings is no less than a prophecy in detail of " *Warfare*

Great," x: 1, covering all Persian, Greek and Roman times, reaching to the last crisis and the last deliverance.

This solemn word is too much for the trembling prophet to endure. If indeed he had been comforted and strengthened somewhat by the angel's word and touch, yet deeply affected by what he now heard, he seems to relapse. The thought of further tribulation for his people overcomes him. He becomes dejected again and "dumb." "When he (the angel) had spoken such words to me, I set my face to the ground, and I became dumb," x: 15. A second time the angel commiserates his frailty and touches his "lips," signifying that he wishes him to speak. The prophet opens his mouth and pleads in plaintive tones his incapacity, "O, my Lord, by reason of the vision my pains came upon me, and I retained no strength. For how can the servant of this my Lord talk with this my Lord, for, as for me, no strength has remained in me, no breath left in me," x: 16, 17. Stricken prophet! Old man, weak from years and from fasting, overpowered by the sight above the Hiddekel, and now weighted afresh with the burden of Israel's future woes, how could he "talk"? A bruised reed and smoking flax, trembling, flickering, bent, breathless and powerless, how demean himself otherwise than in silence, as befits the sorrowing, or how charm into cheerfulness the countenance made sad, or into utterance the chords made mute, by the vision and the voice? "I was dumb, I opened not my mouth, because thou didst it!" A third time the angel touches him and addresses him. "O man, greatly beloved! Courage! Peace be unto thee! Be strong and be strong!" Behold how angels salute the suffering saints of God!—"Ish hemdoth! Tiryeh lo! Shalom leka! Hazak ve-hazak!"—words powerful enough to comfort the saddest, encourage the faintest and doubly confirm and strengthen the weakest. Almighty energy revived his almost exanimated frame, sent new pulses through his blood and stiffened into strength his palsied limbs. The color returns to his face. "Be strong and be strong!" Courageously he "talks." He is ready now to receive the Revelation of the "Tsaba Gadol"—the "Warfare Great." "Let my Lord speak, for thou hast strengthened me," x: 19. And yet the angel would be certain that the mind of Daniel is clear and his memory still faithful to its function. " Knowest thou wherefore I am come to thee ?" x: 20. Rememberest thou the words I spake before the second touch? my mission? the object of my coming? the victory won over the evil angel-prince of Persia? x: 14. Satisfied that Daniel's mind is clear, the angel resumes his exordium, broken off by Daniel's weakness, and meant as a preliminary word to his revelation of the " Warfare Great." Doing so, he continues to comfort and strengthen the prophet by making known two things, viz:

(1) That, as in the past, so in the future, Daniel's people are under the special guardianship of the angels of God. In the midst of their trials, angelic power shall defend the faithful. For this reason, Gabriel informs him that he must " return " to the Persian court to maintain the advantage already gained, x: 13, and continue to " fight with the angel-prince of Persia," x: 20, during the whole period of the Persian supremacy, and so incline the kings of Persia to favor Israel—a fact made evident in all the Persian history and particularly so in the times of Esther. He adds, however, that there will be a time when, after he is gone away and is at his post of watchfulness, another enemy, the evil " angel-prince of Grecia shall come," x: 20. The Persian supremacy will pass away, the Jews shall fall under Greek dominion and again experience tribulation. Nevertheless, the angel will stay long enough to " show," i. e., explain, to the prophet " what is noted in the Scripture of Truth " concerning not only the times of Persia and Greece, but the end of Roman times also, even the end of the " Warfare Great." He further adds that, although the sufferings of the Jews will be severe, yet the outcome will be victory for the people of God. All the more evident is this since but twenty-one days ago, he, Gabriel, stood up against the evil angel-prince of Persia and foiled the intrigues at the Persian court, x: 13; Michael, his only help, and "none but Michael," the archangel and guardian prince of Israel, was needed then or would be needed hereaf-

ter, to "exert himself against these," i. e., the powers of Persia and Greece, or against the "Powers" in the closing struggle of the "Warfare Great," x: 21. No human allies will be needed even in Israel's last extremity. Still further, the angel reminds the prophet that, in a great crisis only four years ago, he, Gabriel, Michael assisting, x: 13, " stood up in the first year of Darius, the Mede, to strengthen and confirm " that weak-minded vacillating monarch, Dan. vi: 4-27, against the machinations of the satraps, stopped the mouths of the lions in the den where Daniel was thrown, delivered Daniel and caused his promotion under the Persian empire; in fact, that two angels of God, Gabriel and Michael, had been all-sufficient to sway the minds of both Cyrus and Darius to execute God's judgment on Babylon and defend triumphantly the interests of Israel. The inference is irresistible that, in coming days under the Greek tribulation, and in the "Great Tribulation" that will close the Gentile times, xiii: 1; Rev. xii: 7; Zech. xii: 8, Israel will not be overwhelmed by the "Powers," nor forsaken by a covenant-keeping God. Jacob's hope will not be in human allies, always a curse to him, but in the "Lord of Hosts" alone. Hereby he recalls to the prophet the memories of the Hebrew history. What allies, in any crisis, ever saved Israel from their enemies? What victories did Israel ever win by foreign aid? What battle ever lost when Gabriel and Michael "stood up" in Israel's behalf? One angel, alone, smote the firstborn of Egypt; another laid low in a single night the entire army of Sennacherib. Was it not enough that the "Captain of the Lord's Host" appeared to Joshua? What allies had the Judges? The murmurs of the Red Sea, the tumbling walls of Jericho, the sun standing still over Gibeon and the moon in the valley of Ajalon, can these be forgotten? The glittering hosts of Mahanaim, whose quivers are filled with lightnings and whose step is in the thunderstorm, are more than a match for all the helmeted batallions of all the "Powers." "Courage, Daniel. Be strong and be strong!" No fear for the future! Of Israel it is said, "The Eternal God is thy Refuge and underneath are the everlasting arms, and He shall thrust out the enemy before thee"—Greek, Cossack, Turk or Persian—"and shall say, Destroy them! Happy art thou, O Israel, O people saved of the Lord who is the Shield of thy help and the Sword of thine excellency!" Deut. xxxiii: 26-29 Thus in "words" and in substance, not less than by "touches," does the angel revive the memories of the past, kindle the hopes of the future and reinvigorate and comfort the mind of the prophet.

(2) The final comfort given is the solemn Sanction of the angel, soul-assuring and inviolable, to all the revelations Daniel has received, and to the "Book" in which, from the first, he had recorded them. He calls **Daniel's** book the "*Kitab Emeth*" or "*Writing of Truth*," i. e., "True Scripture," and not fiction, x: 21, and in xii: 4, calls it "Hassepher," "The Book." This "Writing of Truth" is not any unwritten book of God's decrees, nor of His providence, nor is it the "book of life," nor of "God's remembrance," nor any archives of angels in heaven, but is the visible and manual "Scripture" of the revelations given and recorded by Daniel in human alphabetic characters, Hebrew and Aramaean. It was something in Daniel's possession—a "Sepher," or "Book" which, when completed, was to be placed among the "Sepharim" or canonical "Books" of the Jewish people, like the "Sepharim" or "Books" in ix: 2, of which "Hassepher," "the Book" of Moses was one, Exod. xvii: 14; Dan. ix: 11, 13. Already, from B. C. 603 to 533, the prophet had received various revelations, viz.: those in chapters ii., vii., viii. and ix., and with the histories connected with them, i., iii., iv., v., vi., had faithfully recorded them in "the Book," xii: 4. He "wrote" them, vii: 1, at the time of their occurrence, as did other prophets, Isa. vii: 3; Jer. xix: 14; Hos. i: 2, and "shut up the vision," viii: 26, and he tells us, as a prophet, and in view of his account, that what he wrote was "Truth," not fiction, and "Truth" given by an angel from heaven, and by the Spirit of God, in answer to prayer, ii: 17, 18; ix: 4; not a human invention, or production of his own will, or private interpretation of the mind of God; nothing of a psychological genesis, or even of a logical con-

clusion from any premises, nor a pious imagination, but an "Apocalypse," a "Secret Revealed" by the "God of Heaven," ii: 18, 22, 27, and much of which he could not understand, viii: 27. These revelations contain the forecast outline history of the World-Power and of the Jews, with a chronological clock of the Ages down to the Second Advent of Christ—an apocalypse in which the Holy Land, the Holy City, and Israel, the Holy People, endure persistently, from first to last, in spite of all adverse fortune, reserved for a glorious destiny in the "Time of the End."

And now the angel comes to add one more "Revelation" and "Word of Truth," showing more particularly certain great events in Persian, Greek and final Roman times, to be added to Daniel's "Book," so completing it, sealing it officially and transmitting it to be read and studied in the "Time of the End," xii: 4. This final revelation the prophet solemnly declares is "Truth" because the angel so declared, x: 1-21. Gabriel also calls Daniel's whole "Book" a "Kitab Emeth," a "Writing" or "Scripture of Truth." Thus, from chapter i. to xii. inclusive, all is "Truth," not fiction. By friend and foe alike, the unity of the book and its authorship is conceded. Upon the supposition of the author's piety and honesty, his repeated statements that the predictions were a "revelation" from God at the dates and places specified, and that an angel from heaven pronounced the words he brought, to be "Truth," and Daniel's book a book of "Truth," its prophecies to be fulfilled only "after many days," x: 14; xii: 4; upon this supposition the modern critical hypothesis, that it originated near 400 years after Daniel was dead, and was composed by a Maccabean novelist, is eternally excluded. Otherwise, no man more wicked, sacrilegious or insane, than he who, making such statements as the author of this book has made, and knowing them to be mendacious, would palm them off as true. Doubly insane, and cruel with a mocking sympathy, for writing a book like this, January, B. C. 164—as the critics say—*after* the tribulation was past and gone, December, 165 B. C.—the Temple cleansed—in order to arm beforehand and comfort with a fiction, God's people, in view of that same tribulation yet to begin B. C. 168!—still more, attributing the book to Daniel who, for the Maccabean writer, was no more than a myth! Therefore, did the Holy Spirit use, purposely, the designation "*Scripture of Truth*," warning against the false criticism which, in all ages, would assail the "book," and especially in ours, when the time for its last fulfillment approximates. Knowing that the scoffer would come in the last days, curling his crest against the Pentateuch, the Prophets, the Sacred Books of History, and eminently against the Book of Daniel, the wisdom of God fore-issued this divine declaration against the unbelief that would account it a "fiction," and so would fortify God's people everywhere in opposition to a scientific skepticism that sports with a "Revelation" from heaven, an angel-spoken "word of Truth," recorded by a holy "prophet," and sanctioned by Christ and His apostles. "O, Daniel, greatly beloved, be strong and be strong!"

" The Eastern Question is not a question of to-day, nor of yesterday. When history first began to be written, it was already there. When it is re-opened, all the world is concerned. It is Occidentalism in its inevitable conflict with Orientalism. Who is to be the champion or leader of Occidentalism, now—the Anglo-Saxon or the Slav? The world is arraying itself in two grand camps. It is no longer a question who shall hold Constantinople, or control the Suez Canal, or command the pass of Thermopylæ, or dictate the oracles of Delphi. It is the old question, stated now in terms of greater things. The battle opens on the same old field, but the habitable globe is involved. Islam was the reaction against Alexander's inroads, and Turkey tarries in Europe only because the forces of Occidentalism are not united."
—Wheeler.

Chapter VIII.

DANIEL, CHAPTERS X-XII.—TSABA GADOL. WARFARE GREAT. MACCABEAN TRIBULATION.

In chapter xi. the angel resumes and unfolds the prophetic history of the Medo-Persian and Græco-Macedonian empires, and, after a transition-section, in which both type and antitype are blended, springs from the "Time of the End" of the 3d empire to the "Time of the End" of the 4th, i. e., from Antiochus Epiphanes to the last Antichrist. Such the manner of prophecy. By this means he brings the close of his "Revelation" concerning the "Warfare Great" into harmony with the close in ii., vii. and ix., and terminates in xii. his amazing apocalypse of the future of the Jews and of the kingdoms of the world. Chapter xi., therefore, busies itself with (1) the Ram and Rough Goat of viii., expanding their history; (2) with Two of the Four Horns by which the Notable Horn in viii. was succeeded; (3) with the Little Horn that rose out of one of the Four, viz.: with Antiochus Epiphanes; (4) with the Little Horn that shall rise among the final Ten Horns of the 4th empire, viz.: the last Antichrist represented here as "the King," xi: 36, the Antitype of Antiochus. Thus the angel "shows," i. e., explains, by amplification, "what is written in "the Scripture of Truth." It is not possible to imagine a more powerful proof of the truth of our thesis. The "Warfare Great" continues till closed by the Destruction of the Antichrist. The Millennial Kingdom follows when "war shall be no more." The two ages cannot run parallel. What we are now to consider in this long and difficult chapter, is the events of Persian and Grecian history, which lead up to the Maccabean persecution; then, in the next article, pass to the Antichrist, his last campaign, the Great Tribulation, ending in xii. with the Resurrection of the holy dead, Israel's deliverance, and the "blessed" time of the kingdom. First, however, a critical word.

Modern criticism has specially attacked this chapter, (1) on account of the minuteness, multiplicity and exactitude of its details, and (2) on account of its perfect historical fulfilment, as far as xi: 35, and partly as far as xi: 39. It is regarded as a spurious production, the work of a Jew who, under the mask of prediction, wrote the history of his own times, nearly 400 years after Daniel was dead, attributing the same to the prophet of the exile who, for him, had no existence.* The clearness and precision of the prophecy are used as arguments against its genuineness and authenticity, and the perfection of the prophecy is made a ground of objection against its inspiration. This modern reproduction of Porphyry, "the bitterest enemy of Christianity," A.D. 233-303, 1500 years ago, met its unanswerable refutation in the same antiquity from the pens of Jerome, Eusebius, Apollinarius, Methodius, Chrysostom and others, as it has again from the most eminent scholars who have replied to the modern assault.

The criticism is worthless when once the reason of the prophecy is remembered, in connection with the fact that precisely for want of further details the vision in viii. was "not understood," viii: 27: that, because of the suspended work at Jersualem, the prophet had "mourned and fasted" and seemed

---

*The criticism decides that there is nothing genuine in x-xii: except xii: 1-4, and annexes these four verses to ix. That is, all after ix, save these verses, is a "Maccabean interpolation!" And ix and xii: 1-4 end with Antiochus! It is worthless. Ecclesiasticus, B. C. 180, or 16 years before B. C. 164, when the critics say Daniel's book was composed, recognizes Dan. x: 13, 20, and imitates the texts. The Septuagint, begun B. C. 281, or 117 years before 164, recognizes the whole book of Daniel. Meinhold has critically proved that the book was in existence from B. C. 250-300 before Christ. But, more than all, by friend and foe alike, the unity of the authorship of the book is confessed. The concession to the critics, here, by Zöckler in Lange, is unfortunate. Kamphausen has trumpeted it most vigorously.

to think that the prediction in ix. might not be fulfilled, x: 2, 3; and that having now received the details he declares that he came to "understanding of the vision," x: 1. If such statements are the fabrications of a novelist it is a crime to retain the book in the canon, and, moreover, the whole New Testament eschatology founded upon it is false. They are not fabrications. The reason of the prophecy is all-sufficient. It was in the purpose of God that prophecy should cease with Malachi, and that during 400 years, next ensuing, no prophet should arise to guide God's people in a crisis that threatened to sweep away their new-built city, temple, religion, and even their existence. What wonder, then, that, commiserating the plaint of the prophet who desired more details concerning the future, and knowing well the thunderbolt that would strike the Jews for their apostacy, the Lord, in xi., should repeat and amplify what had been begun in viii., just as He repeated and amplified in viii. what had been begun in vii. and ii.? What wonder that He should thus forewarn the faithful against the sophisms and seductions with which the spread of Greek culture would ensnare them, and by the very details of forerunning events cause "them of understanding among the people," xi: 33, to see approaching danger, and so prepare and arm the faithful with the courage and the constancy that made the Maccabean victory so glorious? The forecast events, as year after year, they were realized in history and the day of trouble drew near, could only incite those "who feared the Lord to speak often one to another," Mal. iii: 16, and confirm their own and their children's faith. And as to the far-off "End" on which the hope of Israel rested, what other termination could be given to this prediction of the "Warfare Great," than that which crowns the whole complex prophecy of this "Book" with Israel's ultimate and full deliverance, connected with the Resurrection of the holy dead at Messiah's Second Coming? In both respects, xi. and xii. are an illustrious proof of the love and care of God for His people, a monument of His unchanging faithfulness to all generations. The objection to minuteness and multiplicity of details may be brought with equal force against the prophecies in ii. and vii. concerning the close of the 4th empire, and in ix. concerning the chronology and close of the 70 Weeks. It is wholly worthless. It would rule out the apocalypses of Ezekiel and John, and the minute predictions of all the prophets.

It is no man-made narrative, under the mask of prophecy, we have here, but true prediction, the tone, gaps, leaps, style and manner of prediction, its organic and typical relations. It is a prophecy of "Warfare Great" not only between the nations, but between Israel and the nations. There is not, in this chapter, a line, movement, campaign, alliance, intrigue, succession, victory or defeat, by sea or land, that does not in some way, affect the fortunes of the Jews and Palestine. There is not a movement of the Jews that does not in some way affect the empires and the kingdoms of this world. It is a long "Warfare," whose final action is decided alone by the Second Coming of Christ; a "Warfare Great" made necessary by the laws of history, the moral order of the universe, but, more than all, by the Kingdom of God and the relation of Israel and the Nations thereto. With clairvoyant gaze, the eyes of the angel see the world-movements of Persia and Greece, from East to West and from West to East, and of the kingdoms of Syria and Egypt, from North to South and from South to North, involving Europe, Asia and Africa, Palestine now quivering like an aspen leaf in the wind, now crushed like a grape cluster in the winepress. A deep philosophy of history is here, a mystery great, an age-long contention by rival powers for Palestine, involving a Jewish History that even Hegel confessed could not be explained on principles of natural evolution, a riddle whose solution is Israel hated by all nations, at last the master of all. The angel sees in the situation at the close of the 3d empire a type of the situation at the close of the 4th, the Jews being the last bone of contention among the "Powers." He shows how the nations hold each other at arms' length while professing friendship; how vain are the intrigues of kings and courts, the schemes of diplomats, merchants and explorers, revenue raisers and colonizers; how alliances and crowns are no effective pledge of national stability, and armies and fleets no guarantee of national security; how the reasons of defeat or victory lie deeper than tactics and strategy, even in a plexus of causes social, moral, religious, civil and political, all under the controlling hand of God, *and in a purpose of God with respect to the Jewish race which the whole concert of earth's "Powers" is unable to thwart.* He selects and unveils momentous crises and epochs in the drama of the age next following the Exile—pivotal events around which the fortunes of the Jews and Palestine with all its destiny revolve—all of them prefigurations of the last crisis that ends with Israel's victory and the triumph of the Kingdom of God.

The geography of the prophecy is easily determined. It is that of the empire of Cyrus, eight times greater than the empire of Babylon, stretching from Thibet and the Indus to the Mediterranean and Aegean seas, and from the Danube, Black Sea, Caucasus, Caspian and the Jaxartes, to the Indian Ocean, Persian Gulf and the deserts of Arabia and Nubia—the empire of one who struck the fetters from the Jews, restored the exiles and enabled them to build their temple and their city. It is the empire of Alexander who carried his conquests still farther southward to the cataracts of the Nile. It is the empire of Rome extended yet farther westward to the British Isles. It is the territory covered by the Colossus of Gentile politics and power in ii.—the scene of the "Warfare Great." Having glanced at the earlier world-movements East and West and the fortunes of the Jews under Persian and Greek supremacy, the angel specially unveils the movements North and South, his eyes ever resting on the Holy Land, the middle union-point of the three Old-World continents, the envy of all kings from the beginning of the world. Nor even here does he narrow the scope of his vision, as the crisis for Israel comes on. He causes to pass before us the whole East and West, North and South, the Syrian, Egyptian and Roman powers contending in

Asia, Europe and Africa, Scipio in the field, Popilius on the sea; Euergetes marching not merely to Antioch but to the Euphrates and trundling homeward images and statues once the booty of Cambyses. The expulsion of Antiochus the Great out of Europe, the ruin of Epiphanes in Persia, are here, both connected with the fortunes of the Jewish people—a vivid illustration of that "ever-recurring law" of historical movement, which a Rawlinson, Stanley and Creasy have noted—invasion from North to South, and East to West, provoking counter movements, and regularly so at fixed though unequal intervals of time. The Euphrates, Babylon, Persia, Armenia, Syria, Egypt, Asia Minor, Italy, Greece, Crete, Cyprus and always Palestine, are here; the Persian Gulf, the Caspian and Black seas, the Aegean and the Mediterranean, all that pertains to the Turkish empire, are here; the Dardanelles, the Bosphorus and old Byzantium. The shore-line of Palestine the fortresses of Sidon, Gaza, Seleucia, and Pelusium are here; Antioch, Jerusalem, Damascus and Aleppo, the Orontes, the Jordan, the Nile and the Tiber—all clear to him who studies the "meaning" of the vision. We hear, as we read, the shouts of encountering hosts, and see the assaults on beleaguered citadels, the sea-fights at Ephesus and Chios, the battles of Raphia, Magnesia, Mount Panium near the sources of the Jordan, the horrors at Jerusalem, and sit beside diplomats and kings intriguing in their palaces to unite their kingdoms, with Palestine as the dowry of their royal brides. It is the "*Eastern Question*" that is here, a question not limited or local, but ubiquitous, affecting to-day the deepest interests of Russia, England, France, Austria, Germany, Egypt, Greece, Turkey and Palestine, in their relations to each other, to India, China, and Japan, and to Africa, affecting the whole world; an age-long contention between conflicting civilizations, with creeds and forms of government, and prejudices of race and tradition diverse and opposed as the poles; that "*mache athanatos*" of Plato, the "immortal conflict" between truth and error, right and wrong, which endures till a "new cycle" of time shall bring its close. What statesman in any cabinet or chamber of modern legislation has ever lifted his voice to tell the world that, as in Moses, Isaiah, Ezekiel, Zephaniah and Zechariah, so here Daniel has exhibited, in chapters viii. and xi., the "*Eastern Question*" in terms impossible to be misunderstood, or that the waters of the Hellespont, the Ægean and Mediterranean seas, with the Isles of Greece and Asia Minor, and the mainlands washed by them—the storm-centre of the Eastern Question in every age—form for the prophet the geographical theatre of his vision of the "Warfare Great?" or that here the fleets of the nations must meet to sink and sail no more, in that final crisis when "Heaven, Earth, Sea, Dry Land, and all Nations" are "shaken?" It is the light of prophecy that enables us to see and understand the immense significance of the recent acts of the "Powers" in reference to Crete, Greece, Turkey, Armenia, and what the parallel Jewish movements forebode. In the words of a great and deep writer in our day, "International politics, the world over, are resolvable into some form of the Eastern Question. It haunts the history of civilized mankind."

But to come back. It belongs to the very perfection of the prophecy, whose compactness and lapidary brevity are without a parallel, that volumes of detail can be crowded into its exposition. It is a "Scripture of Truth" covering the fortunes of the Jews *in contact with the nations*, from 3d Cyrus, B. C. 534, to 11th Antiochus Epiphanes, B. C. 164, a period of 370 years, together with the scenes and events preceding and during the 70 Weeks in chapter ix., the near horizon of the 3d empire, a type of the far horizon of the 4th.

GENERAL DIVISION.

The division of the chapter is not difficult. It falls into the following sections; (1) verses 2-4; (2) verses 5-9; (3) verses 10-20; (4) verses 21-35; (5) verses 36-39; (6) verses 40-45.

I. Verses 2-4. The Persian and Greek supremacies. The angel first of all unrolls the Persian succession after Cyrus, as far as to the fourth in the line. Three kings, the false Smerdis omitted, shall arise after Cyrus, the fourth one the proud invader of Greece, 11:2. These are

(1) Cyrus to Cambyses, B. C. 538-529.
(2) Cymbyses to Darius Hystaspes, 529-521.
(3) Darius Hystaspes to Xerxes, 521-480.
(4) Xerxes' Invasion in 5th year, 480, a period of 58 years. Overleaping next a period of 148 years, filled by a succession of eight Persian kings, he unveils the empire of Alexander the Great and his counter invasion of Persia and the East, 11:3.

(1) Alexander's empire, B. C. 334-323.
(2) Alexander's death, 323.

Overleaping a period of 21 years, he unveils the quadripartition of Alexander's empire, B. C. 302, into the

DIADOCHIAN KINGDOMS.

(1) Egypt and Palestine ruled by Ptolemy.
(2) North Syria ruled by Seleucus.
(3) Macedonia and Thrace ruled by Cassander.
(4) Asia Minor ruled by Lysimachus.

These four generals of Alexander are called "Diadochi" or "Successors," yet "not of his posterity," 11:4. Of these kingdoms the two selected by the angel for special prophecy were chosen because Palestine lay between them. Under the title "King of the North," i. e., of Syria, seven Seleucid kings, and under the title "King of the South," i. e., of Egypt, six Ptolemies, are included, as follow, according to the times of their reigns:

PTOLEMIES AND SELEUCIDS.

(1) Ptolemy I. Soter, B. C. 323-285; Seleucus I. Nicator, B. C. 312-280—11:5.

(2) Ptolemy II. Philadelphus, B. C. 285-247; Antiochus II. Theos, B. C. 261-246—11:6.

(3) Ptolemy III. Euergetes, B. C. 247-221; Seleucus II. Kallinikos, B. C. 246-226—11:7-9.

(4) Ptolemy IV. Philopator, B. C. 221-205; Seleucus III. Keraunos, B. C. 226-222—11:10-12.

(5) Ptolemy V. Epiphanes, B. C. 205-181; Antiochus III., the Great, B. C. 222-187—11:13-19.

(6) Seleucus IV., B. C. 187-175—11:20.

(7) Ptolemy VI. Philometor, B. C. 181-146; Antiochus IV. Epiphanes, B. C. 175-164—11:21-35.

that is, six Ptolemies and six Seleucids *prior* to Antiochus Epiphanes; twelve in all, or thirteen in all, the reign of Antiochus I., B. C. 280-261, being overleaped and unnoticed.

THE INTERVALS.

Remarkable are the *Intervals* or Gaps in this prophecy of the future from 3d Cyrus to 11th Antiochus Epiphanes, 534-175=359 years. The angel chooses the events he foretells as stepping-stones to the crisis. Prophetic history is one thing, ordinary secular history another. No uninspired writer would write history as here forecast. (1) An interval of 146 years lies between verses 2 and 3, from 5th Xerxes 480 to Alexander 334, including eight Persian kings. (2) Another of 21 years, between the clauses in verse 4, from Alexander's death to the partition of his empire, 323-302. (3) Another of 30 years, between 5 and 6, covering the omitted reign of Antiochus I., 280-261, and on to the alliance with Berenice, 250. (4) Another of three years, between 6 and 7, from the murder of Berenice to the invasion of Syria by her brother, Euergetes, 250-247. (5) Another of 20 years, between 9 and 10, from Euergetes to the sons of Seleucus II., 247-227. (6) Another of 13 years, between 12 and 13, from the defeat of Antiochus III. at Raphia to his second invasion of Syria, 217-204. (7) Another of eight years, between 17 and 18, from the alliance with Cleopatra to the last campaign of Antiochus III., 198-190. The sum of the *Intervals* is 241 years, out of a period of 359 years covered by the prophecy. The *great interval* of 2061 years already gone between verses 39 and 40, will be seen hereafter. No "historian" would write history in this way. No "forger" would. The intervals are proofs of the supernatural origin of the prophecy. The angel unveils the

WARS OF SYRIA AND EGYPT.

The warfare wages from Ptolemy I. and Seleucus I. to the death of Antiochus Epiphanes, 11:5-35, B C. 306-164, a period of 142 years, somewhat more than the whole of the 3d and somewhat less than the half of the 2d century before the First Advent of Christ. The angel gives us a picture of the " Warfare Great " at the close of the 3d prophetic empire, the struggle of the Northern Power to gain Cœlo-Syria, Palestine, Phenicia and Egypt, then Macedonia and Asia Minor, in order to form one undivided empire, and so control the world's commerce and acquire supremacy over the three great continents of Europe, Asia and Africa, the type of a scheme yet to be, under the last Antichrist before the Second Advent of Christ.

II. Verses 11:5-9, B. C. 306-247, a period of 59 years, from Ptolemy I. and Seleucus I., " one of the princes " of Ptolemy, and founder of the Syrian kingdom, 11:5, to the first invasion of Syria by Ptolemy III., 11:7. Overleaping the reign of Antiochus I., 280-261, or 20 years, the angel foretells the disastrous alliance between Syria and Egypt, by the betrothment of Berenice, daughter of Ptolemy II. to Antiochus II., Antiochus divorcing his wife in order to unite the two kingdoms with Palestine as the dowry of Berenice; the scheme ending in the assassination of the latter, 11:6. He foretells also the invasion of Syria under Seleucus II. by Ptolemy III., "a branch" out of Berenice's " roots," i. e., by her own brother, sprung from the same parents, in order to avenge her death; an invasion reaching to the banks of the Euphrates, Ptolemy returning with " captives," " gods " and " gold and silver vessels," and surviving Seleucus four years, 11:6-9, B. C. 247.

III. Verses 11:10-20, B. C. 227-175, a period of 52 years. (1) Overleaping 20 years, 247-227, down to the " sons " of Seleucus II., viz.: Seleucus III., 227, and Antiochus III. the Great, 224, the angel foretells the invasion of Egypt by the latter and his overwhelming defeat at Raphia by Ptolemy IV., a victory, however, thrown away, 11: 10-12, B. C. 217. (2) Overleaping 13 years, called " certain years," 217-204, the angel unveils the second invasion of Egypt by Antiochus III., his stupendous victory over Ptolemy IV. at the battle of Mount Panium, near the sources of the Jordan, the élite of the Egyptian army unable to withstand him, his recovery also of the fortress of Sidon and the " fenced cities," and his conquest of Palestine, " with destruction in his hand," 11:13-16, B. C. 198. Irresistible force, a rich military chest, and strong allies should accomplish this. But more, the " Robbers " of the Jewish people, the " Violent among the Jews," the revolutionists of the Holy Land, should league themselves with the King of the North to aid him, *hoping thereby to win the independence of Palestine, but signally fail.* Hereby they should only bind on themselves the Syrian yoke, pave the way for the horrors to come under the Greek Antichrist, and so, without intent, help " fulfill the vision" of the " Warfare Great," 11: 14.

(3) After an imposing military demonstration there should be a second alliance between Syria and Egypt, a scheme again for the union of the two kingdoms, based on what Eastern monarchs would call " equitable negotiations " (not " upright ones "), all the more so since Egypt should be in her conqueror's power; the scheme this, viz.: the marriage of Cleopatra, the daughter of Antiochus, to Ptolemy V., in order to betray Egypt into her father's hands, a scheme foiled by her wifely fidelity to her husband; Cleopatra or ruin, the " equitable negotiations!" 11:17, B. C. 195. (4) Finally, Antiochus should undertake an expedition against the coast islands of Asia Minor, B. C. 190, but suffer a fair and honorable yet lasting defeat by Scipio Asiaticus at the battle of Magnesia, losing also his fleet at Ephesus, and thus, punished for his insults, be driven in retreat toward his own stronghold, compelled to surrender all his European possessions, his eastern ones also west of the Taurus, forced out of Europe by the Romans, loaded with indemnity, killed while plundering the temple of Jupiter at Elymais, and so disappearing forever from human history. 11:18, 19, B. C. 187. His successor—Seleucus IV., a " Revenue Raiser " causing Helioderus to go through Palestine,

and attempting to plunder the temple,—should enjoy a brief reign, and suffer by poison at Heliodorus' hands a death as ignominious as that of his predecessor, 11:20, B. C. 175. Thus, in his own way, in 11:5-20, the angel foretold the founding of the Syrian kingdom, 11:5; unveiled two diplomatic scenes, one in the palace at Antioch, 11:6, the other in the palace at Alexandria, 11:17, one invasion of Syria, 11:7-9, two invasions of Egypt and the conquest of Palestine by the King of the North, 11:10-12, 13-16. Also his last campaign and ignominious end, 11: 18, 19, with that of his successor, 11:20—the whole intended to lead up to the advent of the "Madman," or Greek Antichrist, viz.:

ANTIOCHUS IV., EPIPHANES.

IV. Verses 11:21-35, B. C. 175-164. Of this wild beast in human form the angel foretells that a "Vile" or "Contemptible Person" should, in the place of ("the state of") Seleucus IV. stand up in his pride, a younger son of Antiochus the Great, born B. C. 221, dying B. C. 164, the "Little Horn" in 8:9, 20 years a hostage at Rome, and without title to the throne, and should, at the age of 58 years, effect a successful *coup d'etat*, usurping by craft the Syrian crown, 11:21, B. C. 175; that, under him, the same playing fast and loose with truth and treaties, which distinguished his house, and now prevails in modern times, should continue, the same diplomacy in foreign affairs, the utter absence of good faith and presence of dissimulation, the pretence of peace while preparing war, the promise of reforms for Israel while effecting none, the practice of menace, intrigue, and force, to secure dynastic interests, a policy in which financial and political would be the first and justice, truth, humanity and righteousness, the last considerations—that, true to the traditions of this house, he would establish his kingdom (1) by leaguing with apostate Jews, Palestine now in his possession, breaking a pre-existing covenant to give the Holy Land to Egypt's queen as her dowry, and in which Ptolemy Philometor was "prince of the covenant," 11:

22, repelling by superior force "the arms of a flood;" Ptolemy's invasion of Syria to enforce a treaty right, and entering into a new treaty; and, that "after the league made with him," he, Antiochus, would "work deceitfully," 11:23; (2) by taking advantage of the wars in Macedonia, Greece and Southern Europe, he would endeavor to conquer Egypt, uniting both kingdoms in one, then Macedonia, Thrace, Greece and Asia Minor, so forming one mighty empire out of all, controlling the Mediterranean and acquiring supremacy over the three continents. The angel predicts that his

CAMPAIGNS AGAINST EGYPT

would be three, and in the following order, viz.:

(1) The *First Campaign* would be a crafty entrance into Egypt with a small force, "in time of security," marching along the rich provinces of Lower Egypt—the Nile Valley—coming up as far as Memphis, simulating friendship yet plundering the country, and, in order to become "strong" with the Egyptians, distributing wealth and spoil to the people, contrary to the custom of his house, and plotting against the fortresses, 11:23, 24, B. C. 173.

(2) The *Second Campaign* would be in force, courageously, defeating the great army of Ptolemy betrayed by his own courtiers into the hands of Antiochus; that, then, forming a new treaty, one king in the power of the other, "both these kings' hearts would be to do mischief," both "speaking lies at one table," yet unsuccessfully, because God had set a time-limit to their intrigues. The angel here draws a picture of modern diplomacy also, true to the life. He paints Gentile politics and power in living costume, the code and cunning of the great Colossus, the inner life of the Beasts, 11:25-27, B. C. 170.

(3) The *Third Campaign* should be in force again, but disastrous to Antiochus, since Popilius Lœnas and the Roman fleet from the naval stations at Cyprus and Crete—"the ships from Kittim"—would compel him to vacate Egypt at once and try his hand elsewhere, 11:29, 30, B. C. 168.

Still more, the angel predicts that his

would be two, and in the following order, viz.:

(1) The *First Campaign* would be upon his return northward from his Second Expedition against Egypt. Furious because of distraction and excited by rumors of revolt in Jerusalem, he would assail the "Holy Covenant"—a technical expression for the Holy City, Temple, People, Worship and Mosaic institutions—invading the Holy Land, devoting to destruction 80,000 Jews, taking 10,000 prisoners, rifling the temple of 1,800 talents equal to $3,250,000, set up a High Priest to suit himself, the mitre, robes and breast-plate of Aaron already sold for 440 talents, 150 more given him for the right to erect a Greek Gymnasium to please young men of Jerusalem weary of their covenant with God. Thus should he "do" and go home to Antioch, 11:28, B. C. 170; I. Macc. i: 16-28; II. Macc. v: 11-21.

(2) The *Second Campaign* would be upon his expulsion from Egypt by the Roman fleet under Popilius, 11:30, when, humiliated, and raging like a madman, he would return northward, with indignation against the "Holy Covenant," and, in league with the apostates, devote 20,000 more to massacre, pollute the bulwarked sanctuary of God, abolish the Daily Sacrifice, set up "the Abomination causing desolation"—a pagan altar on the altar of Jehovah—violating mothers and daughters and hanging infants, increasing by corruption the number of apostates and giving orders to his generals if failing to Hellenize the Holy People, then to "root out the seed of Abraham," "root out their religion," "root out the whole race of Jews" and "make Jerusalem a common burying-ground," 11:31, 32. All which he would "do" or attempt to "do," B. C. 168-165; I. Macc. i: 29-64; iii: 32-37. The climax of horror was reached 15th and 25th December, B. C. 168. The vision of it is given in chapter viii: 9-14, 23-25.

But, though ground between contending empires, God would not forsake His people. His covenant stands fast. Evermore there shall be "a remnant according to the election of grace," a company of overcoming souls, faithful to death, ordained to wear a crown brighter than David wore and jeweled with gems more lustrous than the stones on Aaron's breast. If Antiochus can "*do*," God's people also shall '*do*." The angel foretells

THE MACCABEAN TRIBULATION.

He depicts the unsurpassed courage of a holy Mattathias and his five sons, among whom Judas Maccabæus, the "Hammer" of God—a Charles Martel before his time—and all his Asmonean heroes should stand forth strong in the strength of God, resisting the commandments of the Greek Antichrist— God's own, who, through faith should "obtain a good report," when persecution would be the greatest, the tyrants rage the hottest. "The people who know their God shall be strong and *do!*" 11: 32. Soul-thrilling is the record of their deeds, in 1. Macc. ii: 1-70. He predicts that the holy Teachers, the "*Maskilim*," or men of understanding, should instruct the people to stand for the truth, God, and the religion of their fathers in the midst of captivity and martyrdom by flame and sword, spoiled of all things, their only raiment sheepskins and goat-skins, their home the battle-field, their shelter the dens and caves of the earth; that a little band of pious souls, the faithful "*Chasidim*," would rally to their help, when all seemed lost; that a crowd of cowards, deserters in time of danger, hypocrites and flatterers in time of victory, would cleave to them; that among the slain should be some of the brave hero-leaders who would win the martyr's crown; that God's design was to "try, purify and make white" His loved ones, show to the world the indestructibility of grace, the power of faith and patience of hope, and that neither tribulation nor distress, nor persecution, famine, nakedness, peril or sword, could separate them from His love; and, finally, that though severe, the tribulation would be short, even "for an appointed time"—the 1150 days mentioned in viii: 14. So does the angel unveil the "Warfare Great" at the close of Old Testament times. That the illustrious heroes of the Maccabæan age were sustained by the

Hope of the Resurrection, which their holy prophets, from Moses to Daniel, had set before them—yea, from Abraham's day—their history most touchingly attests. Thrilling, beyond description is the story of the martyrdom of the Maccabæan mother and her seven sons—a story without a parallel for pathos and effect upon the heart, save in the case of Him who was the Author and Finisher of their faith. The "Seven," tortured and slaughtered, one by one, before the eyes of her who bore them and nursed them in their infancy, *died with her under God's covenant of everlasting life*, their noble mother cheering and sustaining them amid their agonies, then crowning the aceldama with her own triumphant death. With what calmness, holy resolution and courage of faith, they met their fate! "Thou, O persecutor, takest us out of this present life, but the King of the Ages will raise us up to life everlasting"— an allusion to Dan. xii: 1. "These bodies, this corruptible, we lay down for the sake of His laws, hoping to receive them again." This they knew, that "God will restore to His saints their bodies when He shall raise to life the dead men of this nation, even the slain of His people"—an allusion to Isa. xxvi: 19. Sublime in moral heroism are the words of the seventh son, the other six already weltering in their blood: "And thou, O godless wretch, of all men most abominable, be not lifted up. *Our brethren, having now suffered a short pain, have died under the covenant of everlasting life*, but thou shalt receive, through the judgment of God, the just punishment of thy presumption." Already the fourth son had as calmly and solemnly spoken, "*It is good being put to death by men, to look for hope from God, to be raised again*, but, for thee, there shall be no resurrection to eternal life"—an allusion to Isa. xxvi. 14. Then, lastly, the immortal mother who, in the ecstasy of immolation poured forth the full tide of her unbosomed love and faith, and, slaughtered, fell on sleep to wake with her sons in the resurrection of the just. "Blessed are the dead who die in the Lord," Rev. xiv: 13; 2 Macc. vii: 1-12; 5 Macc. i: 13. Thus did the Old Testament saints look to the second coming of Christ with an intensity of faith and ardor of expectation, that puts to shame the attitude of the Christian church to-day, with reference to that sublime and glorious event.

The holy Apostle Paul has embalmed the memory of these martyrs of the Law, and extolled their exploits with the unction of his inspiration. His heart heaves and his pen burns as he presents them to us for our imitation, crowned by the example of the blessed Jesus. "They waxed valiant in fight and turned to flight the armies of the aliens," as did Judas Maccabæus, scattering at one time 9,000 of the foe with only 1,500 men, at another 110,000 with only 8,000, the battle-cry on their lips, "*God our Help!*" "*Victory from Jehovah!*" "*The Kingdom Forever!*"—proof that the modern maxim, "God is on the side of the strongest battalions" is a lie! "Out of weakness they were made strong." "They were tortured, *not accepting deliverance* (as was the fact with the mother and her seven sons) *that they might obtain a better resurrection!*" Others had trial of cruel mockings, yea, moreover, of bonds and imprisonments. They were stoned, they were sawn asunder, they were slain with the sword. They wandered about in sheep-skins and goat-skins, being destitute, afflicted, tormented, *of whom the world was not worthy!* They wandered in deserts and in mountains, and in dens and caves of the earth! And all these"—the Old Testament heroes of the faith—" having obtained a good report through faith, received not the promise (of life everlasting, never to die), God having provided some better thing for us (even Christ at both His comings) *that they, without us, should not be made perfect*" Heb. xi: 34-40.

These glorious martyrs of the Law at the close of the 3d prophetic empire—twice immortalized in the Scriptures—the prophet Daniel teaches us are the fore-runners of martyrs yet to be, at the close of the 4th empire, under the last Antichrist, Dan. vii: 25; ix: 27; xii: 1, 7. The apostle Paul set them before the New Testament saints as examples to inspire their courage and lead to imitation of their fortitude—" a cloud of witnesses," then beholding and now beholding our warfare and our race. He adds to them "*Jesus*," the Christian protomartyr, the Author and Finisher of the "faith" by which those heroes obtained a good report.

By such examples and the love of Christ, that "cloud" has been expanded to 20,000,000 martyrs more in New Testament times, the latest the brave Armenians who were "slain with the sword" rather than abjure their faith and accept the creed of Islam. The holy John assures us that the early Christian martyrs, also, were the forerunners of martyrs yet to be in the Time of the End, who will cheerfully drink—as did they—the Cup the Saviour drank, and be baptised with the baptism He was baptised with. And foremost shall be their glory, as foremost was their suffering. In that galaxy of saints shine a Stephen, Peter, Paul and James; a Polycarp, Ignatius, Irenæus and Justin; a Wickliffe, Huss and Jerome of Prague; a Wishart and Hamilton; a Rogers, Cranmer, Latimer, Ridley and holy Bradford; with millions more, the victims of Antiochus, of Nero, of Torquemada, the Duke of Alva, Claverhouse and "Abdul the Damned"—a happy fellowship, whose effulgence in the resurrection shall correspond to the suffering by which they testified their loyalty and love. To comfort such, in view of the tribulation to come upon them, every apocalypse in both Testaments was given, without exception. To be among that blessed company, Paul desired that literally he might "be made conformed to the death of Christ, if by any means he might attain to the resurrection out from among the dead" Phil. iii: 10, 11, and nobly won his desire. 2 Tim. iv: 6. Of such, with special emphasis—sharers with the Maccabæan heroes—the Holy Spirit has said "the world was not worthy"—peerless souls whom God Himself has "counted worthy of the Kingdom of God," Heb. xi: 38; II. Thess. i: 5; while the "timid and unbelieving," who "love their lives" and seek to "save" them, shall "lose" them and have their portion among "them that are without," Rev. xxi: 8; xii: 11.

I saw, far down he coming time,
The fiery chastisement of crime,
With noise of mingling hosts, and jar
Of falling towers and shouts of war;
I saw the nations rise and fall
Like fire-gleams on the whitened wall;
I saw them draw the stormy hem
Of battle 'round Jerusalem.
Who trembled a my warning word?
Who owned the prophet of the Lord?

O prophet of the beating heart,
For God's great purpose set apart,
Before whose far-discerning eyes
The future as the present lies,
Beyond a narrow-minded age
Stretches thy prophet's heritage;
Through heaven's dim spaces, angel-trod,
Through arches 'round the throne of God!
Thy audience, worlds!—all time to be
The witness of the *Truth* in thee!
—WHITTIER.

Chapter IX.

DANIEL, CHAPTERS X-XII.—TSABA GADOL. WARFARE GREAT. TYPE AND ANTITYPE. EASTERN QUESTION.

The previous article dealt with the angel's words, concerning the "Warfare Great," as far as to the Maccabean period, viz., to xi: 35. The present deals with the remainder of xi. in connection with xii. The first thing here is

THE TRANSITION-SECTION.

V. Verses xi: 36-39. The death of Epiphanes is not recited at the close of xi: 30-35, B. C. 164, as it was given already in viii: 25, in the words "he shall be broken without hand." The silence is doubtless due to the fact that type and antitype are blended in "the King," xi: 36, continuing together through the section, until the one is displaced by the other at xii: 40. The exit of "the King," the Antichrist, is expressed in the words "he shall come to his end and none shall help him," xi: 45. "His end" here, is "his end" in ix: 26, i.e., the end of the "prince that shall come."

The vital question that decides the division of the chapter from xi: 21, onward to the end, is how much refers to Antiochus, and how much to the Antichrist? We encounter it at verses 21, 36, and 40. It is (1) whether from 21 to the end of the chapter, all relates to Antiochus; or (2) all to the last Antichrist; or (3) all to both; or (4) whether 21-35 relates to Antiochus alone, and 36-45 to the Antichrist alone; or (5) whether 40-45 relates to the Antichrist alone. These views exhaust the history of the interpretation. The first was held by Porphyry in ancient times,—and is held by the higher critics. The second was held by Jerome and some of the church fathers, the *Interval* between Seleucus IV., xi: 20, and the Antichrist being placed between 20 and 21. The third view was next held by Jerome also, Theodoret and others, two senses, the literal and typical allowed in order to include both Epiphanes and the Antichrist. Only in this sense was it that Jerome asked "Suppose these things *are* said of Antiochus, what harm comes to our religion?" The fourth view, viz., partly to Epiphanes, 21-35, and partly to the Antichrist, 36-45, was that of the learned Jews of Jerome's time, and which he himself was inclined to adopt. The fifth, viz., only 40-45 relates to the Antichrist, arose after the rise of Mohammed, and is adopted by some Romanists, some Protestants, and some of the Greek church. It regards Mohammed in the line of his successors, as the Antichrist, on the year-day theory.

As to the first view—all to Antiochus—it is excluded by the fact that nothing in the career of Antiochus corresponds to this campaign of 40-45; that Porphyry's assertion to the contrary is void of all support; that the fancy that the three campaigns of Antiochus against Egypt, and the two against Palestine, in 23-35, are here "*recapitulated*" is absurd, as Jerome himself discovered, since never at any time did Antiochus march through Palestine, as "the King" here does xi: 41, to invade Egypt, but only entered Palestine on his "return" from Egypt to Antioch, xi: 28, 30,—besides never having "the Lybians and Ethiopians at his steps." As to the second view, —all to the Antichrist—it is excluded by this, that the "Vile Person," xi: 21, is the immediate successor of Seleucus IV. in xi: 20 B. C. 175., i.e., stands up "in his estate," therefore cannot be the last Antichrist at the close of Gentile times. There is no interval, therefore, between 20 and 21. As to the third view—all to both—it is excluded by this, that the features peculiar to the Antichrist, and not found in Antiochus (and such are admitted, especially his self-exaltation "above every god,") cannot be common to Both. As to the fourth view, viz., partly to Antiochus, 21-35, and partly to the Antichrist, 39-45, it is certain (1) that the term "the King" is here first used absolutely, apart from the qualifying adjunct, "of the North," and is connected immediately with a description of absolute atheism in its extremest form, which was not true of Antiochus; (2) that, in verse 40, the pronoun "*him*" in the clause "push at *him*,"—and "*him*" in the clause "come against *him*,"—and "*he*" in the clause, "*he* shall enter," all refer to "the King" in 36, the antitype of Antiochus, as do all the pronouns "*He*," "*His*," "*Him*," in all the verses following. Keil, holding the common view, has endeavored to dispute the above, but unsuccessfully against Kliefoth, who with others has victorously defended it: (3) that the "Warfare Great" ends only with the final deliverance of the Jews from the grasp of "the King" in 36, and with the resurrection of the holy dead, xii: 1, at the coming of the Son of Man, and the King's destruction, vii: 13; (4) that "the Time of the End" xi: 40, is identical with "at that time" in xii: 1, and therefore, "the King" in 36, is the "*Him*," "*He*," "*His*" in 40-45, who is destroyed at the second coming of Christ. *A greater than Antiochus is here*! The identity of this blaspheming atheist with the last Antichrist is established by Paul, 2 Thess. ii: 1-12, and by John, Rev. xiii: 5-7, incontrovertibly. Therefore did Hippolytus, the ablest and first real exegete of the early church, say: "Here is the Antichrist in xi: 36, 37." So did the Jews believe, and Jerome say of them, "The Jews maintain that the things here spoken relate to the Antichrist," adding further, "Our writers hold that the things here predicted relate to the Antichrist,—which, indeed, we also understand of the Antichrist." As to the fifth view that *only* 40-45 refers to the Antichrist, it is excluded by the above considerations, while yet it remains true that 40-45 refers *solely* to him and not to Antiochus.

The only question, therefore, is this, viz., if 36-39 is the transition-section, including a double personality, type and antitype in one description, where is the Interval between these two persons, i.e., between Antiochus and the Antichrist. Is it between 35 and 36, or 39 and 40? The answer made by the most patient specialists, and supported by the strongest arguments from men of opposite schools is for example that "the section, xi: 40-45, cannot be explained of Antiochus, in any way, and the Interval must lie between verses 39 and 40." (Dornstetter.) "The transition is at verse 36, and the interval lies between 39 and 40." (Tiefenthal.) Even Cornill, like Kuenen, Hitzig, Bevan, Behrmann, confesses that the section cannot be referred to anything known in the history of Antiochus. "I hold such an explanation to be impossible. It is excluded by the structure of the whole chapter which gives a clear chronological succession of campaigns and events from Cyrus to Antiochus. A leap *backwards* at xi: 40, in order to make a *resume*, is unknown to prophecy and inconceivable at its culminating point. The words 'And in the time of the End' denote progress in events, not regress in discourse, and are decisive against it." (Cornill.) Nor, again, can 40-45 be a fourth campaign of Antiochus, since the tyrant was expelled from Egypt, by Roman force, B. C. 168, and "ever after, Egypt was under Roman protection" (Welzhofer), until it was "deeded as a farm, by will, to the Roman people and in vain was sought to be revived to Cleopatra by Caesar and Antony," (Mariette). Moreover, the battle of Pydna, B. C. 168, shattered forever the Syrian power. What then? Shall we say, as a last resort that 40-45 is the dream of a Maccabean writer, not yet informed of the death of Antiochus, and forecasting an imaginary future for him? Porphyry spurned that idea, "Such exposition is the last resort of rationalistic criticism." (Wolf). "The probability of a *resume* is an improbability, the dream of a possible fourth campaign is the dream of an impossibility, and the resort to an imagination of a Maccabean Jew is only what we might expect from a criticism which itself is a dream" (Herzfeld). It remains, therefore, that 40-45 is a true prediction, and that the interval between Antiochus and the Antichrist, lies between verses 39 and 40. That interval stretches from B. C. 164 to A. D. 1898, and is 2,061 years, or 237 years greater than the interval in ix: 26, between A. D. 70 and 1898; an interval of 1,827 years. At xi: 40, we take farewell of Antiochus forever, and are transported into the "Time of the End" of our present age. Here, we rest with confidence, as to the

THE TIME OF THE END.

Dan. xi: 35; Dan. xi: 40.

Maccabees.  Antiochus.
Time of the End.

B. C. 168-164.
Dan. viii: 10-13.
Dan. xi: 21-31,
1150 days.

The Great Interval.
From B. C. 164 to A. D. 1898, 2061 years, and on to the Time of the End.

	The Blessed Time 1335 days. 1290 days. End of the Week.
3½	1260
Time of the End.	
3½	1260

Dan. xi: 40-45; xii: 7, 11; Dan. viii: 25; ix: 27; Deut. xxxii: 39-43; Joel iii: 9-17; Isa. lxvi: 1-5; Ezek. xxxviii: 1-23; xxxix: 1-29; Ezek. xxxvii: 1-28; Zech. xii: 1-14; xiv: 1-5; Our Lord, Matth. xxiv: 15-43; xxv: 31-46; Paul, 2 Thess. ii: 1-12; 1 Thess. iv: 14-17; John, Rev. xi: 2, 3, 7; xii: 6, 14; xiii: 5; xix: 11-21.

1260 days.

The Course of Empire overleaped from B. C. 164 to the Second Advent.

TYPE AND ANTITYPE.

1. The Double Personality, the King. Dan. xi: 36

2. The Transition-Section. Dan. ix: 36-39.

3. The Great Interval Between. Dan. xi: 39, 40.

4. The Time of the End. Dan. xi: 40-45.

interpretation. Jerome's words are conclusive of the mature judgment of the early church. "Our writers hold that the things here predicted relate to the Antichrist." Fraidl's words are conclusive as to the judgment of the Middle Age, "The judgment of antiquity was that of the centuries following." Düsterwald's words are conclusive as to modern times, "All, save the rationalists, hold that verses 40-45 pertain to the Antichrist." As to the contents of the section before us, we come, now, to the

PHOTOGRAPH OF THE ANTICHRIST.

It surpasses that of Antichus in viii, bad as that is, and transcends all historical accounts of the Syrian tyrant. The angel paints in bold relief the three predominating characteristics of "the King." (1) His atheistic self-deifying egotism and blaspheming mouth. Epiphanes, indeed, stood up against the "Prince of princes," Israel's Jehovah, and opposed him, viii: 25, but it is not said that he exalted himself "above every god," or blasphemed the "God of gods," and refused to "regard any god," as is said of "the King," in xi: 36, 37. Here is an atheism so absolute as to smite every Pantheon in antiquity, every ethnic god, as well as Jehovah. Epiphanes, however, was not "*Atheos*" in an ethnic sense. "*Theos*" belonged as a title to his line, as "*Divus*" did to the Cæsars. He worshipped Olympian Zeus, set up his statue in Jerusalem, made presents to the god of Tyre, and created a temple in Antioch to Capitoline Jove, well known to his fathers. Livy describes him as diligent "In deorum cultu." His ambition was to root out Judaism and instal the Greek Pantheon in its place, and everywhere. Very differently "the King," in 36, exalts himself "above every god," reckless of "any god," and with eruptive mouth, face skyward, explodes his blasphemies against the "God of gods," the only true God. He speaks marvelous things against the "God of gods." This, to the life, is the "Little Horn" in vii: 11, 25, who "speaks great words against the Most High." He is Paul's "Man of Sin," 2 Thess. ii: 4, "who exalteth himself above all that is called God, or is worshipped," and will sit in the temple of God, showing himself that he is God," a thing Epiphanes did not do, nor any Cæsar. He is John's personal Beast who "has a mouth speaking great things and blasphemies," lifting his "mouth in blasphemy against God, to blaspheme His name, His tabernacle, and them that dwell therein." Rev. xiii: 5, 6. It is in verses 36, 37, at the head of this transition-section, Paul and John both find the final "Man of Sin," the "Beast," "the Antichrist," the "Horn," in Dan. vii: 8. (2) His imbruted soul, dehumanized and dead to all the tenderest affections of human kind, disregarding even woman's love,—"*hemdath nashim,*" (compare 2 Sam. i: 26), her desire of husband, home, maternity, the babe on her breast, her children, her daughter's sanctity, the endearments of domestic life, and, like a Moslem or a Mongol, a Sultan or Khan, devoting all to outrage, agony, and massacre. It is not a Syrian god or goddess that is meant by the phrase "love of women," nor celibacy, nor illicit love. So far from this, Antiochus was the father of a family, left his son Antiochus V. as his successor to the throne, and moreover, consorted publicly with the lewdest characters: Only in so far as his debaucheries were a disregard of woman's purest love, does the description here apply to him. (3) His adoption of a new god, in spite of his atheism, and for the sake of his followers as a stimulus to their military ardor, and a means of propagating his religion, viz., "*Allah Maozim,*" the *god of fortresses,*" or "*strongholds,*" placing here his confidence, whether in the strongholds of the Orontes, Nile, Euphrates, Tigris, or Bosphorus,—in Syria, Egypt, Macedonia, or Asia Minor,—(the parted empire of Alexander)—honoring "Allah" with "gold, silver, precious stones, and costly things,—a god unknown to his ancestors and whose religion he would propagate by the sword, procuring for his strongholds garrisons of people who acknowledged his strange god, increasing them with glory while putting to the sword all others, causing them to rule over the many, and because needing money for war, dividing the land he conquers, for the sake of gain." This the meaning of this difficult verse. Such the three great characters of "the King": The first was not seen in Antiochus to the extent here predicted. The second was seen, in his butchery of infants in Jerusalem, his treatment of the Maccabean mother and her sons, and his inhuman conduct everywhere. The third was seen in the confidence he placed in fortresses, and in the propagation of his religion by the sword. But yet, the full reality of all awaits the future and the final Antichrist. And, now, overleaping the great interval between verses 39 and 40, we come to the close of the fourth divided empire, and, the

ANTICHRIST'S LAST CAMPAIGN.

VI. Verses xi: 40-45. It is only in his military character the Antichrist is here presented, and it is only a section of the world-wide "Warfare Great" that is here given; that which pertains to the final struggle of the Jews for the re-possession of their land, and their final deliverance from Gentile power. The time is called the "Time of the End."

In whatever sense the words "at that time" in xii: 1, are taken,—a sense determined by the events described in 1-3, in the same sense the "Time of the End" in xi: 40-45 must be taken, because the "Time of the End" here, is "that time" there. The two are chronologically one, and the events of xi: 40-45 contemporate with those in xii: 1-3, the Deliverance of Israel and the resurrection from the dead directly connected with the destruction of "the King," xi: 45. No interval exists between xi: 45, and xii: 1. The "Time of the End" here, is not the "Time of the End" in xi: 35, and viii: 25, viz., that of the third empire, the Greek, but is clearly that of the fourth in its ten kingdomed state, the Roman. Nor is the expression "the Time of the End" the same as the "End of Time." It does not denote the end of history, nor of the planet, nor of nations, but the end of our present age, the 70th week itself in ix: 27, the last half of which is seen in vii: 25, and xii: 7. It is the time when the Antichrist will make a "covenant," or "treaty," with the Jews, granting them a *modus vivendi*, in their own land, with civil rights, and permission to revive their ancient worship, then suddenly soon after because of some important event in their history which threatens his own empire, perhaps their effort to gain their independence, or the conversion of the remnant, violate his "covenant," ix: 27, and "on wing of abomination," become their bitterest enemy, seeking their extirpation. By such means he accelerates his own destruction. Coincident with his last campaign is the first campaign of "Gog and Magog," led by the "Prince of Rosh, Meshech, and Tubal," and connected with the defeat of both Gog and the Antichrist, and with the restoration of Israel. Ezek. xxxviii: 1-23; xxxix: 1-29; xxxvii: 1-28.

The "Time of the End" is of the intensest interest, as it brings the end of the "Warfare Great," with the momentous events that follow. The angel predicts that, of all the "Powers" then in the field, *three* shall be prominent, (1) the "King of he South," who is not Ptolemy Philometor, but the power holding Egypt, the horizon of the South in the last days extending to the Nile-sources, as in Isa. xviii, and Zephaniah iii; (2) the "King of the North," who is not Antiochus Epiphanes, but the power ruling the North, the horizon extending beyond the Caucasus, as in Ezek. xxxviii; the East reaching beyond the Euphrates, as in Revelation xvi, the West beyond the Mediterranean, again as in Ezek. xxxviii; (3) "The King" of xi: 36, the antitype of Antiochus, viz., the Antichrist; that in "the Time of the End," the power ruling the South, shall "push" at "the King" of xi: 36, that is, cross swords with him, (compare viii: 4, 6), and open the great campaign; that the power ruling the North,—mighty, abundant in horses, wheeled armament, and ships, a great naval and military power, strong in cavalry,—shall come cycloning "against him," the same "King" of xi: 36; that, notwithstanding these demonstrations, "the King" will mobilize his forces, "enter into the countries" round about, "overflow" them with his troops, and "pass over" into Palestine "the glorious land," and that "myriads shall be overthrown" (see xi: 12); in short, that entering Palestine from the north, his line of march will be southward through Palestine, subjecting the insurrectionary Jews, many here as elsewhere being "overthrown"; that, nevertheless, the transjordanic regions occupied by Israel when they first entered the Holy Land, viz., Edom, Moab, and the chief city of Ammon, "*shall be delivered out of his hands,*"—lands called by Isaiah "the shoulders (i.e., mountains) of the Philistines," occupied in this crisis by returning Israel, (compare Isa. xi: 11-16);—that, notwithstanding this, "the King" shall enter Egypt, and the tribes of North and South Africa shall flock to his standard, and "*Egypt shall not be able to deliver itself,*" and that the treasures of Egypt shall be at the King's command. This, the first result to the power holding Egypt, for "pushing" at the King, viz., its temporary loss, xi: 41-43. The whole description goes to show that the final contest for the repossession of the Holy Land, by the ancient people of God, has come. The angel further predicts that "tidings out of the East and out of the North" (East and North of Egypt) will be the Nemesis that will precipitate the doom of the King,—rumors of insurrections in Palestine and further East, of risings in the North,—some strategic movement also in the East and North by some military power advancing on Palestine, in force, compelling him to go forth," i.e., abandon Egypt and concentrate his strength in the Holy Land as his last hope; and that occupying Jerusalem, by assault, (Zech. xiv: 2), he will plant his military headquarters on Mount Moriah, "the mountain of the beauty of holiness," between the Mediterranean and Dead seas, and there,—at Jerusalem,—"come to his end, with none to help him." xi: 45. Thus, he will perish in the military overflowing,—"in the flood" ix: 26, Isa. lix: 19,—struck by the second coming of Christ. vii: 13, 25, 26, Isa. xi: 4. 2 Thess. ii: 8. Rev. xix: 11.

Still further, the angel predicts that, "*at that time,*" a spectacle unparalleled in magnificence, and followed by events incomparable in importance for the kingdom of God, shall take place; that the "Warfare Great" shall extend itself to the unseen world; that "Michael the great prince that standeth for the children of thy people" (Daniel's people, the Jews), shall "stand over" them, and there shall be "*War in Heaven,*" Rev. xii: 7, a battle of battles in aerial regions between the powers of light and darkness, a conflict of principalities and powers leagued for Israel's destruction, with angelic hosts leagued for Israels defense; an onset by "*Michael and his angels*," against the "*Dragon and his angels*," a warfare against "the hosts of the high ones on high," as well as against "the kings of the earth on the earth," Isa. xxiv: 21; heaven, earth, sea, dry land, all nations, shaken;—commotion above, commotion below, commotion everywhere, and specially in Palestine. Elsewhere, we learn that Michael's standing "over" the children of Israel, is at *the middle of the 70th week*, the time when the "Two Witnesses" are slain, Rev. xi: 7, and the conversion of the Jews is announced, Rev. xii: 10-12, and Michael is victorious over Satan, dejecting him from aerial regions to the earth, Rev. xii: 9. Then the Great Tribulation begins. Rev. xii: 12, Matth. xxiv: 22. This fixes the date of Michael's standing as the date when the Antichrist is forced out of Egypt, a part of the alarming "tidings" being that many Jews have become Christian, a rumor that excites the wrath of the Antichrist, and impels him to "go forth" resolved to break his "covenant" with all Jews and "root out the seed of Israel from the earth." Then he will war not only with the sun-clothed woman, but with the whole body of believers everywhere. The angel predicts that the tribulation will continue three and a half years, Dan. xii: 7, and that, at the close of this period the final deliverance of the Jews shall take place, the resurrection of the holy dead also, and the destruction of the Antichrist, xii: 13, 7. These events so stupendous are inseparable from the second coming of Christ to close the "Warfare Great" and introduce the millennial age. That will be a time which whoever lives or is waked from his grave to see, is a "Blessed" man;—in short, the time when the "Kingdom" of Christ is brought to victory "underneath all heavens." vii: 27.

As to the fulfillment of the vision, enough has been said already, to show its impossibility in the time of Antiochus. Up to 1898, all the prophecies of Daniel save the remainder of the interval from 1898 to the 70th week, and the 70th week itself, have met their literal accomplishment in the exactest and minutest manner. This alone, awaits the future. That it was not fulfilled in the siege of Jerusalem by Titus, is evident from this, that our Lord places the great tribulation here spoken of, Dan. xii: 1, 12, in the future, commencing with the middle of the 70th week, when the "abomination of desolation stands in a holy place," and ending with His coming in the clouds of heaven. Matth. xxiv: 15-31, Dan. vii: 13. The whole tenor of Old and New Testament prophecy seems to fix the time when the "Man of Sin" will "sit in the temple of God," 2 Thess ii: 4, as the time when Satan is dejected from his aerial sphere by Michael, and rumors of the conversion of the Jews reach the Antichrist in Egypt. It is then that Satan enters him and he invades Palestine from the South. Rev. xi: 7; xii: 17; (compare ix: 1-21). It is then that in his madness, he slays the "Two Witnesses," seeks to root out Israel, "sits in the temple of God," Rev. xi: 1, makes war with the saints everywhere, Jews or Gentiles, and inaugurates the Tribulation. Whatever fore-lights of this have been recognized in the Saracenic and Turkish "Woes" upon apostatising Christendom in the Middle Age, and in the capture of Jerusalem by Caliph Omar, A. D. 637, and last of all, by the Turk, A. D. 1187 and 1517, it is still certain that the campaign of the last Antichrist lies in the future. The all-embracing prophecy includes all, and evermore the last is the highest, most exhaustive, and literal fulfillment.

That this last crisis is impending, is undeniable. The whole world is preparing for the last act in the tragedy of the "Warfare Great." Christendom is already one vast military camp and naval depot. The son of Pethuel is again on his watchtower, blowing the trumpet in Zion, summoning the nations to "*come up*" to Jerusalem, and the Lord and His mighty angels to "*come down*" from heaven. Joel, iii: 9-16, has dramatized the scene in the most thrilling manner,—the scene of the advance of the nations, marching to the "Valley of Decision," where the "Eastern Question" will be "decided."

THE LORD.

"Proclaim ye this among the nations. Prepare war. Wake up the mighty men. Let all the men of war draw near. Let them come up. Haste ye, and come, all ye nations round about and assemble yourselves together." This the summons.

THE PROPHET.

"Thither cause thy mighty ones to come down, O Lord!" This the prayer.

THE LORD.

"Let the nations bestir themselves, and come up to the Valley of Jehoshaphat, for there will I sit to judge all the nations round about." This the locality.

THE LORD TO HIS HOSTS.

"Put ye in the sickle, for the harvest is ripe. Come; tread ye; for the wine-press is full, the vats overflow, for their wickedness is great." This the order.

THE PROPHET A SPECTATOR.

"Multitudes! Multitudes! in the Valley of Decision! for the Day of the Lord is near in the Valley of Decision! The sun and the moon are darkened, the stars withdraw their shining. And the Lord shall roar from Zion, and utter his voice from Jerusalem. And the heavens and the earth shall shake; but the Lord will be the Hope of His people, and a stronghold to the children of Israel." This last the consolation.

Such the solemn scene, where the Antichrist is judged and Gentile politics and power go down in blackness and blood. The same scene is given in Isa. lix: 19-21, and lxvi: 5-16; in Dan. vii: 9-14; in Zeph. iii: 8-20; in Zech. xii: 2-14; xiii: 1; in xiv: 1-11. It is given in Matth. xxv: 31-46. It is the scene of the sickle-judgment, and the winepress with "blood up to the horses' bridles" in Rev. xiv: 12-20, and of "Heaven Opened" for the Antichrist's destruction, in Rev. xix: 11-21. It follows the Armageddon rendezvous in Rev. xvi: 12-16, and is the end of the "Warfare Great" when the Son of Man comes to "take away the Sultanate" of the Horn, and "consume and destroy it to the end." Dan. vii: 26. All the prophets, Christ and His apostles, have looked to this "End" of our age.

And the nations are "preparing." History is the afterclap of which prophecy is the fore-stroke; the echo of which prophecy is the voice. The growth of modern armies and the man-killing power of their weapons, the destructive enginery of modern warfare by land and sea, during the last twenty-five years is appalling. The augmented war-material, and armies swollen beyond all precedent, in times of peace, are the omen of disaster to the world. They are the presage of the judgment day on all nations, no arbitration can arbitrate away. The guilt of Christendom must meet its punishment. The condemnation of the "Christian Nations" is their military strength. The *peace-footing* of Italy, to-day, is 1,473,000 men of all arms; of Austria, 2,076,000; of Germany, 4,300,000; of France, 4,300,000; of Russia, 4,800,000:—not to mention Great Britain, Turkey in Europe, Denmark, Sweden, Norway, Belgium, Spain, Portugal, and the millions in Asia and Africa, nor to think of the enormous naval strength of the world. Omit the whole, save the military force of the "Five Powers" on the continent of Europe including Russia, and the peace-footing for A. D. 1897, is 16,049,000 armed men. The "*war-footing*" according to the same budgets, for 1897-'98, is Italy 2,200,000; Austria, 2,518,000; Germany, 7,200,000; France, 4,700,000; Russia's "prospective army," 12,000,000,—a total of 28,618,000 men within the limits of these "Five Powers"—powerless to compel the Turk or each other to justice or humanity. The causes of this vast "military Christendom of the Nineteenth Century" are familiar to all; the advance of science in destructive agencies, mutual distrust of the nations, their rivalries and jealousies, treachery and breach of treaties, balance of power, the peace of Europe, enormous increase of wealth, expansion of commerce, the fact that resistless power knows no moral law, the ambition of Europe to divide the non-Christian nations, partition Asia and Africa, and control the mines and markets of the world, lust for supremacy, want of righteousness, the discontent of the masses, the increase of unbelief and crime, and the corruption of Gentile politics and power. Add to those the apprehension of a collision between the East and West, and the coming struggle with Islam, Judiasm, and each other. The prelude to that will be the apparent harmony of the "Powers" of the world for a period of time,—the "silence for the space of half an hour, in heaven," the "four angels holding back the winds," the solemn hush when the air is breathless and the leaves are motionless; then the thunder-burst of Judgment! At such a time, Israel's claims will come up for settlement such as Europe, Asia, and Africa cannot make.

Prepare war! Come up to the Valley of Decision! It is the "Eastern Question." It was the burning question when Joel spoke, 900 B. C., the burning question now, and now as then the nations are waiting the order to march! It is an old question. Its antiquity remounts beyond the days of Chedorlaomer and Abraham. It existed before Russia, England, France, or Turkey was born—before ever Constantinople, Rome, Alexandria, or London, had a name. It means the conflict of civilizations,—a conflict governed by "the ever-recurring law of history," viz., invasion at stated intervals, from East to West, and reversely from West to East; from North to South, and reversely, till at last the whole world is involved. It was the question that sank the Persian empire and brought to Greece her national existence and her glory:—the question on which a Pericles and Demosthenes exhausted their oratory, and where a Cicero stood in the majesty of eloquence, a Caesar in the splendor of arms,—the question for Antiochus Epiphanes,—the Huns and the Mongols, the Tartars,—Islam!—in every case the "Holy Land" its centre. The middle age saw all Europe precipitate itself on Palestine, only to be hurled back by the Moslem, after 300 years of war. Turn whatever way, it is identified with the fortunes of the Jew. Deeper and broader interests than those of England, France, Russia, Austria, Germany, Greece, Turkey, India, China, and Japan in the oceans, seas, waterways, markets and mines of the world, are involved;—the interests of Israel and of the kingdom of God. The cry of the muezzin sounds daily over two cities of universal fame,—Jerusalem and Constantinople,—where once the Religion of Jehovah and the Religion of Christ ruled supreme, and the Imaum's prayer to Allah ever ascends, "O Allah, destroy the infidels, defile their abodes, and give their women, children, friends and wealth as booty to the Moslem!"—all this with the "consent" and "concert" of the so-called "Christian Powers!" How can the "kingdom" come apart from a judgment day and the decision of the "Eastern Question?" That gifted historian, J. von Mueller, has not said in vain, "No thoughtful man can read history, or look upon the face of Christendom, and not be impressed with the conviction that the same law of righteousness that brought the ancient empires to their end, must prevail at last against the empires and kingdoms now existing." Nemesis must come. And say what men may, the battle opens in the same old centre, the Aegean Sea, and the relation of the Holy Land and Israel, geographically and politically, as well as religiously, must assert itself, as before, the more the "Warfare Great approaches its end. Nor is there anything in international politics anywhere that does not lead to this centre, even as the Roman roads all led to the Golden Milestone of the Forum.

It is not for nothing that the histories of the "Seven Great Monarchies" and the hundred histories of the "People Israel," and of the "Religion of Israel," and the "Explorations in Palestine," have been written in these last days, and the scholarship of modern times been called to exert itself in Old Testament studies as never before. The "Future" has become a theme of exciting interest. What means the unexampled interest, to-day, in the "Maps and Survey of Palestine," in such books as "The Recovery of Jerusalem," the "History of Jerusalem," "Palestine under the Moslems," "The City and the Land," "Judas Maccabæus and the War for Independence," "The Latin kingdom of Jerusalem," all by the first scholars of our generation? And what the reversal of the English policy towards Turkey, and of the Russian also, each occupying the place the other did, five years ago? What the scenes in Mediterranean waters, the unparalleled growth of the Zionist movement, the lectures in European Universities on the "Jewish Problem," the "Societies" among Christian peoples for the conversion of the Jews; the absolute control of the finances of the nations, by the Jews, and their influence over science, literature, journalism, the seats of instruction, and the international politics of the Old World? And what the threatening attitude of the East and West, the South and North, and the alliances of the "Powers?"

It is with some providential intent the labors of a Curtius and Grote, a Stanley and Rawlinson, a Mueller and Weltzhofer, a Meyer and Brandis, have drawn attention to the "laws of historical development," and shown how the destiny of the Jews affects the destiny of all nations, and that "in the near future, the world may expect to see the operation of the law, more powerfully than ever." The "Powers" will not be allowed of God to continue their concert of crime perpetually, for their own benefit, and the hindrance of the kingdom of God. The rivalries of the Greek states, after Alexander's death, left the Eastern Question unsettled for many generations, Palestine passing from one power to another. After the "push" of Europe against the Moslem, Jerusalem, regained, was lost by the rivalries of Kings, Dukes, and Barons, unworthy of the valor of a Tancred and Godfrey. After the defeat of the Turk before the walls of Vienna, again the rivalries of European sovereigns left the question unsettled, remaining so to this day. Doubtless, God's hand was in this, as well as Satan's and the hand of man, for the "*End was not yet.*" More development, more missionary work, more preparation for the solution of so vast a problem, were required:—more atrocity in demonstration of the unchanged selfishness of the "Powers," more ripening in sin and disregard of moral righteousness. But now, "the time appointed" plumes its wings. The power holding Palestine must prepare for the power ruling the South to "push at him," and the power of the North to "come against him," and both for the holder of Palestine to resist them, and all mankind for "the Kings from the East, and of the whole world (the Roman) to gather together to a place called in the Hebrew tongue Armageddon (Har-Magedon)."

Rev. xvi: 12-16. Zech. xii: 11. That conflict will decide all questions forever; and Israel redeemed, delivered and re-established in their own land, as the first "Righteous Nation" on earth, Isa. xxvi: 1-24; Rev. xv: 3-8; will be the solution long-desired;—the end of the "Warfare Great";—the bond and union-point of international amity, peace, and righteousness—all peoples one people, all nations one nation, all governments one government, all religions one religion, and "*War no more!*" The nations will have had experience enough of this! Then Jesus Christ will be recognized as the "Only Potentate," "The King of Kings and Lord of Lords." Zech. xiv: 9. Rev. xi: 15. And the terrible, yet immortal battle-field on which that issue will be decided, and that result achieved, will be the *Reservation* the Most High chose as His own when—long before Abraham was,—He divided to the nations their inheritance, and limited the boundaries of the peoples relatively to the land appointed for the twelve tribes of Israel. Deut. xxxii: 8. Such, the importance of Palestine, the Jew, and the "Warfare Great," for the triumph of the kingdom of God. From that early moment the "Eastern Question" became a necessity. Its solution is before us.

"Then shall be great tribulation, such as was not since the beginning of the world to this time, no, nor ever shall be. And, except those days should be shortened, no flesh should be saved; but, for the elect's sake, those days shall be shortened." Matt. xxiv: 21, 22.

"Then shall the righteous shine forth as the sun in the kingdom of their Father; who hath ears to hear, let him hear." Matt. xiii: 43.

"Beloved, think it not strange concerning the fiery trial that is to try you, as though some strange think happened unto you. But rejoice, inasmuch as ye are partakers of Christ's sufferings, that when His glory is revealed, ye may be glad with exceeding joy." 1 Pet. iv: 12, 13; i: 7.

"When the Lord shall build up Zion, He shall appear in His glory." Ps. cii: 16. "Appear to your joy." Isa. lxvi: 5.

"THY WORD IS TRUTH,"
John xvii; 17.

Chapter X.

DANIEL, CHAPTERS X-XII.—END OF THE WARFARE GREAT. THE GREAT TRIBULATION. RESURRECTION. DELIVERANCE.

The chapter falls into three divisions: (1) the Conclusion of the prophesy, xii: 1-3; (2) The Completion of the Book of Daniel, xii: 4; (3) the Epilogue or closing Vision, xii: 5-13.

(1) The Conclusion of the Prophecy, xii: 1-3. These verses disclose in what way the constancy and faith of God's people will be tried in the final crisis, by what means the Lord will separate converted Israel from their apostate brethren, Isa. lxvi: 5, and how he will break in pieces the oppressor and redeem from deceit and violence the souls of the poor and needy, Ps. lxxii: 4, 13, 14. The fate of Israel and the world will not be decided by the diplomats and kings of Europe, Asia, and Africa, nor by the bankers of Antwerp, Berlin, Paris, London or Vienna, but by the hand of God. The doctrines of the "Balance of Power," and the "Sceptre of Mammon," will perish together. It will be decided at Jerusalem by the Coming of the Son of Man. The solution of what is called the *Eastern Question* requires a higher power than all the baffled sovereigns of the world, a solution only possible upon the overthrow of all the Gentile Powers themselves, of the corrupt forms of religion by which they are supported, of antichristianity everywhere, and of Antichrist, the last leader of Satan's kingdom on the earth. Whatever power the Jews may have acquired by means of their wealth, influence and alliances, among the nations, in the last times, or in Palestine, will be unavailing here. The struggle to gain their independence while in their unbelief will be signally defeated. It is not by

force of arms, alliances or wealth that Israel is delivered, but by the wonder-working power of God, when their own power is utterly annihilated. Deut. xxxii: 36; Dan. xii: 7. This final act in behalf of the faithful is connected with the resurrection of Israel's holy dead, waked from their graves to meet and greet the delivered ones, and to shine as the sun and the stars in the Kingdom of God. What we have here is

(1) The Definition of the "Time" of these events. It is "at that time," xi: 40, when the Antichrist camps on Mount Moriah, xi: 45, hence neither in the times of Antiochus, nor of Titus, since it is immediately followed by the "Great Tribulation" that next precedes the Second Coming of Christ. Dan. vii: 13, 25; xii: 1-3, 7; Matt. xxiv: 15-29; II. Thess. i: 6, 7; ii: 1-12; Rev. xiii: 5; xix: 11-21; xx: 1-6. It will be "such a time as never was" prior to A.D. 33, when our Lord made this statement, therefore not in the times of Antiochus; "no, nor ever shall be" prior to the days immediately before His Second Coming, therefore not in the times of Titus. The character of the time is faithfully delineated by our Lord as corresponding to Antediluvian and Sodomite times. "As it was in the days of Noah," and of "Lot," Luke xvii: 26-37. The Gospel will have gone, as a testimony, to all nations, and Christendom, the field full of Tares and Wheat, will be burdened with "scandals" to be "taken out" by the sickle of judgment. Matt. xiii: 41. Modern Culture and Civilization will have done their best and worst, and amid antichristianity, lawlessness, church-defection, and a world in war, Israel's problem will demand solution.

(2) The intervention of Michael in behalf of Israel. "At that time, Michael, the great prince standing over the children of thy people (the Jews), shall stand firm," xii: 1. By Michael is not meant the "Angel of Jehovah," nor "Jesus Christ," but the guardian angel-prince of Israel, who with Gabriel exercises a protectorate over God's ancient people. He is the "archangel Michael" who contended for the body of Moses, Jude 9, and who, with Gabriel, "stood up" for Israel in the days of Cyrus and Darius the Mede, and in the days of Anti-

ochus, to give the victory to Judas Maccabæus, Dan. x: 13, 20; xi: 1. Once more he "stands up," "over," and "firm for" converted Israel, "the holy people," xii. 7; "these my brethren," Matt. xxv: 40; the 144,000, Rev. vii: 4-8; xiv: 1-5; xii: 10, 11; Isa. lxvi: 5, i. e., "the people of the Saints of the Most High," vii: 27. Here again we have a glimpse into the angel world. Satan is still the "god of this world" (age), and " prince of the power of the air," and has the right to "accuse" before God the Jewish people as apostates from their covenant so long as they remain in unbelief, and even to "accuse" believers before God, because of their sins. Job ii: 1-5; Zech. iii: 1. The significant fact here is that when Michael stands up, at the time specified, Satan and his angels—till then allowed to roam the air—are "cast out" from their ærial spheres and dejected to the earth. Rev. xii: 9. With this dejection of the Dragon the great tribulation begins, the cause of Michael's standing up being Israel's conversion to Christ, at the middle of the 70th week. Rev. xii: 1-11. The ground of Satan's accusation is cut away by the Jewish acceptance of Jesus Christ preached to them by the "Two Witnesses," Rev. xi: 3, and by the Church, to whom the "open door" of missions to the Jews is given," Rev. iii: 7-11; Acts iii: 19-21; Rom. xi: 26. The battle of Michael and his host is, first of all, in the air, where Satan roams and sends his evil angels and his influence to sway the powers of the earth adversely to the Jews. Then there is "War in Heaven," i. e., in the ærial regions. John describes it. "Michael and his angels fought against the Dragon; and the Dragon and his angels fought and prevailed not, neither was their place found any more in heaven." Rev. xii: 7, 8. They are cast down to rage on the earth a "short time," viz., during the last 3½ years of the 70th week. Rev. xii; 12; Matt. xxiv: 22. The conversion of the Jews, at least, of their first instalment, and the dejection of the Dragon, are simultaneous events, at the middle of the 70th week. This overthrow of Satan in the air is the preliminary action on the skirmish line, as it were, the assault of the advanced-guard on the outposts of Satan's kingdom, viz., on "the hosts of the high ones on high," Isa. xxiv: 21. It is intended to clear the air from the evil angels and prepare the region for the Rapture of the Saints at the Coming of Christ in the clouds of heaven.

But if the conflict is ærial, it is also terrestrial, and chiefly in the Holy Land, where "the nations are gathered against Jerusalem." Here also angelic intervention shall occur in Israel's behalf. "Thither cause Thy mighty ones to come down, O Lord!" Joel iii: 11. The "War of the Great Day of God Almighty" includes "the kings of the earth on the earth,' as well as "the hosts of the high ones on high." Isa. xxiv: 21. Angels execute the "Harvest" and the "Vintage" orders. Rev. xiv: 12-20; Zech. xiii: 8; xiv: 5; Jude 15. Great, however, as is the help of Michael, the destruction of the Antichrist is reserved for Christ alone, Isa. xi: 4; II. Thess. ii: 8; Isa. lix: 19, 20; Dan. vii: 13; Rev. xix: 11-21. There is right and propriety in this. It is when the Lord himself appears in person to raise His saints, and smite the Antichrist, that the "Warfare Great" is terminated and Israel is delivered. To Him belongs the victory, the kingdom, the power and the glory.

(3) *The Great Tribulation.* "There shall be a time of Trouble such as never was since there was a nation, even to that same time," xii: 1. Of this, much has already been said. It is that period of affliction described so graphically and so frequently in both Testaments, by Moses, Deut. xxxii: 39-43; by Balaam, Num. xxiv: 23, 24; by Isaiah, xxvi: 8-21; lix: 16-21; lxvi: 5-16; by Jeremiah, xxx: 7; by Ezekiel, xxxviii: 1-23; xxxix: 1-29; by Joel, iii: 9-16; by Zephaniah, iii: 8; by Zechariah, xii: 1-14; xiii: 1; xiv: 1-5; by our Lord, Matt. xxiv: 15, 28; by Paul, II. Thess. i: 6, 7; and by John, Rev. iii: 10; vii: 14; xi: 7; xii: 12; xiii: 1-18, covering the second half of the Apocalypse from chapter xii. to xx. Here is found the formal condemnation of all the modern optimistic schemes, social theories, and wide-spread false teaching, that looks for the reform of the whole world and conversion of the nations before the Second Coming of Christ. If we ask the Prophets, Christ and His Apostles, *what they expected in the Future*, after the

Gospel seed had been scattered over all the earth, their reply will be found to be one and harmonious. By the side of the Wheat, Satan's seed, the Tares, will occupy the field of the world "together" till the Lord comes. During the Times of the Gentiles Israel will remain in unbelief. Along with the progress of Christianity, externally waxing to a power in the world, and allying itself with governments and states, shall go prosperity, internal corruption and decay, a deepening departure from the faith, as the last times draw near—antichristianity at last ascendant, the world controlling the Church, false teaching, false Messiahs, false culture and civilization, crime universal, the faithful a "little flock" to whom it is "the Father's good pleasure to give the kingdom." The great apostasy in Christendom shall culminate in the Antichrist, and bring the crisis of the "Warfare Great," viz., the "Great Tribulation," the world still "lying in the Wicked One." They looked for all this, and for the return of the Jews to their own land, their conversion in the midst of the crisis, and the Second Coming of Christ to put an end to the whole disorder and bring His Kingdom of righteousness and truth to victory. No other future than this is found in the Sacred Scriptures, save the Millennial Age and the final New Heaven and Earth, both which follow the Advent of the Son of Man in clouds. The triumph of the Kingdom comes only to those who, faithful to Christ, pass through this Tribulation, and, sealed by His Spirit, are "overcomers" who have "gotten the victory over the Beast and His Image, his Mark and the Number of his Name," even as before in early times, Rev. xv: 2; xx: 4. The unwritten in the Book of Life "worship the Beast" and perish in his punishment. Rev. xiii: 8. The conversion and reform of the whole world before the Second Advent is a human fiction, contradicted by both Testaments.

In Daniel's Book the Tribulation, though universal, is confined to the Jews and the Holy Land, the election out of Israel being prominent, as in Rev. vii: 4-8, but not the election out of the Gentiles, who yet pass through the same Tribulation, Rev. vii: 9-17. Territorially, the vision covers Europe, Asia and Africa, within the limits of the old Roman empire, yet Palestine is the centre of the drama. For the Jews the Holy Land will be a furnace seven times hot, and a lion's den. As in Maccabean days, they shall fall " by the sword, by flame, by captivity and spoil." Tried the faithful will be, as were the first Christians, as were the martyrs in Papal times, as were the faithful Armenians in our own day. Tried they will be by apostates of their own race who will cast them out, as the Jews go on building their Temple, Isa. lxvi: 1-5; Rev. xi: 1-3; and by the Antichrist, doubly enraged because of their conversion on the one hand, and the effort of apostates on the other to gain the independence of Palestine. Both these events are the cause of the Antichrist's breach of his covenant, of his sitting in the Temple as God himself, demanding homage from all on pain of death for disobedience. Tried they will be by the Rabbinism of the magnates among them, who seek to develop Judaism in opposition to Christianity, ejecting them from their fellowship, ostracised socially, destroyed commercially, persecuted personally, and, if scorning to be bribed, then betrayed, massacred, and left unburied in the streets—victims, not only of the sword of the Ottoman, but of the "Cherem," or "curse," of the Jew, pronounced upon them. Isa. lxvi: 5; Rev. xiii: 7-10.

(4) The Deliverance. " Thy people shall be delivered," xii: 1, i. e., at the close of the Great Tribulation, xii: 7; vii: 25-27; ix: 27. Here is proof conclusive that the final gathering of living Israel, and the resurrection of Israel's holy dead, are contemporaneous events at the close of the Great Tribulation, Dan. xii: 1-3, and that " our gathering together unto Christ " is at the same time-point of Israel's Deliverance, viz., at the close of the 70th week. II. Thess. ii: 1-3. This promise of Deliverance of the " Remnant " is ancient as Moses and runs through both Testaments. Not exempted from trial, or even martyrdom, yet the " Remnant " shall not be destroyed. Sealed of God, kept safe from the power of temptation, delivered out of all their troubles, as were their fathers before them, they shall be overcomers through the blood of the Lamb. "Alas,

for the day is great, so great that none is like it; it is the time of Jacob's trouble but he shall be saved *out of it*." Jer. xxx: 7. Accounted worthy to escape the licentiousness, drunkeness, surfeiting, cares of this life and snares of the antichristian time, and the judgments to fall on the ungodly, they shall stand, a faultless company, with their Redeemer, on the earthly "Mount Zion," where He promises to come to them. Isa. lix: 20; Rom. xi: 25, 26; Rev. xiv: 1-5.*

The deliverance will be miraculous, (1) by the personal appearing of the Son of Man, first of all in the clouds of heaven. Dan. vii: 13; (2) in the next place, "His feet shall stand on the Mount of Olives," and a way of escape for the Jews be provided by earthquake shocks, sundering the mountain,

*Remarkable is the space given to Israel in the Revelation by John. Elect Israel is sealed, Rev. vii: 48. The "*Little Book*" in x: 8, contains the fortunes of the Jews in the Time of the End, when the "mystery of God" foreshown to Daniel and the prophets concerning Israel's rejection and recovery, and the overthrow of the Kingdoms of this world, is completed—the *Little Book* symbolising the contents of the following chapters. The 70th Week, and Scenes in Jerusalem under the Anti-Christ, enter at xi: 1, and continue through, with other events, to xx: 1, i. e., through the last 1,260 days. All from xii: 1 to xx: 1 is the last 1,260, i. e., is the seventh trumpet, which is the seven vials. The Beast, in xi: 7, is the Antichrist. The Sun-clothed Woman, in xii: 1 is the Daughter of Zion, the Jewish Church, seen in her whole history at both advents. The 144,000, in xiv: 1-5, are delivered Israel, the same as in vii: 4-8, but safe with their Redeemer returned to them on the earthly Mount Zion, at the close of the Tribulation. The vision is proleptic. In xv: 2-4, the martyrs of Israel are harping in heaven, even as the martyrs and confessors of the church are seen in heaven, in vii: 9-17. In xvi: 16, is Armageddon in Palestine. In xi: 18; xiv: 13-16; xvi: 15; xx: 3-6; are the Second Advent, the Resurrection of the holy dead, the Reaping of the living saints, the enthronement. In xiv: 17-20; xix: 11-21; the Valley of Jehoshaphat, the Blood-Bath, the Destruction of the Anti-Christ, the Deliverance of Israel, at Jerusalem. In xix: 1-9, the Hallel over the ruin of Babylon and the Marriage-time of the Jewish wife, long separated from, but now returned to her husband. Isa. lxii: 3-5. Hos. ii: 19-23. In xx: 9, is Jerusalem the "Beloved City," the metropolis of the millennial age. Such the place of Israel in New Testament prophecy, in the "Time of the End," and millennial age.

Zech. xiv, 10; (3) by the tripartition of the city previously, its fall of "one-tenth" of it, and the engulfment of "7000 men of name," the supporters of the Antichrist; Rev. ii: 13; (4) by the destruction of the Antichrist and his hosts "outside the city," Rev. xiv: 20; Dan. ix: 27; vii: 26; xii: 7; 2 Thess. ii: 8; Rev. xix: 11; (5) and, as stated, by the coming of the Lord to "Zion," the last military station where the Antichrist encamped, Dan. xi: 45. It will be an elect deliverance even of "as many as are written in the book," Dan. xii: 1; "the holy, every one written among the living in Jerusalem," Isa. iv: 3; the surviving "We who are alive and remain unto the coming of the Lord," even as in the case of Gentile believers, who have just been caught away, 1 Thess. iv: 17. It will be a spiritual deliverance of Israel new-born and penitent, accepting Christ and trusting for pardon through His blood, Zech. xiii: 1; xii: 9-14; Ezek. xxxvi: 24-29; Acts iii: 19-21 (R. V.); Rom. xi: 26; Isa. lix: 20-21. It will be a political deliverance from subjection to the Gentile Powers, to restoration of long lost sovereignty, and of an absolutely independent kingdom which no sword or diplomacy shall ever wrest from their possession, —a kingdom in which Judah and Israel shall be one and undivided forever, Zech .xii: 3; Ezek. xxxvii: 22—an Israelitish kingdom, the centre of Messiah's kingdom, wide as the world, Luke i: 32, 33; i: 70-74. It will be a jubilant deliverance, the ransomed of the Lord returning to Zion "with songs and everlasting joy upon their heads," Isa. xxxv: 10. It will be a deliverance, God-glorifying and irreversible. "They shall dwell in the land, even they and their children, forever," Ezek. xxxvii: 25, God's sanctuary among them, He their God and they His people—His Name "magnified among all nations." Ezek. xxxvii: 27, 28; xxxviii: 23; xxxix: 27-29; Dan. ix: 24. If the Tribulation is great, the Deliverance is greater still. It gives birth to the first time in history when God's name is universally "hallowed" by the nations, and profanity expires,—and when the will of God is "done on earth as it is in heaven," Rev. xv: 4. Of such importance is Israel for the kingdom of God.

(5) The Resurrection of the Holy Dead. Not only shall living Israel's election be delivered, but the holy dead be waked to share the joy. Decisive and clear are the words of the angel, "*At that time*," when Israel is delivered,—"many shall awake (literally, be separated) out from among the sleepers in the earth-dust; *these* (who awake at that time) shall be unto everlasting life, *but those* (who do not awake at that time) shall be unto shame and everlasting contempt," xii: 2. The "those" include two classes (1) the wicked, long-buried in the earth, (2) the slaughtered wicked, still unburied on the field, "an abhorrence to all flesh," Isa. lxvi: 24; Rev. xix: 17-21; Ezek. xxxix: 11, 17-20. A simultaneous resurrection of all mankind, good and bad, is nowhere taught in the Scriptures. It is the resurrection of the holy, and of Israel's holy dead that is here predicted, as in Isa. xxvi: 19, and the non-resurrection of the wicked, "*at that time*," Isa. xxvi: 14. The resurrection here taught is the "First Resurrection," Rev. xx: 3-6; that of the already spiritually raised, John v: 24, 25; that of "the just," Luke xiv: 14; the "out-resurrection," Phil. iii: 11; the hour when Old and New Testament saints are together "made perfect" in their communion and in the consummation of their blessedness, both waked from their graves by the voice of the Son of God. Heb. xi: 35, 40. No greater epoch has earth ever known. Its *time-point* is given with the utmost precision in the Scriptures. It is the time-point of the Second Advent for the salvation of the righteous and destruction of the wicked, even as at the one time-point Noah and his family entered the Ark, and the ungodly perished in the Flood; and Israel was redeemed when Egypt was whelmed in the sea; and the Church fled to Pella when Jerusalem was destroyed. It is a time-point for both Judgment and Salvation. Asaph calls it the "shining" of the Lord, Ps. l: 1-6. Isaiah calls it His "Appearing," lxvi: 5, in order to raise the holy dead, deliver Israel, destroy the Antichrist, and bring to victory the kingdom. Five times in the Old Testament this illustrious *Parousia* of Christ is described as (1) the Coming of the Son of Man in the Clouds of Heaven, Dan. vii: 13; (2)

of the Conqueror from Bozrah, descending over Edom, Isa. lxiii: 1-6; (3) of the Coming of the Lord to Olivet, Zech. xiv: 5; (4) and to Zion, Isa. lix: 20, and (5) in Clouds for both Judgment and Salvation, Ps. 1: 1-6; xcvi:13; xcvii: 2-8; xcviii: 1-9; cx: 1-7; lxxii: 2, 4, 9-14, 18, 19; cii: 13-17. Not less great does it appear in the New Testament, and precisely for the same events, with others added. Ten times again this *time-point* is fixed at the close of the Great Tribulation, and is described (1) as the Lord's Coming *with* His Saints, the Holy Angels, *for* His Saints the Holy Living and the Holy Dead— a " Gathering of His Elect ," universally, involving first of all, the resurrection of the holy who sleep in the dust of the earth, then the rapture of these and the Holy Living ones, and their meeting of the Lord in the air Matth. xxiv: 29-31, 40, 41; xxv: 1; these scenes, followed by the deliverance of converted Irael,—" these, my brethren," Matth. xxv: 40, the Judgment of the Nations, xxv: 31-46, and the welcome to the kingdom; (2) as the time-point for "Our gathering together at Christ," 2 Thess. ii: 1, "in the air," 1 Thess. iv: 17; (3) as the *"thief-time,"* Matth. xxiv: 43; (4) as the Coming to judge the World-Power, Rev. vi: 12-17; (5) as His Coming under the Seventh Trumpet, to vindicate the holy dead by their resurrection, Rev. xi: 15-17, 18; (6) as His Coming to reap the holy living, Rev. xiv: 14-16; (7) and at the *"thief-time,"* Rev. xvi: 15; (8) and after the Sixth Vial, Rev. xvi: 12; (9) and to destroy Babylon, Rev. xvi: 19; (10) and the Antichrist, Rev. xix: 11-21; (11) and to enthrone and reward His Saints, Rev. xx: 1-6. So great is this greatest of all time-points in the history of the world, when the Jews are restored, and Gentile politics and power are destroyed, and the holy dead are waked from their graves. From Moses to Malachi, and from Matthew to the Apocalypse by John, the Resurrection of the Sleeping Saints is placed at no other epoch than the close of the " Tribulation Great," and of the " Warfare Great."

The idea, therefore, of a Secret Parousia for the resurrection of the holy dead, prior to the appearing of the Son of Man in the clouds of heaven at the close of the tribulation, is contrary to the Word of God. To this time-point of the revelation of Christ in His glory, to raise the dead, deliver Israel, and destroy the Antichrist, the hope of both Old and New Testament saints, was directed. Matth. xxiv: 29-31, 40-44; 2 Thess. i: 6-10; ii: 1-8; 1 Thess. iv: 14-17; Rev. xi: 17; xiv: 13-20; xix: 11-21; xx: 1-6; xvi: 15; Dan. xii: 1-3; Matth. xiii: 40. In view of that hope, Old Testament martyrs, accounting themselves dead even before the tyrant had struck them, refused to "accept deliverance" at the cost of foreswearing their faith. The New Testament martyrs did the same. The "better thing" they grasped by faith was the "better resurrection," when both, washed in the blood of Christ, Heb. ix: 15, should together be perfected, body and soul, in the likeness of Christ, at His second coming, and satisfied, Ps. xvii: 15; l: 3-6; Dan. xii: 1-3; Matth. xxiii: 40; xxiv: 29-31. One in Christ, and one with each other, both saved in the same way. God foresaw and provided the plan concerning us, "that they *apart from us*, should not be made perfect." Heb. xi: 35, 40. Moses and Paul, Isaiah and John, are one in Christ.

(6) The Splendor of the Risen Saints. They that be wise shall shine as the brightness of the firmament, and they that have turned the many to righteousness, as the stars forever and ever," xii: 3. The angel employs two words nowhere else found in the Old Testament, (1) *Hayi Olam*, life everlasting. *i. e.*: to die no more, and (2) *Hizhir*, shall shine, from *Zohar*, splendor. This last one is beautifully rendered by the German word *Himmelglanz*, the gleam of Heaven. Moses describes the firmament as a "sapphire pavement" beneath the feet of the God of Israel, "the body of heaven in its clearness," Exodus xxxiv: 10, and Elihu compares it to a "molten mirror," shining with undimmed resplendency. Job xxxvii: 18. Ezekiel describes it as "an appearance of brightness as the look of the brightness of burnished gold," Ezek. viii: 2. To the golden sheen the angel adds the incandescent glory of the "stars," literally of the "glitterers." Our Lord and Paul allude to these expressions in their brilliant language when speaking of the resurrection and its different degrees of glory,

Matth. xiii: 43; 1 Cor. xv: 41. An instance of the reality, we have in the Transfiguration of the Lord in the "holy mount," when His face did shine as the Sun, and His raiment was white as the light," Matth. xvii: 21, "white as snow and glistering," Mark ix: 3; Luke ix: 30. What the angel teaches is that the wise shall shine like the crystal sheen of a sunlit firmament, and the converters of the many to righteousness shall glow with the glitter of the stars in a cloudless canopy. Still more, their effulgence shall be eternal—a glory unobscured forever, xii: 3. This their *Zohar*. Degrees of glory there will be, even as the three in Orion's belt excel in magnitude and glory the lesser stars of the constellation. The transfiguration of the living will equal that of the dead. The Lord extends the splendor to all the "righteous." Matth. xiii: 40. Allusion is here doubtless to the Maccabean teachers of the law, in xi: 33-35, but the prophecy includes the whole sacramental host of God's elect, who share the glory ready to be revealed. All who are instrumental in the salvation of the many will be clothed with a surpassing brightness. Eminent, the martyrs of Jesus will shine, saints who have not deemed as dear to them their lives, for Jesus' sake. Rev. xx: 4; xiv: 13; 2 Thess. i: 5; Heb. xi: 35-39; Rev. xii: 11; 2 Tim. iv: 6-8. Such the "out-resurrection." Phil. iii: 11. If a splendor so great and enduring, for the body alone—even to be glorified like Christ, whose brightness Paul tells us eclipsed the noonday sun—is the reward of a Tribulation so brief, then indeed the sorest afflictions are but as the puncture of a pin, and the longest but as a moment—not worthy to be compared with the " far more exceeding and eternal weight of glory." Rom. viii: 18. Earth never wore a diadem so royal as that composed of risen saints. The eloquence of all antiquity, or modern times, has furnished no description equal to this conclusion of the prophecy; a scene so imposing, majestic and impressive; so sanctifying and sublime; so solemn and subduing! We have seen the rainbow braided on the brow of the dying storm, but here a glory-crown of saints, the jeweled diadem of God, is placed upon the head of the dark Tribulation itself—a vision that can never vanish from the soul of the believer. How quick the transit from the cross to the crown, from shame to honor, from suffering to glory! The end of the "Warfare Great" is the outburst of an illumination which celebrates a victory for the Kingdom of God that is everlasting. Time cannot dim its brightness. Eternity will only enhance its greatness.

II. The Completion of Daniel's Book. The great prophecy of Daniel is now ended. The whole future has been disclosed to the Second Coming of Christ, and now the angel issues his order to the prophet. "But thou, O Daniel, shut up the words and seal the Book, even to the time of the end." xii: 4, i. e., (1) to the end of the third empire, and (2) to the end of the fourth. By the "words" is meant the words of the last revelation just given, viz., chapters x, xi, xii: 1-3. By the "book," the whole Book of Daniel, from first to last. By "shut up the words" is meant, bind them with the rest of the parchments, as part of the Book. By "seal the book" is meant, attach to the roll the official seals of its authentication, and deposit the same in the archives of the Jewish nation, as part of Holy Scripture. Preserve it for the warning and comfort of God's people. This does not mean that its contents shall remain inaccessible to the High Priest or to teachers of the people. The order relates alone to the preservation of the original text. It was the custom of the prophets, before binding the separate parchments, to transcribe copies for the public use, from which still others were transcribed by official hands, under penalties for error. Thus the Book of Daniel descended to the Jews, in a standard text, with which all copies could be compared as the near "time of the end" approached. The order of the angel implies no less than this, that Daniel was the author of the whole book, most of which was written during the exile, and its finisher in post-exilic times, during the Persian reign.

III. The Prediction of the Study of the Book in the "Time of the End." "Many shall run to and fro, and the knowledge shall be increased." Dan. xii: 4. This explains the reason of the order. A *long period* will intervene between now and then, and only then will the contents of the book be completely understood, therefore "seal the book," that a sure and standard text may be preserved. Proof conclusive, again, that the book was written long before the Maccabean times. That it existed then and was studied with unabated interest, is established by indisputable testimonies. That it is studied to-day, yet more than ever, is a sign of the nearing "time of the end." By the words "run to and fro" is meant, not "modern locomotion," nor "missionary enterprise," nor "rushing here and there," but the diligent perusal of the book with intensity and earnestness, by the method of turning forward and backward its pages, comparing prophecy with prophecy, in order to understand its contents. The angel means that, as the "time of the end" approaches, whether the near or far horizon, "multitudes" will devote themselves to a study of the book, and come to the "inner perception" (the knowledge) of its meaning. Light will burst forth as Israel's day draws near. The definite article " the," before the word " knowledge," in the original text, is conclusive against the idea of modern locomotion and knowledge of every kind. It means the knowledge of the prophecy.

IV. The Epilogue or Closing Vision. xii: 5-13. With the termination of the order, what we have is

(1.) The sudden change of the scene; and not without some deep significance. The linen-clothed-man reappears, hovering over the Hiddekel to which the name of the Nile—"Yeor"—is given, as if to remind Israel that hereafter, in the crisis it shall be again as it was "in the day when he came out of Egypt." Isa. xi: 14-16; xix: 21-25; xxvii: 12, 13. Besides Gabriel and Michael, "two others" appear in the scene, one on this, the other on that side of the river. Clearly, they are introduced as two witnesses of the oath about to be made by the linen-clothed man. Expositors differ greatly as to who these "two others" or "after ones" are, whose names are purposely withheld, and whose position alone is indicated. As *angels*, they are supposed to be Michael and Gabriel—an impossibility, since they are expressly called "two others," (2) as two of the holy watchers over Israel, but of rank subordinate; (3) as the "two" who afterwards appeared at the sepulchre of our Lord, and again as sent from the ascension-cloud to comfort the apostles. As *men*, they are supposed to be either (1) Enoch and Elias, or Moses and Elias, foretold to appear at the time to which the vision here refers, therefore "the two witnesses of me," of whom the Lord speaks as testifying to the Jews in the first half of the seventieth week, Rev. xi: 3, viz., the "two" who appeared on the Mount of Transfiguration, Luke ix: 30. Most regard them as angels. The question still remains an open one.

(2) The dialogue between the linen-clothed man and one of the "two"—a conversation introduced for Daniel's benefit. One of the "two" asks the linen-clothed man "How long shall it be to the end of these wonders?" xii: 6, i. e., "how long from the invasion of Palestine by the Antichrist, xi: 40, to the Resurrection, the Deliverance, and the Kingdom and Glory? The two-fold answer is (1) that "a time, two times, and half a time," 1260 days, shall be the length of the time, and (2) that the end will be signalized by the fact that whatever "power" the Jews may have in the last days, it shall be broken, the Jews helpless in the hands of the Antichrist, with whom they make alliance. Anti-semitism will wax to triumph among the "powers," in spite of the counter movement to rehabilitate the Jewish state. Deut. xxxii: 36-24; Dan. xii: 7. Both hands uplifted to heaven, the Linen-clothed Man swears in the presence of the "Other Two," and "by Him that liveth forever," that not one syllable of the prophecy shall fail, but that all shall be accomplished. The last Invasion of the Holy Land shall take place, the Great Tribulation shall come, the Jews shall be driven to the wall, Michael shall stand up, the holy dead shall be raised, Israel be delivered, and the Antichrist destroyed. *By the life of God, these things shall be so!* This is tremendous adjuration. See Deut. xxxii: 40-43; Rev. x: 5-7. It was not without intense significance the angel had

said in viii: 26, that "the vision is truth;" in x: 1, that "the word is truth;" in x: 21, that Daniel's book is a "Scripture of truth;" and declares in xi: 2, "I will show thee the truth." And not without the same deep significance does he further admonish the prophet, yea, command him, to "close the words," and "seal the book," xii: 4, and declares them "closed and sealed till the time of the end," xii: 9. Yea, more, he crowns the whole with an oath, "by the living God,"—both hands held up—that all these things shall be accomplished," i. e., *that none of them is fiction!* In the name of all that is sacred and solemn, why does the angel thus repeat himself, exhausting all sanctions, angelic human and divine? If the writer of the book is not a pious impostor, the whole book is true as God is true, and not a Maccabean novel, as our modern Higher Critics would have it. No other book in all the Bible, save John's apocalypse, has such a weight of attestation, Rev. xxii: 18, 19. The "Vision" is "Truth," the "Revelation," the "Writing" of it, the very "words," the "book" itself,— all is "Truth," God-sent, angel-given, Spirit-breathed, everlasting "Truth," closed, sealed, authenticated, and attested by angels, sworn to by the Lord Himself, and transmitted to our times to be studied with the intensest interest. Had criticism any conscience or fear of God before its eyes, it would quail in the presence of such transcendent confirmation. God the Almighty, thundering from heaven, could give no stronger demonstration of its verity. It has the sanction of Father, Son, and Holy Ghost, angels, prophets, Christ and His apostles, to its Chiliastic doctrine, and is established by no less than 2,500 years of human history.

(3) The Perplexity of the Prophet. "I heard, but I understood not. Then said I, O my lord, and what shall the *Afterness* of these things be?" xii: 8. What was it he did not understand? Expressly, he declares, he "understands the vision," x: 1. What perplexed him was the definition of the time, given by the Linen-Clothed Man in xii: 7. His soul had been riveted upon the Maccabean persecution, xi: 30-35; the tyrant's

character, xi: 36-39, and the invasion of the Holy Land, xi: 40-45. He knew that the "Time" of that horror was to be "2,300 evening-mornnig," or 1,150 days, 8: 14. But now the announcement of the time, as 1,260 days, xii: 7, confounded him. He could "not understand" how 1,150 could be 1,260, or how the "Little Horn" of the third empire could be the "Little Horn" of the fourth. No Higher Critics were present to show him how things so different are identical! Intent only to hear the angel talk, he had failed to see the *double personality*, type and anti-type, in xi: 36-39, or understand that the great *Interval* lay between verses 39 and 40, and so missed the transition from the one to the other; from the third empire to the fourth. Therefore the "1260," xii: 7, confounded him. Confident that the vision in VII was "truth," he leaves the mystery to God, and to the ages, to solve his perplexity, and only begs to know what the *"afterness"* of the 1260 shall be? the *"afterness"* of the "wonders" in xii: 1-3—what shall follow the Resurrection and Israel's deliverance. It is one of *our* questions to-day. Curious of the future, his pious interest would keep the angel talking forever. Let us remember that the prophets are never *"interpreters"* of the visions they receive, or of what is given them to speak to others. This is that in 2 Pet. i: 20, 21. They are simply receivers, announcers, and searchers. Angels, moreover, are not commentators on their own communications, but simply dictators. The mystery of the double personality here, the transition, the interval, was reserved to be developed by our Lord, Paul, and John, 600 years after.

(4) First Dismissal of the Prophet. "Go thy way, Daniel, for the words are closed up and sealed *to the time of the end,*" xii: 9. Tenderly the angel declines to protract the Revelation. He recurs to the thought in xii: 4, expanding it. "Many shall be *purified, and made white, and tried*, but the Wicked shal do wickedly. And none of the Wicked shall understand, but the Wise shall understand," xii: 10. Two classes of persons there shall be in the time of the end, the "Wicked" and the "Wise." The world will not all be converted to Christ. Moreover the

Wicked, in spite of the Day of the Lord, will continue to practice wickedness. The tribulation that refines the saints will only incrustate the ungodly. The fire that purifies the gold will only harden the clay. For that reason the Wicked will neither study nor understand the Book of Daniel, but the Wise will do both. Clear to their "inner perception" will be the necessity of the tribulation to sift God's saints from the world-loving and unbelieving professors of religion, and to test their fidelity.

(5) The Extension of the Time. "And from the time that the *daily sacrifice shall be taken away and an abomination that maketh desolate be set up*, there shall be 1290 days. Blessed is he that waiteth and cometh to the 1335 days," xii: 11, 12. This much the angel concedes to Daniel's further curiosity. The italicised words here, and in the section above, are found also in viii: 12, 13, and xi: 31, 35, where the vision treats of Antiochus. From this fact certain interpreters, both evangelical and rationalistic, conclude that the whole section in xii: 8-13, refers to the times of that tyrant. Undoubtedly, there is an *allusion* here to time past, since the angel has already carried the prophet, in xii: 7, into the remote future. But a prediction of the future in terms of retrospective *allusion* to a prophey, which itself is typical of the far future, in no way loses its own futurity. The common use of the same terms to express different stages in the development of both prophecy and history, is frequent as it is necessary. It springs from the organic and typical relations of prophecy and history alike. One epoch becomes the mirror of another.

Gabriel's answer, in xii: 9-13, to Daniel's question in xii: 8, is a word explaining something of the "*afterness*" of the 1260 days. Moreover, the angel has already told Daniel, in ix: 27, that "a prince to come," at the seventieth week, would come "on wing of abomination," after allowing to the Jews, by treaty, the practice of their "daily sacrifice," and would break their covenant in he middle of the week. The deeds of Antiochus would be repeated, substantially, yet in variant form. "*An* abomination"—not *the* abomination—would be set up, perhaps the image of the Antichrist himself, Rev. xiii: 14. The "time of the end" would be extended first to thirty, then to forty-five days more beyond the 1260. Then the "blessed" time would come. That no "blessed" time, such as is here predicted for Israel, followed the "cleansing of the temple," either 1290 or 1335 days after the act of Judas Maccabaeus, is evident from the Maccabaean history. The citadel remained in the hands of the foe. Two whole years foreign armies, 100,000 strong, assaulted Jerusalem. Alliance with Rome became a necessity for Jewish protection. Israel's apostasy continued and culminated in the crucifixion of Christ, the second destruction of the temple, and dispersion of the nation. The six-fold blessings in ix: 24 were never realized.

Ever more increasingly, the ablest interpreters regard the thirty days, following the 1260, as the period of Judah's national repenatance, Zech. xii: 10-14; xiii: 1, their baptism by the Spirit, the turning of their mourning into joy, and the destruction of the last remainder of Gentile power. The forty-five days, yet further, are regarded as the period of the return of the residue of the "dispersed" and the "outcasts," brought back by Gentile hands after the Judgment-scenes at Jerusalem, and by those who have "escaped" from that catastrophe. Isa. lxvi: 20; Zeph. iii: 10, 19, 20; Zech. viii: 20-23. Here comes the consecration of the wealth of the Gentiles, to rebuild, enlarge, and beautify the Holy City, Isa. lx: 18-22; lxii: 1-12. This the "comfort" for Zion at the close of her long warfare. Isa. ii: 1-4; Mica iv: 1-4, 8, 13; Isa. lxvi: 10-14. Here belong "the times of the restoring of all things," and "the seasons of refreshing," forespoken by the prophets, Acts iii: 19-21 (R. V.) the period of the six-fold blessing ,in Dan. ix: 24, the epoch of the complete reunion of all Israel in their own land, and their recognition, by the nations, as an independent kingdom, the local and sustaining centre of the millennial age. It is the time of the new sunrise over Jerusalem. "Arise, shine, for thy light is come, and the glory of the Lord hath risen upon thee!" Isa. lx: 1. Here belong the multitude of glowing prophecies in the Old Testament, concerning Israel's latter-day glory. "*Via crucis, via lucis! Post tenebras lux!*" It is the motto of all prophecy!

How "blessed" the time will be, and "blessed" the man who lives or wakes to see it, when the Lord will "apppear in His glory and build up Zion," "gathering the outcasts, healing the broken in heart, and binding their wounds," only a pen dipped in prophetic fire can describe. The angel pronounces a benediction and beatitude on the heirs of the kingdom, whom he calls "waiters" for it. And myriads such there are to-day, notwithstanding "blindness in part has happened unto Israel." "Hope springs eternal in the Hebrew breast." There is for Zion a love tender and sacred in the heart of Israel, such as we Gentiles little feel. Magnificent was the unstaggering faith of Sir Moses Montefiore: "I know it! I am certain of it! Palestine, the beauty-land, now desolate ,shall yet be restored to Israel. The Lord has spoken it!" Touching, the words of Judah Hallevi, as he entered the city: "Prostrate thou art, O Zion, but thy glory is forever! The Eternal has chosen thee. We suffer for our sins, but the blessed time draws near when the Lord will appear in His glory. Blessed he who waits in faith to behold thy rising light!" And tender and sweet, and enough to make the heart-strings of a Gentile vibrate, are the words of Judith Mendelsohn, as with tear-washed cheeks she uttered them when taking leave of the city: "Blessed be the Lord, the God of Israel, forever! Farewell, my loved Jerusalem! The fountain of our tears shall ever run in the current of our prayers and our thanksgiving. Peace be within thy walls! One day we shall meet again. The ransomed of the Lord shall return and come to Zion, with songs and everlasting joy upon their heads!" What tenderness! What faith! What hope! What love and devotion! Courage, oh Israel! The Lord will yet have mercy on thee—sinful, but not forsaken! "Blessed be he that blesseth thee, and cursed be he that curseth thee!"

(6) Second Dismissal of the Prophet. "Go thou thy way

til the end shall be, for thou shalt rest." xii: 13. The lingering prophet, loth to leave, is again admonished to retire. It is hard to part. But "Go thou!" The GloriousOne who hovered over the Hiddekel has gone! The "two others" are gone! The vision fades. " Go thou thy way," the way of the righteous. " Go till the end shall be—the end of life, with all its cares—"for thou shalt rest"—a holy repose, entering into peace, thy body in its bed, thy spirit—"walking in uprightness before God." Isa .lvii: 2. Rest till the end of Israel's weary way. Finish thy Book. Discharge what remains of the duties of life. Dismiss all anxious thoughts. Messiah will come, and though rejected, will come again and be accepted. Israel shall be saved with an everlasting salvation, never to be ashamed or confounded, world without end! Be comforted, and " Go!"

(7) The promise of the Prophet's Resurrection. "Thou shalt stand in thy lot at the end of the days," xii: 13. The transition from a reclining posture to one of standing, implies a resurrection. By the term "lot" is meant the portion of the righteous. The allusion here is to the redistribution of the Holy Land, as given by Daniel's contemporary, Ezekiel. Judah's "portion," to which tribe Daniel belonged, lies next to the "Holy Oblation," near the sanctuary from whose threshold the "living waters " flow, and near the "portion of the Prince," under the beams of the Shekinah-Cloud. Ezek. xlvv: 1; xlviii: 8; Isa. iv: 5, 6. By the "end of the days" is meant the end of the 1335—not the time-point of resurrection, but that of the enjoyment of the assigned reward. There Daniel shall "stand," justified, sanctified, glorified, body and soul, a witness of the truth of his predictions. So vanished the vision of the Hiddekel, as a tableau dissolves before the gaze of the beholder, and nothing remains of all that enchanted his eyes. The prophet is left alone—yet not alone, for the sanctity and memory of that scene never faded from his heart. He died in hope of the First Advent to atone for sin, and of the Resurrection at the Second Coming of Christ. How blessed

to him was life's end! How glorious the hope that pillowed his aged head! His body rests to-day among the "sleepers in the dust of the earth," at Shushan. One day, when Jesus comes, he shall rise again, and shine in the glory! May it be ours to share with him that blest transfiguration! His "lot" may not indeed be our "lot," but if we are Christ's, the glory, though of different degree, shall be the same, for " we know that when Christ shall appear we shall be like Him, for we shall see Him as He is!" 1 John iii: 2. This is *"Our Hope."*

"The Age of Gold, which a blind tradition has placed in the past, lies before us. But first a Phœnix death-birth, a Palingenesis. Destruction and deliverance go together. All things wax old and roll onward. Judgment is inevitable. A Millennium or reign of peace and wisdom having been prophesied of old, becomes more and more indubitable. If our era is the era of unbelief, why murmur at it? Is there not a better coming? Thou art not alone if thou hast faith. Hast thou a genuine love of truth? Awake! speak forth what God hath given thee, and what the Devil shall not take away. Higher priesthood than that for the truth has been allotted to no man. Renounce the cavils that darken into doubt and then denial. Face thou the light, since otherwise darkness is cast upon thy sunshine, that darkness the shadow of thyself!"— Carlyle.

Chapter XI.

SUMMATION. OBJECTIONS. CONCLUSION.

What the book of Daniel teaches is that, because of Israel's apostasy, the Jewish state was overthrown and the sovereignty of the Hebrew people, whose great ancestor became "heir of the world through the righteousness of faith," was passed by God's decree to the four empires of Babylon, Medo-Persia, Græco-Macedonia and Rome, and to the several kingdoms into which the third and fourth of these should be divided; and signally so to the "Little Horn" out of the third, a type of the "Little Horn" of the fourth, yet to appear. Thenceforward, during these "Times of the Gentiles," the Jews should ever remain under the Gentile yoke, scattered among all nations, expatriated from their home, without an organized nationality, and only saved from their subjection at the second coming of Christ, upon their repentance and faith, and after sore tribulation. Then, and only then, their lost sovereignty should revert, their kingdom be restored in glory greater than that of Solomon, and made the local and sustaining centre of the kingdom of Christ in victory "underneath all heavens." Thus, the ancient people of God, converted to a "holy people" in the highest spiritual sense, should be re-established in their old historical relations to the nations of the earth, and be as life from the dead to the world.

Many are the important lessons here taught; among them (1) the indestructibility of the Jewish race, as a separate unamalgamated people, a "generation that shall not pass away;" (2) the destructibility and transient character of all the empires and kingdoms of the world; (3) that during the Times of the Gentiles the triumph of the kingdom of God in righteousness and peace, underneath all heavens, is not to be expected; (4) that the restoration of the Jews and the re-establishment of the Jewish state are as little to be expected, until the Jewish people have been turned to faith in Jesus as the true Messiah, and resumed the central doctrines of their ancient creed, as taught in the prophets, and professed by the first disciples in the holy city; (5) that the time-point, or epoch, of the final Jewish elevation is the time-point of the final destruction of all Gentile power, viz., the second coming of Christ.

One by one the prophet sees the ancient empires pass away, beginning with the empire of Babylon, Egypt and Assyria already overthrown. Babylon endures B. C. 625 to 538, or 87 years, and is also overthrown by Cyrus; Medo-Persia 538 to 330, or 208 years, and is overthrown by Alexander; Græco-Macedonia, united, then divided, 336 to 146, or 190 years, and passes to the Roman power. The Roman empire, founded by Augustus B. C. 28, endures in its Western half to A. D. 476, or 494 years, and in its Eastern to A. D. 1453, both divisions broken up into independent kingdoms and dependent states, changed by the sword of the conqueror, and existing in their different relations to the present day; each passing away, like those of Constantine and Theodosius, of Charlemagne and the Othos, of Louis and Napoleon;—the Ottoman, with all the kingdoms of Europe, Asia and Africa, foredoomed like the rest to retire from the scene that the kingdom of Christ may enter victoriously with Israel's kingdom as the centre of the new age. In vain we look, according to the prophet, for the triumph of truth, righteousness and peace, public and private, in this present age. The entrance of Christianity into history, notwithstanding all the blessings it has brought, and the ameliorating influence of its peerless and transforming power,—has not changed the essential nature of the World-Power, destroyed Sin, bound Satan, or brought to victory universal righteousness and peace.

The prophet beholds the conflict ever permanent until it culminates in the closing scenes of the "Warfare Great." He takes account of the kingdoms of this world masquerading in the costume of a nominal Christianity. He sees no hope of the world's deliverance from its evils, under such condition, during the "Times of the Gentiles." He has anticipated the fact that when Christianity should enter history and come to be the religion of princes and the state, in place of Paganism and the old idolatry, it would be embraced, politically, by the Fourth Empire, and the Powers, only to be made subservient to their temporal interests. He foresaw that it would become a military Christianity, a force employed by rulers and legislators, as a means of subjugating nations to their sway, and that, under the pretense of giving the Religion of Christ and a better civilization to the world, it would veil the rapacity and lust of nominally Christian Powers, seeking temporal dominion over the property and lives of men less powerful than themselves, and so "Christianize" the nations. History has verified his foresight, and at no time more openly than now, in the standing armies, and the fleets, of the Christian world. The "Horns" fight each other. That militarism will prevail till Christ comes is the teaching of the prophet. The Roman empire accepted Christianity, incorporated the Ten Commandments and the Sermon on the Mount in the Theodosian code, organized the "Christian Legions," and began the work of "world-reform." What followed, the student of history knows—the Middle Age, the Papal power, the Moslem holding the fairest portions of the earth once Christian, the politics of Europe, Asia and Africa, even now governed by the same motives that governed the ancient heathen empires. The "Church" does not enter the field of the prophet's vision. He is the "Statesman" of Israel and the world. He sees the whole future of Gentile world-power and of Jewish subjugation, and places his hope alone in the coming of Messiah. That is his divine philosophy of history. As for him in the prospect, so for us in the retrospect, the story of the struggle of the nations remains forever the same.

> "'Tis but the same rehearsal of the Past,—
> First Freedom, and then Glory; when that fails,
> Wealth, Vice, Corruption, Barbarism at last,
> And history hath but one page."

The old empires have perished from the earth, and over their dull, dark sepulchres, "*Dead for want of Righteousness,*" is read through the fog that dampens the grave of their glory. Their monuments wake only the reflection that

> "Hardly the place of their antiquity,
> Or note of those great monarchies we find,
> Save in their dust, a verbal memory,
> An empty name is left behind."

So shall it be with modern empires and kingdoms. "Passing away," are the words the winds moan over their dying greatness. Thoughtful men—and of schools the most opposite—a Brandis, Hegel, Rawlinson, Macauley, von Mueller,—a Goldwin Smith and Sybel,—how many more, have recognized the law. They vindicate the prophet's view. One kingdom alone is everlasting.

As to the *nature* of the communication made to Daniel, it was a divine message, mediated by an angel, as was the later case with John, who, however, includes the "Church" in his apocalypse. As to the *form*, it is an apocalypse, or "secret revealed," Dan. ii: 18, 19, an open unveiling of the future, by means of plastic images or symbols presented to the eye, with their divine interpretation to the ear; a series of realities to be fulfilled in history, in order and succession. As to its *contents*, they are Israel, the nations, the empires and kingdoms of the world, Messiah, and the kingdom of God in conflict until the final victory. As to the *time*, it is the entire march of history from B.C. 606, to the second coming of Christ. As to the *law of its presentation*, it is that of advance to the end, retrogression to the beginning, advance again to the same end, retrogression again to the second empire, and advance again under more minute development, with always something new till the final vision is exhausted. As to the *End*, it is the goal or limit, of Gentile power over Israel, the final triumph of the kingdom of God underneath all heavens, in connection with Israel's deliverance and the resurrection of the holy dead. As to the *Chronology*, it is given in a scheme of seventy year-weeks, with their included intervals, reaching from B. C. 538 to the Second Coming of Christ; with intervals besides in the various prophecies. Chief among these are (1) the Interval between the 3d and 4th of the 70 Weeks; (2) between the 45th and the 70th Weeks; (3) between the 69th and 70th Weeks: the first of these 57 years, the second 2,061 years, the third 1,827 years, already. All from Cyrus, 538 to the Second Advent, is covered by 70 Weeks that enter into all New Testament prophecy, and govern every prophetic utterance of Christ and His Apostles. As to the *political significance of it*, for our times, it contains the whole "*Eastern Question*" in politics, and its final solution. As to the *Jewish aspect of it*, it exalts the importance of the Jew for the final triumph of the Kingdom of God on this present earth. The Book opens with the victorious march of the World-Power, under Nebuchadnezzar, against the Jews, Jerusalem, and the Holy Land, and closes with the last war-march of the same Power under the last Antichrist, against the same people, city, and land, ending in the eternal annihilation of the former, and the eternal triumph of the latter. As to the *sum* of it, it is God's own *Plan* for the development of His Kingdom, crowned with the Second Coming of Christ. Modern World-Reformers may here learn the wisdom of keeping their own theories to themselves, while doing all the good they can.

It has been already noted, and must be borne in mind, that the *Vision of Judgment*, in Dan. vii., is not that of all mankind, quick and dead, i.e., not the Last Judgment, but the Messianic Judgment of the living nations, connected with Israel's restoration, and the resurrection of the holy dead. The "Nations" are not annihilated, but the "Kingdoms" are, and become the kingdom of Christ, the nations still remaining. Rev. xvi: 3, 4; 15-18; Dan. vii: 27; ii: 44. The sovereignty of the Gentiles is indeed taken away, but the "Nations" are saved, through the destruction of that sovereignty. They survive the loss of their dynasties, recognize the supremacy of Israel, and the eternal sovereignty of Jesus Christ. His Kingdom comes, not only as a reign, but as a **realm**, wide as the world. Here are seen the import and solemn grandeur of the advent, for the world, viz., that, whereas, at the first advent only a few beheld the Son of Man, and in humiliation, now, "every eye shall see Him," and in His glory. Then, "All nations shall come and worship before Him." Rev. xvi: 3, 4. The aim of the whole judgment is to *"magnify"* and *"sanctify"* God's great name, "in the eyes of all nations." All the miracles recorded in the historical portions of the Book of Daniel, and the resulting "decrees" of Nebuchadnezzar, Cyrus, and Darius, were designed to be pledges of this. All the predictions fore-announce the same result. The Lord intends to smite the pride of all Gentile politics and power, and overturn all Gentile kingdoms, as in the days of old. He means "to bring down the mean man, and humble the mighty and the eyes of the lofty," so that "the Lord of Hosts shall be exalted in judgment, and God, the Holy One, be sanctified in righteousness." Isa. v: 16. No concert of the *"Powers"* can countervail this oracle, or stay His hand. "Thus," says God, "will I *magnify* myself, and *sanctify* myself, and I will be known in the eyes of many nations, and they shall know that I am the Lord." Ezek. xxxviii: 23; xxxix: 25-29. On such texts did the mind of the Saviour rest, as on Daniel's book, when teaching His disciples to pray, "Our Father who art in heaven, hallowed be Thy name; Thy kingdom come; Thy will be done on earth, as it is in heaven." Matth. vi: 9, 10;— petitions that will never be fulfilled underneath all heavens, till the Lord comes.

It is through judgment this great consummation is achieved. It comes with the solution of the world's greatest problem —that concerning the political condition of the ancient people of God. Like all other prophets, Daniel, under the imagery of the 10 Horns, foretells the final conflict through which Israel's lost sovereignty shall be restored. The conception of a great battle in which the assembled Gentile Powers shall be defeated at Jerusalem, in the end of the age, by the intervention of Israel's own Messiah, is the conception everywhere from Moses to Malachi, and from Matthew to the Revelation by John. The prophet, Daniel presents it under the sublimest and most terrific symbolism, as the closing act in the drama of the "Warfare Great." It is then, when the Cloud-Comer comes, all Gentile empires are broken as a potter's vessel, and Israel's kingdom rises on the ruins of them all.

He is a poor scholar in the study of the Scriptures who has failed to see the deep inner connection between eschatology and the Messiah-doctrine, in both Testaments. A disembodied state in heaven is not the end of the ways of God. The whole earth shall be filled with His glory. Through successive stadia His kingdom comes, with mighty changes among the nations, till the last catastrophe is reached. Men cannot arbitrate the "Day of the Lord" out of the Book of God. We can no more dissociate eschatology from the Messiah-doctrine, than we can dissociate Messiah from the kingdom. His work was not all completed at His first coming. Prophecy provides the ground-lines of the whole movement in connection with a calculus of time that passes from the Old Testament into the New. If it is true that, in science, indestructibility of matter, persistence of force, and continuity of motion, are essential axioms of development, and that the last impetus is from the heterogeneous back to the homogeneous, from diversity to unity, conflict to rest, through age-long transformations, these are no less true of history and the kingdom of God. Long before science announced these, God's Word revealed them, and built all prophecy upon them. Heb. xi: 3. Acts xvii: 26-28. It is to the crisis of the second advent the prophet looks when the world will change front and a new age heave into history. The kingdom is indestructible, the force is persistent, the motion is continuous. The result of the crisis will be the union of Jew and Gentile in the one kingdom of God on earth, discord giving way to peace, iniquity to righteousness, evil to good, and the breath of universal benevolence will salute all mankind. God's name will be "magnified" and "sanctified," "the Name that is above every name," be on the lips of all, and God's will "be done on earth as it is in heaven." To this "one event,"—not "far off,"

—"the whole creation moves!" The plan, the view, the process of becoming, the way, the end, are as "scientific" as they are Biblical.

If therefore, we ask ourselves what the prophet Daniel has done, the answer is easy. He has unveiled the plan of God, foretold the course of empire, and Israel's way, down to the end of our present age, with a glorious kingdom following. As to the "Time of the End," he has predicted, (1) the final partition of the territory of the fourth or Roman empire, an empire still existing in its divided state; (2) the Interval between the first and second comings; (3) the last Antichrist; (4) his deeds and his destruction; (5) the wreck of all Gentile politics and power; (6) the conversion and restoration of the Jews; (7) the resurrection of the holy dead, and final triumph of the kingdom,—all these in connection with the second coming of Christ. This brief summation is sufficient.

"Objections" abundant there are from every side to Daniel's doctrine, which is that of all the prophets, of Christ and His apostles, as to every other doctrine of the Word of God,— "objections" as numerous as they are worthless. It belongs to the truth of God that it always gives occasion for "objections," and is never "received" until the heart is subdued to recognize its authority above the prejudices and the vain interpretations of men. The "difficulty" is not in the head, but in the heart, and its normal disposition toward the truth it dislikes. "Unto the upright there ariseth light in darkness." The chief "objection" is to the "Truth" itself, and here to the truth of the pre-millennial advent of Christ—the "Chiliasm" of Daniel's book, as also of John's Apocalypse—blind to the fact that it is the "Chiliasm" of the whole Bible. To discuss the objections would be to write a large volume. It is not necessary. Truth once established by the word of God, objections are nothing,—least of all the common-place that the pre-millennial doctrine "disparages the means of grace, the mission of the church, and the work of the Holy Spirit,'"— an objection which amounts to this, that the Word of God disparages itself! That the second coming of Christ *precedes*

the victory of His kingdom "underneath all heavens" is as
certain as that the sunrise precedes the day, or that the first
advent preceded the setting up of the kingdom on its spiritual
side in conflict. The *sequence* of the kingdom on the advent
to set it up in conflict in undeniable. The sequence of the
kingdom on the advent to set it up in victory "underneath
all heavens" is not less evident. And as that kingdom in
victory is the millennial kingdom, the second advent is pre-
millennial. The kingdom in victory follows that advent as
inevitably as the fall of the Colossus follows the Stone's
impact on its toes, and as the destruction of the Antichrist
follows the second coming of the Son of Man. Nothing is
more clear. What obscurity of vision not to see that none
of the "objections" made against the *nature* of the advent, the
kingdom, or the thousand years, touch the question of the
sequence of these upon the fact of the advent! Let the kingdom be what it may, its sequence remains undisturbed. Nor
is any truth more clear than this, viz., that no advent of Christ
could be aught else than pre-millennial. "He is before all
things." For he who holds that the "thousand years" have
already been, are now, or yet will be before the second coming of Christ, must hold that the first advent is pre-millennial.
And he who holds that the book of Daniel is truth must hold
that the kingdom "underneath all heavens" follows the second
advent, and the thousand years are closed by the last judgment and final New Heaven and Earth. Did forty advents
and ages exist antecedent to "the thousand years," whose
starting point is fixed by all the prophets, Christ, and His
apostles, at the close of the last great tribulation and Israel's
national conversion, each and all would be pre-millennial.
In any case the advent is pre-millennial. The only escape
is to deny the word of God, and say the millennium may
occur in any age, or that there is *no* millennial age and *no*
sequence in the case, or, like those who were confronted with
the question as to John's baptism, answer, "We cannot tell."
But an intellect that "cannot tell" whether the Colossus falls
before or after it is struck by the Stone, or whether the Anti-

christ is destroyed before or after the coming of the Son of Man in the clouds of heaven, or whether the "kingdom underneath all heavens" is "given to the saints" before or after that impact and that destruction, is incompetent to teach the word of God. The vital question and core of the whole debate is whether the vision in Daniel vii. is a true prophecy and teaches the literal second coming of Jesus Christ. It is not the intellect, however, that denies, but the moral disposition toward the truth,—the prejudice, the preconceived opinion. The fact is that the sequence is denied only because it is seen, and prepossession refuses to admit it. Other considerations, unworthy of a teacher of the truth, prevail with not a few to resist it. The sequence is as clear as a first truth in consciousness,—as "I think,"—"I exist." It is a *datum* in prophecy, something *given*, not left to deduction or induction, an indemonstrable, self-evident and necessary truth in revelation,—not a nebula dimly discernible, but a thing so obtrusively prominent and present, that he who denies it mus' first have extinguished the light, then put out his own eyes. All methods of escape are vain. The "Truth" remains in spite of all. It is curious to say that the millennial age when "war is no more," has been in the past, is now, or ever will be, before the close of the "Warfare Great,"—a warfare extending to the destruction of the Antichrist at the second coming of Christ. It is more than curious, it is comical, to say that the final New Heaven and Earth which, admittedly, come only *after* the second advent, *are* "the 1,000 years" or millennial age, but that the advent is not *pre*-millennial! And worse than all, it is unpardonable to say that, because the Kingdom of Christ is spiritual, it therefore cannot be an outward polity, sovereignty and realm, on this present earth, but must denote the reign and rest of the saints "in heaven," when the prophet expressly declares—an angel prompting him,—that it is "underneath all heavens!" To dissolve the "Kingdom" into spiritual *inwardness* alone, is to deny one half of divine prophecy.

Let it be remembered, then, that the kingdom is an outward

"realm" and "royalty," as well as an inward rule of grace in the heart, and that in it are found "the kings of the earth," and "all nations," reconstructed under the sceptre of Christ "the only Potentate," "King of Kings and Lord of Lords." The proud titles of the ancient monarchs, blazing on the monuments that tell their pride, He takes to Himself, and places their diadems upon His head. The advent of Christ does not mean denationalization. The restoration of Israel's kingdom does not mean a narrow Jewish particularism, but a universalism wide as the world, and of intensest spirituality, righteousness, truth, peace, and holiness. Messiah's kingdom in victory is not His reign over an unorganized mass of spiritual humanity, without a nation or a government, but a kingdom where civil, social, political, municipal, and state relations, in public and private life, will find their highest satisfaction, and where science, art, literature, industry, capital and labor, and even sanitary regulations, will be governed by the letter and the spirit of His gospel. When the Roman empire came to Palestine, it came also to Spain, Gaul, the British Isles, the East, West, and civilized world. So, when the kingdom of Christ shall come in victory to the Holy Land, it will come to all nations. Expressly, the reign of the saints is declared to be a "reign *on* the earth" (not *over* it), Rev. v: 10. God's will is "done *on* the earth." The saints "reign with Christ a thousand years," Rev. xx: 6. It is then "the Lord of Hosts shall reign in Mount Zion, even at Jerusalem, before His ancient ones, gloriously," Isa. xxiv: 23. Once more, Jerusalem shall be the center of attraction. Isa. ii: 2-4; Mic. iv: 1, 2; Zech. ii: 11, 12; Rev. xx: ix. A Shekinah-Light will crown the city. Isa. iv: 1-6. "They shall call Jerusalem the throne of the Lord." Jer. iii: 17. "In that day His resting-place,"—here on the earth,—"shall be glorious." Isa. xi: 10, and "the place of His throne, and of the soles of His feet, and of His holy name," shall be "holy," Ezek. xliii: 7. The city that was spiritually called "Sodom and Egypt" shall be called "Beulah, Hepzibah, a city sought out and not forsaken," Isa. xlii: 4, 12. "The name of the city, from that day, shall be called *Jehovah*

Shammah, the Lord is there!" Ezek. xlviii: 35, Isa. lix: 20; lx: 1, 10, 14, 15, 21; lxii: 1-12. A hundred "objections" may fly forth from their quivers, impotent to pierce the word of God. "The day will declare" the truth, One thing is certain, the spirituality of the kingdom is not destroyed by its terrene locality nor is there any evidence that the King is confined either to a throne in the heavens, or to a throne on the earth. His motion is free. Glorified in His transfiguration, He moved among the unglorified. Risen from the dead, He showed Himself alive to His disciples. Nor were they less spiritual because of His presence among them, "speaking of the things pertaining to the kingdom of God." Acts. i: 3. Our duty is to dismiss all doubts, believe the word of God, and give Him the glory. To do this is an achievement in our present age.

From all that has been said, it is manifest that the Millennial Age does not lie in the "Times of the Gentiles," therefore not in the Church-period at any time. That period is described by our Lord, twice, in the clearest manner, (1) in His Olivet discourse, Matth. xxiv: 4-29; (2) in His seven words to the seven churches of Asia Minor, Rev. ii: 1-29; iii: 1-22; in both cases a period wholly different from the period of the kingdom in victory, Rev. xi: 15; xvi: 2-4; xx: 1-6. If John has used the phrase, "the 1,000 years," it was simply, as Professor Ewald well says, "because it was a technical expression for the glowing period described by the prophets, a name already well-established, steadfast, and a matter of well-grounded expectation." So, Professor Dorner adds, with truth, "Undoubtedly, the thing common to both the Jewish and the Christian apocalypses is the period of the 1,000 years, commencing with the second advent." We need not dwell on this. What we need to guard against is the great error that, because the "Church" is not the "kingdom" in victory, therefore, the kingdom as foretold by the prophets, is not here now, in any sense, but only comes at the second coming of Christ. On the contrary, the Messianic kingdom was set-up, on its spiritual side, at the first advent, in conflict, and we are "translated into it," by renewal from the Holy Spirit and our faith in Christ. It came in the person of Christ, in His blessed Gospel, in the power of the Spirit and in the preaching of the Apostles. It is the sum of all spiritual good, all grace here, with the promise of all glory hereafter. To seek it, is our first necessity. To enter it is our salvation. It is pardon of sin, peace with God, and life-eternal. And yet the conception of the kingdom, in the teaching of Christ, is so great and manifold, that it cannot be defined but only described. No logical definition is adequate. The predicate is too immense. The kingdom is "like" a hundred different things. It has many phases, forms, and spheres. It is inner and spiritual; outer and material; moral and political. It is individual and national. It is earthly and heavenly. It is temporal and eternal. It is mixed and separate. It is past, present, and to come. Circumstantially it is many. Essentially it is one. It is the administration of the rule of God in Christ over heaven, earth, and hell. Its realization, here, is the doing of the will of God on earth as it is in heaven. Incomplete now, it is destined to perfection hereafter. "The 1,000 years" are but its future evolution, mediated by the second coming of Christ. Its conflict now is the postulate of its triumph then. To ablate this "blessed hope" is to call the church to a battle for the world's salvation without the certainty of victory. It is to make Paul's argument in his letter to the Romans, chapters ix-xi; and his exclamation, "O the depths!" the outgush of a deluded mind, and the "Hallelujahs" in John's apocalypse, the wild ejaculations of an excited dreamer.

The light of science should have taught us better. The orderly succession of the ages and sequences of dispensations, in a grand march to ultimate perfection, is a law as absolute as in the cosmos and the kingdoms of nature and of history. Evolution indeed, yet not without divine intervention. Acts. xvii: 26-28. The procession from the rude beginnings of inorganic being to the elementary forms of organized existence, thence more complex in vast unfoldings and transformations, mediated by catastrophe, and the introduction of new forces, is not more true in geology, astronomy, and biology, than in revelation, prophecy, and history. The same law operates in all, that of "development,"—a word that involves three distinct ideas (1) "*tollere*," to take away, or abolish, (2) "*preservare*," to preserve, (3) "*elevare*," to elevate or raise to a higher plane, a higher life, and so bring to perfection. A score of instances present themselves as illustrations of this law,—the growth of the child, the growth of a plant, the growth of a civil constitution, the growth of a doctrine, the growth of a nation to its maturity and highest bloom. What is changing and ephemeral in form, passes away, while what is substantial, essential and enduring, moves onward and upward, through sunshine and storm, ever in conflict, ever opposed, yet finally victorious, "So is the kingdom of God." The conception constitutes the grandeur of the whole book of Daniel, as of all revelation. Of the eternal ages before our present cosmic order, as of the eternal ages after the regenesis of the planet, we can only speak as "ages of ages," infinitely backward and forward. Between these lie the Biblical ages or dispensations, known to history, the antediluvian, the postdiluvian, the Mosaic, the Messianic age in conflict, the Messianic or Millennial age in victory, each of these characterized at its beginning by some self-revelation of Christ, pre-incarnate or incarnate. "The Ultimate Age" we call the "Endless Age," only because the curtain of the future here drops, and the line of succession is concealed from view. And yet it is "unto ages of ages, world without end, Amen!" What cycles lie beyond! How vast the contemplation!—the one great aim of all being the sanctification of God's great name, the immortalization of man, body and soul together, the glory of Christ, the perfection of the planet, "God all in all!" Therefore, to blend in one *historically* what is seen oftentimes in one *prophetically*, is to misuse prophecy, annihilate both time and space, confound the ages and the ends, and disregard the clear distinction between them which later prophecy has made so plain. It is to abuse, by our littleness and short-sightedness, what was meant, on the one hand, to enable us to grasp the total future as a unit, and on the other, to comprehend the ordered and majestic march of the kingdom through different stadia of development, from conflict to victory. It is to lose that sublime conception of the apostle who says that "By faith we understand that the ages were articulated (to each other in succession), by the Word of God, so that the things which are seen did not become from the things that do appear," Heb. xi: 3. The forces and varying forms of all started backward from the infinite past, and reach forward into the infinite future. Herein lies the whole Biblical and scientific strength of the Chiliastic doctrine.

Therefore, at the close of a long life devoted to the study of God's Word, and having prayed that He, who alone can open the eyes of the blind, would vouchsafe that mercy to me, as He did to Bartimæus, and the two wanderers to Emmaus, do I desire to leave on record my unalterable conviction of the truth of the pre-millennial doctrine, a doctrine no other than this, that the second coming of Christ precedes the millennial kingdom "underneath all heavens,"—a doctrine for which the prophet Daniel stood at the Babylonian and Persian courts, winning glory for God, and honor for himself and his friends. It is not that a man's convictions are either the measure or the test of "Truth," or his emotions a proof that his creed is right. The Holy Spirit often dwells in sanctifying power where He does not dwell as an illuminating power in the deep things of God, and time embalms the errors it does not destroy, and creeds are propagated from father to son. But it is that the long, prayerful, and independent study of the truth,—with a sincere desire to know it,—and a heart honest enough to receive it,—does bring with it a self-evidencing and self-interpreting light, by which the truth is sealed to the conscience in the sight of God, with a certitude transcending all conjectures, and superior to all the changes of human feeling,—an "assurance of understanding" in the mystery of God. It is that the truth, like its Author is invincible. The question is not what "views" do I hold, but what "views" hold me, and what their ground, and whence their origin? In the words of Augustine, "it matters not what *I* say, what *you* say, what *he* says, but what saith the *Scripture!*" And as to the "meaning" of the Scripture, which *is* the Scripture, an interpretation that runs organically current, from the Pentateuch to the Revelation by John, and is simply a self-developing statement consistent and harmonious, amid a hundred variations and expansions, each prophet and apostle leading up to the same objective point, and final focus of the truth,—the Master confirming all,—is absolutely infallible, and never can be set aside, so long as the Word of God endures. Like the encircling concave mirrors of Archimedes, so placed as to flash their converging lights in front of them, so stand the books of the Bible,—that effulgent focus, the glorious second coming of Christ. He who fails to see it, only fails because his vision is perverted. The insight of such truth is supplied alone by the "Spirit of Truth" who gave the sacred volume to be the light in all our seeing, and the comfort in all our searching. And, to the writings of no prophet, have the Holy Spirit, the Lord, and His apostles, borne greater witness than to the writings of "the prophet Daniel." If we fail, here, it is because we do not use the Old Testament as they used it, cite it as they cited it, or believe it as they believed it.

Therefore do I deem it loyal to the Truth to testify that in Dan. ii: 44, vii: 27, and in Rev. xx: 1-6, lies the bottom, bedrock, basis, and formal statement of the pre-millennial doctrine, more deep, massive, and enduring than the granite foundations of the earth,—not to speak of a hundred other texts. I deem it "Truth" to affirm that such is the organic connection of both Testaments, and the dependence of the New upon the Old, that the sequence of the kingdom upon the second advent, in Dan. vii, for the Beast's destruction determines forever that the scene of the cloud-seated Son of Man in Revelation xiv., and of the Warrior on the White Horse in xix., are no other than the same as that of the Cloud-Comer in Dan. vii., and therefore, the second coming of Christ is pre-millennial. Heaven and earth shall pass away, but this connection, dependence, sequence and identity, shall not pass away. God's throne is not more firmly established. The almightiness and everlastingness of God's Word are here. Monumental brass, marble, and adamant, will wear away corroded by the tooth of time. The solid masonry of men, the rocks on which man's mightiest architecture has reposed, will become as the shifting sands, and his proudest structures crumble into dust. But this "Truth" shall stand forever. Abused like every other doctrine of the Scriptures, associated with delusions it abhors, error now seeking to enjoy its followship, and now to repel it, wounded in the house of its friends, rejected by those who know the least about it, studied relatively by the few, distorted by the many, victimized to creeds, councils, and special hate, it still lives and will continue to live forever.

"Time writes no wrinkle on its brow."

The "Hope" it whispers has been tested on the plains of Dura, in the fiery furnace and the lion's den, in Maccabean caves, the amphitheatre at Rome, the dungeons of Patmos, the recesses of the Cottian Alps, the Armenian mountains, and wherever the blood of the martyrs of Jesus has been shed. Wreathed with the memories of Olivet, it looks to Olivet in days to come. Twice ten centuries and a half it has been the one bright star that has shone through the gloom of Israel's long night of suffering and expatriation; and now that the brows of the morning are purpling with the tokens of coming day, it beats in Israel's breast with a redoubled pulse. The present age hates it. The self-deluded admirers of human progress turn their back upon it. Sociologists deride it. World-reformers make light of it. The political Zionist hisses at it. The church treats it with indifference, and oftentimes with opposition. Many good men, from motives of policy, avoid it, unable to refute it. It is not popular with the optimism of a false theology and a blooming antichristianity. But in multitudes of hearts it finds a home, and is welcomed as nothing less than the imperishable truth of God.

And this I can truthfully and intelligently say, with eyes resting on the history of the church for eighteen centuries, giving full credit to all that Christianity has done for the world, in the gift of civil and religious liberty, the abolition of gigantic evils, the propagation of the blessed Gospel, in the institution of her immortal charities, and in the education of what the early church believed, and how the doctrine came to be corrupted, and by what devices she was persuaded to revolutionize the faith of that "cloud of witnesses" who were the spectators of her early warfare, and versed in the vain attempts to set aside her testimony; and with perfect understanding of all that creeds, councils and polemists, have formulated, and how both ancient and modern sects have nobly but imperfectly expressed their judgment, and how false teachers have made use of it, and true teachers have been misled, and what dogmatics have objected, and what criticism has to offer, and, better still, what a thorough exegesis has so triumphantly established in the study of both Testaments;—in view of all, and of my account, I desire to utter this confession, that the doctrine that the kingdom of Christ cannot come to victory, "underneath all heavens," till the Lord Himself comes, is the very "Truth" of God. That great and "Blessed Hope," is our hope, that "Faith" is our faith, as it was the faith and hope of all the prophets, of Jesus Christ, and His apostles. It is the only "Hope" of victory for the Church, Israel, the nations, and a groaning world.

So take we leave, for the present, of the great prophet of the exile, whose pages have been to us a light and a comfort in these our "troublous times." And all the more, since God Himself is fulfilling, now, His own word beneath our very eyes, that "sure word of prophecy unto which we do well to take heed." Would that our feeble effort had been worthier of the book and its holy author! All we can do is to close our own words, and seal our own book, yet saying as we drop the pen.

> Blest prophet! second to no seer,
> Whose eyes beheld the coming day,
> To whom the sacred task was given
> To paint the End, and point the Way!

SUMMATION.

The world's whole future thou hast seen,
The march of empires, ages down;
Israel's long pathway to the goal;
Their conflict, victory and crown.

The wars of twice a thousand years,
Five hundred more, and more to come,
Earth's kingdoms scattered like the chaff,
For one alone to find the room!

For Babylon, a place no more;
The Persian, Greek, and Roman line
Egypt and Syria swept away
To set a throne in Palestine.

The blood-stained Horns that gore the world,
The Teuton, Bourbon, bold to scoff,
Islam, Tiara, downward hurled
Braganza, Saxon, Romanoff.

Secrets of terror thou hast told,
Of glory, too, so strange to tell;
Visions beside the rushing streams,
Euphrates, Ulai, Hiddekel;

Time's footfall measured by the hand
That wheels the orbs in orbits high,
The Seasons, Ages, Epochs, Ends,
The calendar of history;

Messiah, first upon the cross,
Then hidden long from mortal view;
Messiah coming on the clouds
To judge the Gentile and the Jew.

The Risen Saints thine eyes beheld,
The Antichrist sent to his doom;
Delivered Israel, new-born, saved;
The " Kingdom, Power and Glory" come!

O prophet of thy people, great!
Above thy grave, to Shushan lent,
Thy *"Kitab Emeth,"* " Book of Truth,
Is thine eternal monument!

In vain the critic plies his art,
To fiction make of heaven-born words
Immortal still the "words" remain
Thine own, the angel's, and the Lord's.

Rest undisturbed, till yonder morn
Awakes the "many" from the dust;
Within thy lot thou then shalt stand
In resurrection of the just.

In brightness, like the golden sun,
And glittering as the largest star,
Splendor shall crown thy labor done,
Nor age-long years its brightness mar.

"*Hayi-Olam*", streaming in from God,
"*Zohar*," the gleam that fadeth never;
Thy portion these, with Jesus near,
Amen! Forever and forever!

Thy Hope our Hope, thy Faith our Faith,
Thy people on our heart in prayer,
One day our eyes the joy will see,
And then with thee the glory share!

APPENDIX.

APPENDIX.

I.
ERROR CORRECTED.

I think the best apology a teacher of the Truth can make for his errors, and the only one, if he is an honest man, is to acknowledge the same. It is with great pleasure I give to the public the subjoined letter from my friend, Prof. George B. Merriman, formerly Professor of Mathematics and Astronomy in the University of Michigan, Ann Arbor, and more recently in the same chair in Rutgers College, New Jersey, correcting two errors of mine in my computation of the 70 weeks of Daniel. Amid the pressure of so many things upon the mind, and the struggle incident to so wide a field of entangling speculation in the study of a theme so difficult, I neglected to allow for the difference between the soli-lunar years of prophecy, as found in Daniel's book, i. e., prophetic years of 360 days each, and Julian years, in which our calendar is made. Instead of adding I subtracted the Dionysian 4 referred to in the calculation. Prof. Merriman has kindly corrected these errors and inadvertencies. The difference of one year in the interval of 57 weeks between the 3d and 4th weeks is merely a difference between current and completed time, affecting in no way the validity of the demonstration. It is a great satisfaction to find the 70 weeks mathematically exact, since, exegetically and historically, nothing is more certain than that B. C. 536 was the starting point of the weeks. The judgment of an authority so careful and competent as Prof. Merriman leaves nothing more to be desired.

CLIFTON SPRINGS, Feb. 3, 1898.

Dear Dr. West:—

Allow me to call your attention to an error in your exposition of Daniel's prophecy, on page 86 in September number, 1897, of "Our Hope." You concede that the 69 weeks, or 483 years, of the prophecy are prophetic years of 360 days each, but you have combined them with Julian years, and, to annul the effect of this error, have, inadvertently, made another by subtracting 4 years, when you should have added them. I think the following is the explanation you intended to give:

Daniel's prophecy of 69 "sevens," or 483 years, when reduced to Julian, or years of civil reckoning, makes 476 years. This period terminates, as you interpret the prophecy, at the birth of Christ, B. C. 4. The time to the year A. D. 1 is evidently 4 years longer than 476; i. e., is 480 Julian years. The prophet, you say, took no account of Ezra's "gap," the interval between Ezra's chapters vi. and vii., or from B. C. 515 to B. C. 457. This interval, reckoned exclusively or in completed time, as was then the custom, is 56 years. By adding this number, therefore, to the 480 years, we have 536 years as the entire period from the starting point of the 70 weeks to A. D. 1. This puts the beginning of the 70 weeks in the very year of the Edict of Cyrus, B. C. 536, and shows the "perfect harmony" you seek to establish between the Biblical and secular chronology.

Very respectfully yours,

GEO. B MERRIMAN.

II.
THE PROPHETIC NUMBERS.
THE 70TH WEEK.

Dan. ix: 24-27, is the *seat and source*—the *fons et origo*—of all the prophetic numbers in both Testaments concerning the "End." Each week is 7 years, prophetic time. The "One Week," Dan ix: 27, is the last of the 70 weeks, and is therefore 7 years. Its first *"Half,"* or $3\frac{1}{2}$ years (ix: 27), is unfilled in Daniel, but filled in Rev. xi: 3, and called "1,260 days." The middle of the week, when the "abomination" is set up, reappears in our Lord's Olivet Discourse, Matt. xxiv: 15, and again in Rev. xi: 7, when the "Two Witnesses" are slain, and is furthermore prominent as the time-point when Israel's conversion is announced and the Dragon is dejected, Rev. xii: 10-12, and is the beginning of the Great Tribulation, Rev. xiii: 5; Dan. vii: 25; xii: 7; Matt. xxiv: 15. The second *"Half,"* or $3\frac{1}{2}$ years, is expressed in various ways, yet all commensurate: (1) As "a time, two times (dual number) and the dividing of a time" (Dan. vii: 25; xii: 7; Rev. xii: 14), a "time" being a prophetic or soli-lunar year of 360 days everywhere in Daniel's book, as when it is said of Nebuchadnezzar that "7 times shall pass over him" (iv: 3), i. e., $3\frac{1}{2}$ "times" are a half-week, as "7 times" are one week. (2) As the 'shortened days" in Matt. xxiv: 21, 22. (3) As a "short time," in Rev. xii: 12. (4) As 42 months (Rev. xi: 2; xii: 5). (5) As the 1,260 days of the sheltered woman (Rev. xii: 6), identical with her "time, times and a half" (Rev. xii: 14). Daniel's weeks are weeks of years, not of days put for years, but of years for years, in the first instance. No "Year-Day Principle" finds any place in Daniel. "Son of Man, I have given thee each day for a year," was not spoken to Daniel, but to Ezekiel. Daniel's "Sevens" are groups of years, not of days. The utmost caution is needful, lest we practice deception on ourselves when using the term "weeks." All the weeks are of equal size, i. e., commensurate, although the two *"Halves"* are not identical. Otherwise, the angel would have told the prophet that in the 69 weeks no less than 173,880 *years* would pass away between the Edict of Cyrus, B. C. 536, and the Birth of Christ, and that the 70th week in Daniel means 2,520 *years*, the half-week 1,260 *years*. Thus, on the Year-Day Principle, the last half ends somewhere about 1846, or 1866, or 1896, or 1897 or 1898, the Middle of the Week being the Edict of Justinian, or the capture of Jerusalem by Omar, or the temporal donation to the Papacy, i. e., somewhere in the neighborhood of A. D. 500-700. *The first half of the last Antichrist's week must, therefore, have begun from 1,000 to 1,200 years before the Antichrist appeared, i. e., the 70th week began more than half a millennium prior to the Birth of Christ!*

III.

TESTIMONIES TO DANIEL, AND TO THE KNOWLEDGE AND INFLUENCE OF HIS BOOK.

B. C. 603. Nebuchadnezzar's first testimony. Daniel 18 years old. Dan. ii: 46-49.

B. C. 598. Ezekiel's first testimony. Daniel 23 years old. Ezek. xxviii: 3.

B. C. 555. Nebuchadnezzar's second testimony. Daniel 63 years old. Dan. iv: 8, 9, 18.

B. C. 538. Gabriel's first testimony. Dan. ix: 21-23. v: 13, 14, 16, 29.

B. C. 538. Darius the Mede's testimony. Daniel 83 years old. Dan. vi: 2, 3, 14, 16, 18-20, 24-28.

B. C. 538. Testimony of the Satraps. Daniel 83 years old. Dan. vi: 5.

B. C. 536. Nitocris, the Queen Mother's testimony. Daniel 85 years old.

B. C. 536. Belshazzar's testimony. Daniel 85 years old. Dan. v: 13-16.

B. C. 534. Gabriel's second testimony. Daniel 87 years old. Dan. x: 10, 11, 19.

B. C. 538-534. Self-testimony of Daniel. Daniel 83 to 87 years old. Dan. vii: 1, 28; viii: 1, 27; ix: 2; xii: 4, 8.

B. C. 518. Zechariah's testimony to the knowledge and influence of Daniel's book: (1) In the "Stone" as Messiah, Zech. iii: 9; Dan. ii: 45. (2) In the "four horns" as symbols of world-power, Zech. i: 18-21; Dan. vii: 7, 13. (4) In the Deliverance of the Jews at the Advent and the setting up of the kingdom, Zech. xii: 11; Dan. xii: 1; Zech. xxiv: 9; Dan. ii: 44; vii: 27. This, more than 300 years before the Maccabean times.

B. C. 468. Ezra's testimony to its influence. Daniel's prayer a model. Ezra ix: 5-7; Dan. ix: 4-8; 300 years before the Maccabees.

B. C. 455. Nehemiah's testimony. The Prayer. Neh. i: 5; ix: 32; Dan. ix: 8; Neh. ix: 12; 287 years before the Maccabees.

B. C. 333. Baruch's testimony in the Persian period. The Prayer. Baruch i:15-22; ii: 1-15; Dan. ix: 7-10, 12, 13.; 160 years before the Maccabees.

B. C. 332. The testimony of Josephus to the exhibition, 332, by Jaddua, the High Priest, of Daniel's prophecy of the Rough Goat to Alexander the Great. Josephus, Antiq. xi: 8, 7. See Farrar's onslaught here. On the other hand, Zöckler's Daniel in Lange, Introd. 25. This, 160 years before the Maccabees.

B. C. 250. Testimony of the Septuagint—begun B. C. 281, finished 247—to Daniel's *whole* book; 86 years before the Maccabees.

B. C. 170. Testimony of the Sibylline Oracles, Book iii: 396, 613, and *passim*, to expressions borrowed from the Greek version of Daniel; 2 years before the Maccabean persecution.

B. C. 168. Testimony of Mattathias, father of Judas Maccabæus, to Daniel and his companions. 1 Macc. ii: 60. This, 3 years before B. C. 164, when the critics say Daniel's book was composed. See Zöckler in Lange, Daniel, Introd., 24, 25.

B. C. 168. Testimony of the expression "Abomination of Desolation" applied, from Daniel's book, to the idol-altar of Antiochus, 3 years before the critics' date of the book, and other expressions. 1 Macc. i: 54; Dan. viii: 11.

B. C. 132. Testimony of Ecclesiasticus, xxxv: 18-20; xxxvi: 1-16; Dan. ii: 35, 45; vii: 25; xii: 7.

A. D. 33. Testimony of Jesus Christ, *passim*, the title "Son of of Man," "Coming in Clouds," the "shortened Days," the "Great Tribulation," the "Abomination of Desolation," the "Resurrection," the "Splendor" of the righteous , the "Times of the Gentiles"—"unto the End." Luke xxi: 24; Dan. ix: 26. "Daniel the Prophet," Matt. xxiv: 15; xxvi: 64; xxiv: 4-31; the Deliverance of Israel and Judgment of the Nations, the Kingdom, xxxv: 31-46; Dan. ii., vii., ix., xii.

A. D. 53. First testimony of Paul. 2 Thess. ii: 4-8; Dan. viii: 12; xi: 36; 2 Thess. i: 6-10; 1 Thess. iv: 17; Dan. vii: 13; xii: 1-3. See Matt. xxiv: 29-31.

A. D. 66. Second testimony of Paul. Heb. xi: 33-38; Dan. iii: 25; vi: 22; xi: 33-35.

A. D. 67. Peter's testimony. 1 Pet. i: 10-12; Dan. ix: 2; xii: 6-12.

A. D. 75. Testimony of Josephus. Antiq. x: 11, 14; xi: 8; xii: 7.

A. D. 95. Testimony of John, in the Apocalypse—*passim*, "Behold, He comes in clouds," the "Beast," the Horns," the Antichrist, the "Great Tribulation," the "Conversion of the Jews," the "Resurrection," the "Deliverance of the Jews," the "Judgment of the Nations," the "Kingdom." The date A. D. 69 or 70, assigned by the Higher Critics as that of the Revelation is indefensible.

It was impossible that the Book of Daniel could have been introduced into the Jewish Canon in Maccabean times, or later. The right of introduction belonged to the prophets, who were the historiographers also of the Jewish nation. The Canon,—notwithstanding all that the Higher Criticism has to say,—was closed by Ezra, Zechariah, Haggai, and Malachi, and the prophets passed away. No new prophet arose to guide the people of God. Nor did the Jews ever violate their national usage as to the introduction of a new book into the body of their Scriptures. As to the order and place of the books, many different classifications were made, in later times, for various reasons, some good, some bad. In one, the Prophets and the Hagiographa are in the same division. In others they are separate. At one time, Daniel is placed among the Prophets, because of so much prophecy in his book. At another time, he is placed in the Hagiographa, because of so much history in his book. In the Septuagint he comes after Ezekiel. In the Moseretic text he is put in the Hagiographa. Our Lord puts him among the prophets. The "Testimonies" to the pre-existence of Daniel's book, both internal and external, are irrefutable.

IV.
DANIEL, THE FATHER OF UNIVERSAL HISTORY.

To Daniel we are indebted for the formula, *"Times and Seasons,"* which occurs so frequently in the Old and New Testaments, since his interpretation of the dream of the Chaldean king. In the Chaldee dialect he calls them *"Iddanayya"* and *'Zimnayya,"* translated in the Septuagint, Theodotion and the New Testament, as the *"Chronoi"* and *"Kairoi"* appointed of God. Thus, of God Most High, the prophet says He changeth the *"Iddanayya ve-Zimnayya,"* and "removes and sets up kings; He giveth wisdom to the wise and knowledge to them that know understanding." Dan. ii: 25. In Dan. iv: 25, "Seven *Iddanin"* pass over Nebuchadnezzar, each *"Iddan"* a year. In vii: 25, the period of the Great Tribulation is divided into 3 periods of "a Time, two Times and the division of a Time"— *"Iddan, Iddanin, U'phlag Iddan,"* i. e., 3½ years, or the "Hali-Week" in ix: 27, and xii: 7. In vii: 7, the lives of the Beasts are prolonged a "Season" and a "Time," a *"Zeman"* and an *"Iddan."* In the Hebrew dialect the formula is *"Mo'adh, Mo'adhim, ve-Khetsi,"* xii: 7, "a Time, Times and a Half." With direct reference to these expressions, our Lord, in the New Testament, speaks of the whole period of the subjection of the Jews to Gentile power as the "Times of the Gentiles"— the period from the Babylonish Exile to the Second Coming of Christ, and particularly from the Destruction of Jerusalem by Titus. Luke xxi: 24. So, in Acts i: 17, "It is not for you to know the Times or Seasons which the Father hath put in His own power." In Acts iii: 19-21, Peter urges the whole House of Israel to repent and believe in Christ, in order that God the Father may send back Jesus Christ to them from heaven, whom heaven must retain until the promised "Seasons of Reviving" and "Times of Restoring" come from the Presence (or Face) of the Lord, pointing thus to the Old Testament predictions of the conversion and restoration of the Jews, in conection with the Second Coming of Christ. In Acts xvii: 26, Paul tells the Athenians, when speaking of the historical development of the Gentiles, the periods, epochs and crises in their progress, that God "hath determined the Times before appointed and the bounds of their habitation." So in 1 Thess.

v: 1, he tells the Thessalonians, when speaking of the Day of the Lord and the Times and Seasons connected with His Coming, that "of the Times and the Seasons" he has no need to write to them, for they themselves "knew perfectly" that the Day of the Lord would "come as a thief;" knew all concerning that Day and the Times and Seasons also from the book of Daniel, from the Lord's Olivet Discourse, and from his own instructions. So, in John's Apocalypse, these "Times and Seasons" and the "Day of the Lord" enter into the conception of the whole drama, and are distributed into different series of sevens, connected with the development of events under the fourth prophetic empire. The words *"Mo'adh"* and *"Mo'adhim"* are, besides being used of "Times," applied constantly to the stated religious "seasons" of the Jewish ritual, and represent definite portions of time measured by the sun and moon. Ex. xii: 10; xxiii: 14; Num. ix: 12; Gen. i: 14. An *"Iddan,"* a *"Zeman,"* a *"Mo'adh,"* are each a definite, appointed portion of time, and are called in general a *"Chronos"* or a *"Kairos."* At the same time they are employed in an indefinite sense elsewhere in the Scriptures, long or short, as the case may be, the "Seasons" and the "Times" often coinciding with each other, the "Times" including the "Seasons." As definite, they are chronologically determined in the Scriptures so far as their own measure is concerned. Others, indefinite, are indeterminable. In both cases they are in the power of the Father; in the one case to make them long or short, as He pleases; in the other to locate them in history, where He will, in their relation to the other times, whose measure is undefined. History alone can solve this location and relation. Thus, the period in the words, *"after* those 62 weeks Messiah shall be cut off" (Dan. ix: 26), and in the words, "unto the end," are both *chronologically* indefinite. History determined the measure of the first by the length of our Lord's life, viz., 33½ years, and history will determine the second, of which 1897 years have already passed away. While no one is forbidden to "search what time and what manner of time" the Holy Spirit has foretestified concerning "the sufferings of Christ and the glories after these," yet here is the loudest warning against the adventurous efforts of time-reckoners, whether astronomical or chronological, who would fix the year, even the day, when the Lord will come, and against that equally erroneous view that, ever since His Ascension, He might have come "any moment," or may so come now. Although there are definite times and seasons, or opportunities, yet there are indefinite also, in the government of God, which is not that of mechanical stoicism, or fixed fate, but is a wise and free government, directed at all times by His sovereign will. How long the Interval between the 69th and 70th weeks shall be is known only to God, and is in His power. Just when the "Times and Seasons" connected with the restoration of the Kingdom to Israel shall set in is contingent on the time when the Antichrist shall come, and this is unrevealed. Therefore, to His disciples the Lord said: "It is not for *you* to know the 'Times or the Seasons,' which the Father hath put in His own power," because the location of the definite ones depends upon the determination of the indefinite, whose measure is unrevealed. On the other hand, so far as the measure and relation of the final "Times and Seasons" to the Day of the Lord and the Coming of Christ are concerned, the Thessalonians knew them "perfectly," for they are connected with the 70th week in Daniel. It is from Daniel the whole terminology and periodology of prophecy in the New Testament come. He is the father of it all. Solemn "Times and seasons" there have been in the past, are now, and will be again, and to these our study is divinely directed.

Therefore, in view of all, has "Daniel the prophet" acquired for himself the enviable title, *"Father of Universal History."* By means of his predictions we are not left in ignorance of the end of our present age, nor of the way to it. How far we have come, what lies behind us, what is before us, and, in general, how approximately near we are to the end, is here revealed. The "Times and Seasons" represent the political and religious periods, ages, centuries, epochs and crises of world-history and of the development of the Kingdom of God on earth. Of such *"Times,"* or *"Iddanayya,"* appointed of God, were the Patriarchal times, the 430 years' sojourn in Egypt, the 40 years' wandering, the period of the Judges, the 490 years' monarchy, the 70 years' captivity and the 70 weeks' prophecy. Of such *"Seasons"* were Abraham's call, the descent into Egypt, the Exodus, the building of the first Temple, the disruption of the kingdom, the going into and return from exile, the building of the second Temple, the First Advent of Christ, the Day of the Crucifixion, Pentecost, the second destruction of Jerusalem. "Times and Seasons," represent the vicissitudes of kingdoms and nations and of the people of God in all their history, and look to the final "Times and Seasons" when the sure word of prophecy shall be fulfilled. They signify the fact that the whole course of history has been mapped out according to a divine plan, and that the ages and ends, the periods and epochs, were determined, whether definite or indefinite, long or short, as the will of God dictated, and that, thus arranged, the whole was revealed to Daniel.

The profoundest writers have not been slow to recognize this great truth. The "Scheme of the Four Empires" and the kingdoms sprung from them, with the entire pathway of Israel to the end—the whole theological conception of history—was regarded as a divinely revealed outlook for the future, and ruled the Christian Church, from the beginning to the rise of Rationalism in the 17th century. Herein, viz., in the fact that it has a *Teleology*, or definite *End*, it differs from all uninspired history, ancient or modern—that "End" the Kingdom of God in universal victory. It was the first total conception of history ever made known to mankind, a conception on which Paul built his magnificent oration to the wise men of Athens. The great historians, Gatterer, von Mueller, Schlosser, all adhered to the four-empired view of the world's development, in its relation to the Jewish people. Against all Rationalism the view held its ground, that Israel is the centre of all history by divine appointment, and that the destiny of Israel decides the destiny of the nations. Heinrich Leo, unable to penetrate the deep mystery of Israel's mission and relation to the world, rejected the four-empired view, in order to work out a universal history on an ideal evolutionary scheme according to natural law. In like manner Hegel, at the beginning of the present century, though unable to account for Israel's history by means of natural evolution, yet dreamed that he had devised a perfect scheme of universal history, which Vatke, his disciple, adopted and applied to the Old Testament, as a hundred others have done since his day. The importance of Daniel's view, however, still asserts itself, since it is from this view alone we learn that the Fourth Prophetic Empire, the Roman, though wounded, is still existing, and will exist, revived, before Christ comes. Luther was perfectly right in believing, from Daniel's book, that "the Fourth Empire must remain till the last day." In like manner, Orelli truly says, "The Colossus still stands." Calvin's wrong view that the destructive "Stone" which shatters the Colossus was Christ in His First Advent and establishment of the Christian Church—a view adopted by Mede, as again by many others, and followed by so many, the view of Rome, was defended not on exegetical grounds, but on polemical, in order to meet the equally wrong view that the "Kingdom of God" is not here now, nor wi'l be until the Lord comes, and also to counteract the fanaticism of various sects in Reformation times, who held that it ought then to be set up by force of arms. For want of a thorough knowledge of Eschatology, the only way to refute the wrong view was to "spiritualize" the prophecies!

Nevertheless, the four-empired view has a charmed life. None could deny its influence over Christ and His disciples. The whole Olivet Discourse is based upon it. Peter's Pentecostal second discourse rests its appeal to the Jews on the same view. Paul's appeal to the Athenians has it for its ground. In John's Apocalypse his Roman Empire is the legs and feet of the Colossus. At Jerusalem, on Mar's Hill, in Patmos, it gave scope, magnificence and power to every apostolic utterance. Augustine, Orosius, Vico, Bossuet, all recognized it as the only true guide for the historian. It was the accepted frame of universal history all through the Middle Age. It was the soul of the "Chronicon" of John Carion, worked over and edited by Melanchthon, 1532, and again issued, enlarged and improved by Melanchthon, in 1556. No work ever exercised a greater influence during the Reformation of the 16th century than the great work of Sleidan, *"De Quatuor Monarchiis,"* no less than 70 editions of which were called for and sold. Bodin's "Method for the Comprehension of Universal History," 1566, followed in the steps of Sleidan, and in 1672 Köber, in his "Dissertation," could still ask, "Who that writes history and chronology to-day stops short of the Four Empires as the goal of his endeavor?" It was Keller (Cellarius), in 1685, who first pushed aside the monarchy Colossus, in order to introduce his three-fold division of history, viz., "ancient, mediæval, modern." Still, the view of Daniel holds its ground among all believing writers on the world's progress and destiny. The supreme importance of the "Scheme of the Four Empires" lies in this, that it is a divine Apocalypse of the future, a telescope that penetrates through the entire vista of world-history, and brings to view the end of our age in the most vivid colors, and in symbols the most gorgeous and terrific. It is a light for the "Times of the Gentiles," for Israel and the Church, revealing the government of God over all history, and supporting the hope of the believer as no unprophetic history could do. It looks to a "Fullness of the Gentiles" and of the "Times of the Gentiles," a "Fullness of Israel," the overthrow of all anti-Christianity, all Gentile politics and power, and the victory of the Kingdom at the Coming of Christ. The New Testament simply unveils still more than the Old the events connected with the development of the Fourth Empire. We cannot do without it. A Müeller, Brandis, Baumgarten in his splendid volumes on the Acts of the

Apostles, Luthardt in his "Doctrine of the Last Things," Tiefenthal in his recent work on ":Daniel," Düsterwald in his "End-Time Kingdom," D'Envieu, in his immense four-volumned work on "Daniel the Prophet," in fact, all expositors of Daniel, save the Rationalists, are a loud concert of praise to the grandeur and truth of its representations and its world-wide significance,

V.

RELATION OF DANIEL'S PROPHECY OF THE FOURTH EMPIRE TO THE OLIVET DISCOURSE AND THE APOCALYPSE.

The prophet Daniel spreads before us the entire times of the Gentiles, Babylonian, Medo-Persian, Græco-Macedonian and Roman, with the kingdoms sprung from the third and fourth empires, from B. C. 606 to the Second Coming of Christ. As to the *Fourth Empire*, the Roman, he gives: (1) The birth of Christ, A. D. 1; His Crucifixion, A. D. 33½; the destruction of Jerusalem by Titus, A. D. 70; (2) the Great Interval of the Roman times of the Gentiles to the 70th week, and (3) the 70th week itself. He thus covers the whole time between the First and Second Advents. That Interval lies between the 69th and 70th weeks, and includes the birth, death and ascension of the Son of Man and destruction of Jerusalem. Or, if starting from that catastrophe, it lies between A. D. 70 and the 70th week.*

Our Lord, in Matt. xxiv., xxv., and parallels in Mark and Luke, resumes all this, and, building on Daniel, enlarges the prophecy, *assigning the Church to her place, alongside of Israel*, the one carrying the Gospel to the nations, the other remaining in unbelief during the Interval. The period of 33½ years from His birth to His crucifixion lay behind Him when He uttered His Discourse. The whole period from His death to His Second Coming stood before Him. He characterizes the Roman "Times of the Gentiles" as the period of Israel's rejection and the cross-bearing of the Church; a period for the development of the world-power, false Christs, war, missions, persecution, famines, pestilence, apostacy; all manner of calamities. To paint in, here, a millennial age of universal righteousness and peace is an impossibility. There is no room for it. The Lord has positively excluded it.

The Apostle John, in his Apocalypse, building both on the Olivet Discourse and Daniel's prophecy, as well as on other prophecies, gives us, again, the same Interval of the Roman Times of the Gentiles and the 70th week, with the Church, Israel, the world-power or kingdoms of this world and the Kingdom of God. He separates artistically all the events of the future in outline, and, with the lucidity of exposition and perfect symmetry of arrangement, displays the whole course of

*See Dan. ix: 24, 27.

the Church and of the world-power in four great series or groups of sevens, viz., the 7 Epistles to the Asiatic churches, the 7 seals, the 7 trumpets, the 7 vials, with an episode, or pause-vision, between the 6th and 7th places in each series—each series ending with the Day of the Lord and the Second Coming of the Lord; the *Theme* of his book, announced in Rev. i: 7, "Behold, He cometh with clouds!"

The 7 Epistles unfold the great interval of the Roman times of the Gentiles on its *ecclesiastical side*, giving in separate letters to the churches the different phases of Christianity in the first century, all typical of the different phases of Christendom till the Lord comes. They represent the Church development and the doom of its last prevailing form, even to be "spued out" of the Lord's mouth. The 7 seals cover the same interval, and give us the *civil and political side* of the same period, the development of the world-power, proceeding from a state of temporary peace near John's time, going forth externally, "conquering and to conquer" through scenes of bloodshed and woe, and also the hostility of the world-power toward the Church, her martyrdom and the doom of the world-power itself at the Second Coming of Christ. The 7 trumpets, entering later, yet covering a large part of the same interval, give the judgments of God upon an apostatising Christendom, while still the work of missions continues, and, after the conversion of Israel, ending with the overthrow of the kingdoms of this world, their conversion to Christ, and the victory of the Kingdom of God at the Second Coming of Christ. The 7 vials, entering last of all, are the judgments under the 7th trumpet, and run on to the same end; judgments specially quick and intense on the Antichrist and his kingdom during the Great Tribulation. The *Climax*, or *Summit-Section*, here is Rev. xi: 15-19, *which contains, proleptically, all that is afterward more minutely developed from xii. to xx: 6.*

The characters in this great "Drama of the End" are (1) the true election out of Israel, the sealed 144,000; the sun-clothed woman, or Jewish Church, whose history at both Advents is given; (2) the Dragon dressed in the uniform of the Roman empire; (3) the Roman Beast and the false prophet, his whole history, pagan, papal, infidel, given in the symbols; (4) the false Church, the harlot and her daughters, everywhere; (5) the true Church, or suffering saints of God, whose "patience and faith are tried;" (6) the personal Antichrist, or "8th head"; (7) the worshippers of the Antichrist; (8) the ten horns or kingdoms springing from the Roman empire; (9) Israel's martyrs in Heaven by the glassy sea; (10) God, Jesus Christ, the Holy Spirit, angels and demons.

As to the progress or development of the Apocalypse, Chapter i. is general introduction with the fundamental vision of the whole book, the Christophany, the commission to write and explanations of the vision. Chapters ii. and iii. are the 7 Epistles to the churches. Chapters iv. and v. are scenes in Heaven at the Ascension of Christ to His Father's throne, the delegation to Him, formally, of all power by the gift of the 7 sealed Book of the future amidst a universal jubilee. Here is the source of *"Old Coronation."* It is Ephesians i: 19-23, in symbols. It is not the Second Advent, but the Ascension, and Coronation, six weeks after Gethsemane and Calvary. Chapters iv. and v. are General Introduction to all the Seals, Trumpets and Vials, just as i. was General Introduction to the Whole Book. On this follows the opening of 6 seals in Chapter vi. Between the 6th and 7th seal is the episode, or pause-vision, given for comfort to the Church and in contrast with the awful scenes in the seals preceding. Here the dramatic progress is suspended. In great typical symbols, or ideal frames, the different phases of the future are represented, all the events corresponding to each symbol entering into that symbol, from John's time to the Second Coming of the Lord. Chapters viii. and ix. resume the progress and give 6 trumpet-visions, which *are* the 7th seal developed. Again, between the 6th and 7th trumpet comes the next episode, in Chapters x. and xi., where the Rainbow-Angel (Christ) gives the open "Little Book," containing Israel's fortunes in the time of the end, into the hands of John, whose commission to "prophesy again" is executed by the Two Witnesses. *Here enters the 70th week, as given in Daniel, only more largely filled out with the Antichrist and scenes in Jerusalem under the Antichrist during the building of the Temple.* In xii. we have converted Israel, the Jewish Christian Church of the "Time of the End," Michael standing up, as in Daniel. Chapter xiii. is the Great Tribulation. Chapter xiv. is the programme chapter, giving, proleptically, (1) a picture of delivered Israel after the Tribulation, their Redeemer come to them on the earthly Mount Zion, and (2) the call of the Gospel to the nations, the last warning to all apostates, the climax of the Tribulation, the harvest and the Vintage at the Second Coming of Christ. *The time is under the 7th trumpet, or 7 vials.* In xv. we have a special introduction to the vials, Israel's martyrs in Heaven preluding the victory of the Kingdom of God and the universal conversion of the nations. In xvi. the 7 vials pour the 7 last plagues upon the Antichrist and his kingdom, finishing the mystery of God, and bringing in the Kingdom of God in victory, amid cosmic convulsions and judgments unknown before. The *Episode* between the 6th and 7th vials so rapidly affused, is the brief word in Rev. xvi., *15, 16, announcing the near, imminent and impending Advent of the Lord for His saints at the "thief-time,"* and repeating the admonition, given by Himself previously to the Church, in Matt. xxiv: 42-44, *"Behold I come as a thief! Blessed is he that watcheth and keepeth his garments, lest he walk naked, and they* (the *Antichristian worshippers) see his shame."* It is the time of the gathering at Armageddon, Antichrist gathering his hosts, Christ gathering His own.

Chapters xvii. and xviii. are explanatory of Babylon and the Beast, i. e., apostate Christendom, and its relations in the last time, and paint in drastic colors the fall of Rome. Chapter xix. brings the loud "Hallelujahs" and the announcement that the time for the marriage of the Lamb to His long-divorced but now repentant "wife," the Jewish Church, has come. The same chapter gives us again the Second Advent and the destruction of the Antichrist at Jerusalem, as at the close of xiv. Chapter xx: 1-6, gives us the binding of Satan, and *resumes* the Resurrection, given in xi. and implied in xiv., in order to associate the same with the kingdom of the 1,000 years. All that Joel, Isaiah, Daniel, Ezekiel and Zechariah have spoken concerning the Valley of Jehoshaphat, the Mount of Olives, Zion, Jerusalem and Israel, the Antichrist and the nations in the last crisis is here involved. John expressly adds Rome, Armageddon and Jerusalem. As in Daniel, so in John's Apocalypse, the *two cities* around which the whole Revelation revolves are Jerusalem, and Rome the capital of the Fourth Empire. John expressly emphasizes Rome, Jerusalem, Armageddon and the Valley of Jehoshaphat, which he calls the "winepress outside the city." As in the beginning of the Christian age, Jerusalem fell and Rome arose to be the central city of the Christian age for a 1,000 years, so at the end of our age Rome shall fall and Jerusalem "arise" and "shine," the central city of the millennial age. How completely the rôles are reversed in the providence of God!

Thus the great peculiarity of the Apocalypse is precisely that of Daniel and the Olivet Discourse, only drawn out more at length, viz., that when we think we have reached the "End," still "the End is *not yet,*" since the "End" has its own development. When we came to the End in Dan. ii., still it was *not yet*, but a new series of visions developed as in vii. And so again in the succeeding prophecies. So was it in the Olivet Discourse. When we came to the period of universal war, and supposed the "End" had come, still the End was *not yet*, but only the "beginning of sorrows." And when, again, we reached the extension of the Gospel to all nations, still the End was further developed by a retrogression to the middle of the 70th week, thence advancing to the *Parousia* itself. So it is with the series of the 7 Epistles, 7 seals, 7 trumpets and 7 vials. *By an ingeniously divine arrangement the whole drama of the future is disposed into different series of seven visions each, the 7th in each case blooming into a new series, until the 7th vial, the "Vial of the Consummation," is reached.* Two of these series are parallel, the remaining two entering *en echelon*, each later than the other. Nothing is clearer to him who unstands the structure of the Apocalypse than its organic relation to the Book of Daniel and the Olivet Discourse. That Discourse is the link between them. Daniel's prophecy of the Fourth Empire furnishes the ground lines for both, the frame into which both are set. Daniel's 4th Beast is John's Roman Beast. The 10 Horns in Daniel are the 10 Horns in John. The "Little Horn" in Daniel vii. is the personal Beast who ascends from the abyss in John, Paul's "Man of Sin," "the Antichrist," "the prince to come" in ix: 27, "the king" in xi: 36, 40-45, the Beast in Rev. xiii: 5; xi: 7, and xvii: 8; the "8th head" in xvii: 11, the personal Antichrist being the whole Beast itself, the one in whom the whole Antichristian empire in Europe Asia and Africa is centred in the last times. Israel, in Daniel, is both apostate Israel, and the 144,000 of elect Israel in John "the People of the Saints of the Most High." The 70th week in Dan. ix: 27, is the 70th week in Rev. xi: 2, 3, 7. The 1,260 days of Great Tribulation are the "shortened days" in Matt. xxiv: 21, 22, and "short time" in Rev. xii: 12. Michael standing up in Dan. xii: 1, is Michael standing up in Rev. xii: 6. The "these my brethren" in Matt. xxv: 40, are the "our brethren" in Rev. xii: 10, 11, the "People of the Saints of the Most High in Dan. vii: 27. The Son of Man coming in the clouds, Dan. vii: 13, is the Son of Man in the clouds, Rev. i: 7, and xiv: 14, and in Matt. xxiv: 29-31. *The resurrection of the holy dead, Dan. vii: 2, 3, is the resurrection in Matt. xxiv: 30, 31, followed by the rapture, xxiv: 40-44; i. e. the resurrection in Rev. xi: 18; implied also in Rev. xiv: 13*, the reaping of the living saints, Rev. xiv: 14-16, and their enthronement in Rev. xx: 3-6. The destruction of the Antichrist and his allies, Dan. vii: 25, 26; xii: 7, is the destruction in Rev. vi: 15-17; xi: 18; xix: 11-21; xiv: 20, at Jerusalem. *The kingdom in victory underneath all heavens, Dan. vii: 27; ii: 44; is the kingdom in Matt. xxv: 34, and in Rev. xi: 15, and xx: 6, and xii: 10.* The conversion of Israel, Dan. ix: 24, is their conversion in Matt. xxiii: 39, and in Rev. xii: 10, 11. Such is the organic unity of these three great predictions in Daniel, Matthew and John. If the Vision of Judgment, Dan. vii., is not a prophecy of the literal Second Advent of Christ in person, to set up His millennial kingdom in triumph over all the earth, but is mere "judicial poetry," the authority of Christ and His Apostles and the whole New Testament eschatology are wrecked. The literal Second Coming is annihilated by every figurative and spiritualizing process of interpretation. In the Apocalypse the *Advent* is represented in various ways, under various symbols, in order to express its relations to the various characters and events of the closing scene at the end of the age. *It enters the drama no less than 7 times:* (1) After the 6th Epistle, in its relation to the out-spued Church of the End-Time; (2) under the 6th seal, in its relation to the doom of the world-power; (3) under the 7th trumpet, in its relation to the resurrection of the holy dead; (4) in the programme-chapter, in its relation to the reaping of the living saints and their separation from the wicked thrown into the winepress; (5) in the vial-visions, after the 6th vial, in its relation to the gathering at Armageddon; (6) again under the vials, in its relation to the destruction of the Antichrist at Jerusalem, a special picture connected with the binding of Satan, the resumption of the resurrection, to which is added the enthronement of the saints and the 1,000 years; (7) in the epilogue, in its relation to the theme of the whole book. *In all these representations the time-point of the Advent for the Church is the close of the Great Tribulation.* Such the law and the structure of the Apocalypse, in perfect harmony with the Olivet Discourse, Daniel and all the prophets—from Rev. iii. to xx. There is no Advent of any kind, anywhere, for any purpose, in all the Bible, save the First Advent, prior to the close of the Great Tribulation, i. e., prior to the *"thief-time."* The *"thief-time"* in Rev. xvi: 15, is the *"thief-time"* in Matt. xxiv: 44.

And now as to John's development of Daniel's 70th week. That week enters in Rev. xi. Chapter xii. shows the conversion of the Jews, as xiii. shows the empire of the Beast and the Great Tribulation, which extends to xx. Chapter xiv. after an anticipating scene of new-born Israel, with their Redeemer come to them on the exalted earthly Mount Zion, gives us a view of the state of the world during the last generation of men who survive to see the Advent, and of the last events before the Advent itself. It is the "Time of the End," when it will be as in Noah's day, the time also of the ascendancy of Antichristianity in Europe, Asia and Africa, its world-wide power felt in every nation under heaven, the time of politically dechristianized Christendom, the time when the Jewish problem, the fate of the Antichrist and his allied kings, the fate of the Holy Land, of the nations and of the Kingdom of God on earth must be decided. Apostate Judaism in league with Mohammedanism, both against Christ, will have hastened the end, and the rupture between the Antichrist and Israel will have hastened the final crisis. In the general programme of the end (xiv.) John sees, in a special group of 7 visions, 6 officiating angels and the "*Son of Man*" in the clouds of heaven. The first three are announcers of the Divine will. The last three are the bearers of Divine orders from God the Father to the Son of Man, who has now descended from heaven and is now cloud-seated in the air. Between the groups the Advent takes place. The programme stands thus:

(1). The first angel announcing the Gospel. xiv: 6, 7.
(2). The second angel announcing the fall of Babylon. xiv: 8.
(3). The third angel announcing the doom of apostates. xiv: 9-11.
(4). THE VISION OF THE PAROUSIA OF THE SON OF MAN. xiv: 14.
(5). The fourth angel bearing the order for the harvest. xiv: 15.
(6). The fifth angel, coming and waiting. xiv: 17, till
(7). The sixth angel comes and orders the vintage. xiv: 18.

In other words, John sees the Zenith-Angel flying in the path of the sun, uttering the last call of the Everlasting Gospel to the nations, the Judgment, and urging men to repentance. He sees another angel in the air proclaiming the doom of Rome, the corruptress of all the nations of the earth. He sees another still, and hears him threatening divine wrath on all apostates of the Antichristian time. It is the climax of the Tribulation. It is God's last merciful and faithful appeal even to an antichristian world, the angels symbolizing those whom God will raise up as messengers to make the last call of His mercy to mankind in this present age, and the last faithful warning of the Lord's Coming and impending Judgment. The martyrs are falling, the last blood-witnesses of Jesus. Interposed is a benediction from heaven, upon their graves: "*Blessed are the dead, the slaughtered ones in the Lord, from now on; Yea saith the Spirit; that they may rest from their labors;*

for their works follow with them." xiv; 13, 13. The time-point is immediately before the Advent. *"From now on"* they are blest, because their works meet now their full reward. It means their resurrection. Any moment, then, the Lord may come. And He comes! John sees what Daniel saw, and the Lord Himself foretold, *"One like the Son of Man on the clouds,"* but "having on His head a golden crown (the crown of life, symbol of the resurrection) and a sharp sickle in His hand." It is Matt. xiii: 39-43. And now that Christ is cloud-seated in the air, the order-bearing angels bring to Him the word from God the Father to commence and execute the judgment. With loud voice the Harvest-Angel delivers the command to Him who sits on the cloud. *"Thrust in the sickle and reap, for the harvest of the earth is over-ripe."* Man's wickedness is great, and the time to separate the holy living ones has come. The earth is reaped, the wheat separated from the chaff, and, with the holy risen ones, both are raptured to meet the Lord in the air. It is after the 6th vial. It is Armageddon-time. It is Matt. xxiv: 40, 41. Next, John sees the Vintage-Angel descending from the Temple in Heaven, yet waiting till the Altar-Angel follows and cries with loud voice again to the cloud-seated Son of Man, *"Thrust in thy sharp sickle and gather the clusters of the vine of the earth; for her grapes are fully ripe."* The earth's corrupted vine is reaped, its clusters piled into the winepress of the wrath of God outside the city of Jerusalem. The blood flows up to the horses' bridles, discoloring the streams and rivers, bridle-deep, 1,600 furlongs off. It is the land of Palestine that is the theatre of war. The scene is the Valley of Jehoshaphat, that Joel saw, as did Isaiah and Zechariah. It is the settlement of what we call the "Eastern Question" in the "Great Day of God Almighty;" the same judgment pictured further on under the Rider on the White Horse from an opened heaven. Such the programe-chapter developing the events of the 70th week, first mentioned in the prophet Daniel.

After a special introduction to the vials, Chapter xv. comes the final group of 7 visions, the vial-visions in Chapter xvi., showing the mode in which what was programmed in xv. is fulfilled. The first 4 vials, poured upon the earth, sea, river sources and the sun in Europe, Asia and Africa, poison the waters so needful for man, and infect the atmosphere and land with plagues made terrible by the scorching heat of the sun. It means great naval and military warfare, East and West alike; the hot, bleak mountains and the arid sands burning the feet of antichristian hosts, and scorching their heads; where water is, yet "not a drop to drink," the carnage is so great; the world still impenitent and still blaspheming. The 5th vial spreads darkness over the seat and the kingdom of the Antichrist, darkness thick as that of Egypt; Jerusalem is darkened, as at the Crucifixion. Sun, moon and stars refuse to shine. In the East the Euphrates is dried up under the 6th vial, to speed the march of the allies of the Antichrist to Armageddon. The kings of the whole earth, now quarreling among themselves, meet, with their armies, in the Holy Land for the last struggle. Rev. xvi: 12-16. *"Behold, I come as a thief! Blessed is he that watcheth." It is the Advent, the Resurrection-Time.* Then the 7th vial, "the Vial of the Consummation." *"Done!"* The last act of the tragedy of the Warfare Great is completed, amid atmospheric phenomena of rapidly alternate heat and cold, earthquake, cosmic phenomena, Olivet sundered, Holy Land upheaving and subsiding, cities falling, mountains disappearing, islands fleeing away, Rome's place subgulfed, hailstones a talent's weight smiting the foe, the wicked calling on the rocks to hide them from the face and the wrath of the Lamb. Specially, and after the explanations given in Chapters xvii. and xviii., John hears the thundering *"Hallelujahs"* in Heaven over the fall of apostate Christendom, and the announcement that the time of the marriage of the Lamb to His long-divorced but now repentant "wife," New-Born Israel, has come. The vision closes with the picture of the Antichrist's destruction (Rev. xix: 11-21), the binding of Satan and the resumption of the resurrection scene in order to connect it with the kingdom of the 1,000 years. Rev. xx: 1-6. So ends our present age. So comes the Kingdom of God to victory under all heavens. The Colossus has become as "the chaff of the summer threshing floor." The nations, purged by judgment, and destruction of the wicked who have failed to see the hand of God and refused to listen to the last call of the Gospel, are saved. It is God's "strange work." "I will sing of judgment and of mercy; unto thee, O God, I will sing!" Ps.ci: 1. Thus has John unfolded and filled, in detail, the Vision of Judgment seen by Daniel in Chapter vii., and expanded in our Lord's Olivet Discourse. The unity of prophecy is indestructible. A millennial age before the Lord comes is impossible. Only through the Messianic Judgment can the world ever attain to an age of universal righteousness and peace. This, the **concert of all the prophets, Christ and His Apostles.**

VI.
GOG AND THE ANTICHRIST.

Ezekiel's great prophecy, Chapters xxxviii. and xxxix., exhibits the war march of the northern power, in the last days, against Palestine, for the purpose of acquiring wealth and territory, the Jews having returned in large numbers to their land, dwelling peacefully, and engaged in agricultural and commercial pursuits. It is a state of things impossible except by consent of the Ottoman power. The line of Gog's march is from north to south, then, turning westward, crossing the Euphrates, moving through Syria toward the Holy Land; yet southwardly also, gathering the nations around him as he goes, and subsidizing to his standards the Ethiopians and the Lybians, i. e., the tribes of North and South Africa. On the western side of Palestine he moves from the Crimean region, the land of the Gomer, or the Gimirrâ of the monuments, the Kimmerians or Gomerites, and doubtless through the Dardanelles to the Ægean Sea and the Mediterranean, turning eastward to Palestine, with his ships of war. His march is challenged by Arabia and the Mediterranean nations, including the British Isles, as they were included in ancient times in the term "Tarshish," which passed from its local significance (Tartessus opposite Gibraltar) to a wider one, involving the whole commercial trade of the West upon the Middle Sea. In concert with these are their colonial dependencies, represented as the "young lions," i. e., the princes or rulers who govern them.

The prophecy of Ezekiel is based, historically, on the fact of the previous invasion of Palestine by the Scythian hordes from above the Caucasus, in the days of Josiah; in consequence of which the name "Scythopolis" was given by the Greeks to "Bethshean" (Beisan), where the Scythians camped at the eastern end of the plain of Esdraelon, not far from Megiddo or Har-Magedon. It relates to the far future, and foretells another invasion of the Holy Land, "in the latter days," by the same great northern power, strong in horsemen and in vessels of war. Interpreters have seen in the invasion of Palestine by Antiochus Epiphanes a preliminary fulfillment of the prophecy. Others have seen a yet stronger fulfillment in the invasion of the land by the Moslem, and again by the Turk. Both these views are fanciful, since neither Antiochus, nor the Moslem, nor the Turk, ever had an army such as is here, composed of many nations, nor moved as Gog moves, nor did they ever meet his fate. Moreover, the time of the fulfillment of the prophecy is strictly the time of Israel's last Great Tribulation and re-establishment in the Holy Land. Clearly, this war-march is pre-millennial, not that described in John's Apocalypse, and contemporates with the last campaign of the Antichrist. Dan. ii: 40-45. Both Daniel and Ezekiel see *the same end* of Israel's conflict; the difference this: That, whereas Daniel's vision is confined to the cultured nations within the limits of the old Roman territory, Ezekiel's has to do with the semi-civilized and barbarous nations and tribes outside the cultured centre of the Old World. The two visions, therefore, given by these two prophets of the exile embrace the three continents of the Old World, their relations to the Jews in the "latter years" and the final struggle of the ancient people of God. That Gog's march is, first of all, *pre*-millennial is evident from Ezek. xxxviii: 16, 21-23; xxxix: 21-29.

The question of critical interest is this: Is Ezekiel's "Gog, the prince of Rosh, Mesheeh and Tubal," the same as the "Little Horn" in Daniel vii., the "prince to come" in ix., and "the king" in xi: 36-45? An eminent writer on the Book of Revelation, Prof. Fehrmann, of the University of St. Petersburg, Russia, asserts the identity, saying "Gog is the Antichrist" *(Offenbarung, p. 143)*, and, like Kliefoth, of Mecklenburg, Germany, pleads this in the interest of *post*-millennialism. I cannot so understand it. There are similarities between them, in their relation to Israel and the Holy Land. But similarity is no proof of identity. Antiochus, Gog and the Antichrist cannot be identified as one. The differences are great. The Horn in Daniel belongs to the Roman Empire in its final form. Gog belongs to the Caucasus and dwells in the high north, outside that empire. Ezek. xxxviii: 15; xxxix: 2. Gog makes no covenant with the Jews. He does not slay the "Two Witnesses," nor inaugurate the "Great Tribulation." His march is challenged, which is not the case with the Antichrist. He descends from the steppes of Europe and Asia, gathers the nations in his train, compelling some against their will, and compelled to be a "guard" over them, lest they are induced to turn against him. Satirically, the prophet bids him "beware." Like the Antichrist, he is full of Antisemitism, a hater of Israel since God declares, "O, Gog, I am against thee!" As the power ruling the north, he "comes against" the Antichrist. Dan. ii: 40. The Antichrist's destruction is at Jerusalem (Dan. ii: 45), Gog's grave is in the Valley of the

Crossers over, East of the Mediterranean Sea," the Valley of Megiddo, the plain of Esdraelon. Ezek. xxxix: 11. Joel sees both Gog and the Antichrist, sees both the "Valley of Decision" and the "Valley of Jehoshaphat." His word for "multitudes" in the "Valley of Decision" is "Hamonim" (Joel iii: 14), and Gog's "grave" is called "Hamon-Gog" (Ezek. xxxix: 15), and his memorial city "Hamonah." Ezek. xxxix: 16. Both and his memorial city "Hamonah." Ezek. xxxix: 16. Both Gog and the Antichrist, though from different motives, are against Israel in that day, and God is against both.

From all it seems evident that Gog is not the Antichrist, and that the invasion of Palestine by Gog follows its invasion by the Antichrist, and occurs under the 6th vial, when the kings not only from the East, but "of the whole world," are gathered at Har-Magedon (Armageddon). Rev. xvi: 14-16. The last campaign of the Antichrist is in Dan. ii: 40-45; that of Gog is in Ezek. xxxviii: 4-12, 15, 16. The result in each case is the destruction of both, the deliverance of Israel, the victory of the kingdom and the sanctification of God's great name among all nations. That is the end of the "Warfare Great,"

VII.
CANON FARRAR AND THE BOOK OF DANIEL.

In his late work on the "Book of Daniel," found in the "Expositor's Bible," the Very Rev. F. W. Farrar, D. D., F. R. S., Dean of Canterbury, Archdeacon of Westminster and late Fellow of Trinity College, has the following:

"*If our Lord and His Apostles regarded the Book of Daniel as containing the most explicit prophecies of Himself and His Kingdom, why did they never appeal or even allude to it, to prove that he was the promised Messiah? How came it that neither Christ nor His Apostles ever once alluded, or even pointed, to the Book of Daniel and the Prophecy of the Seventy Weeks, as containing the least germ of evidence in favor of Christ's Mission, or the Gospel preaching?*" *Book of Daniel, pp. 103, 104. (1895).*

This is simply the reproduction of Kuenen in his "Prophets of Israel," a work he ordered to be suppressed as death drew near. The assumption is that no such appeal was made, and the conclusion is that the Book of Daniel has nothing to do with Jesus Christ, or with any events under the Roman Empire. Such the Higher Criticism! The assumption and conclusion are alike false. Both Christ and His Apostles "alluded," "appealed" and "pointed" to the Book of Daniel and his 70 weeks' prophecy, and many times, in proof of His Messiahship. That book was the most popular and best read book of all the Old Testament in the days of Christ. The Jewish nation, the High Priest, the Sanhedrin, all regarded it as Messianic. The burning question of the day was the Messiahship of Jesus. "*Art thou the Christ?*" Many other proofs He adduced from other books of the prophets in connection with His person, words and works, yet to none did He appeal more powerfully than to those in the Book of Daniel. The great polemic between Himself and the Jews involved that book, and especially the 70 weeks' prophecy; since, according to that prophecy, Messiah must have "come" and been "cut off" between the building and destruction of the second Temple. It is our contention with the Jews, to-day, the very centre of our demonstration, that "*Jesus*" is "*the Christ*,"—a *suffering Messiah*, risen, ascended to Heaven, and to come again in the clouds of heaven. Either "*Jesus*" is the "*Messiah,*" or the Book of Daniel is false, and the books of other prophets also. His birth is set at the close of the 69th week. Gabriel, moreover, who gave that prophecy, had come to preside over its fulfillment, announcing the birth of "Prince Messiah" as that of "Christ the Lord." The proofs of the falsity of Canon Farrar's assumptions are abundant:

1. *The debate of Jesus with the Jews*, recorded in John. As Messiah, asserting His judicial supremacy and authority to hold the Messianic judgment and bring to pass the resurrection and the life, which Daniel predicted (Dan. xii: 2, 3; vii: 13). He said: "I am the Resurrection and the Life." John xi: 25. Still more: "The Father judgeth no man, but hath committed all judgment to the Son, and hath given Him authority to execute judgment because He is the Son of Man;" i. e., because He is the One described in the Vision of Judgment in the Book of Daniel. Again, "The hour is coming, and now is, when the dead shall hear the voice of the Son of God, and they that hear shall live," John v: 22, 25, 27—a fact fulfilled in the resurrection of Lazarus and at the crucifixion, and yet to be fulfilled in the last day. The "appeal" is direct to Dan. vii., with which Dan. xii. is inseparably connected. All the reader has to do is to attach Dan. xii. to the close of Dan. vii. and see the connection. So well was the allusion known, that to have *named* the Book of Daniel would have been no less superfluous than to tell us to-day that the recital of the resurrection of Lazarus may be found in the Gospel of John. From the vision in Dan. vii. the title "*Son of Man*"—"*Bar Enash*"—given to Messiah, was taken and used by Jesus, the Jews and the Apostles, 84 times in the New Testament. The appeal to the Book of Daniel to prove that Jesus was the "Son of Man" and "Son of God," i. e., Son of the "Father," the "Ancient of Days," and therefore "Messiah," and that to Him the judgment the resurrection and the life were committed, could not have been more direct. The Jews so understood it, and "marveled" that the Nazarene assumed to Himself prerogatives pertaining only to God. It asserted no less than the supernatural constitution of the person of Messiah as both God and Man, and, therefore, of Jesus Himself. Jesus did "appeal," "allude" and "point" to the Book of Daniel in proof of His Messianic claims. It is a Messianic book, and does predict events under the Roman or Fourth Prophetic Empire, in spite of the Critics, and of Farrar, their second and third hand imitator and repeater.

2. *The answer to the High Priest.* In a paroxysm of rage the High Priest, contesting the claims of Jesus, vociferated, "I adjure thee by the living God, that thou tell us whether thou

be *the Messiah, the Son of God!"* Caiaphas himself is alluding and pointing to Dan. vii. as well as to other prophecies. Could the answer be misunderstood? "Hereafter ye shall see the *Son of Man* sitting on the right hand of power, and coming in the clouds of heaven." Matt. xxvi: 63, 64. Vain the effort of the critics, saying that the *name* of the book is not mentioned. The whole Sanhedrin understood it, and condemned Him to death for blasphemy. It is needless to say that Jesus *identified* Himself with the "Son of Man" in that judgment scene. That He did so in His Mount Olivet Discourse, two days previously, is self-evident. Matt. xxiv: 29-31.

3. Again, did our Lord never once "appeal," or so much as "allude" or "point" to the 70 weeks' prophecy? "These are the words I spake unto you while yet I was with you, that all things must be fulfilled which were written in the Law of Moses, and in the Prophets, and in the Psalms, *concerning Me.* Then opened He their understanding that they might understand the *Scriptures,* and said unto them. Thus *it is written,* and thus it behoved Messiah to suffer and to rise again from the dead the third day. And, beginning at Moses and *all* the Prophets, He expounded unto them, *in all the Scriptures,* the things concerning *Himself."* Luke xxiv: 27, 44, 45. Here is a dispute between us and the Jews. They refuse to admit a suffering Messiah. Only 5 days before this exposition He had dignified Daniel as "Daniel the Prophet," and, in keen foresight of the Higher Criticism of our times, as well as in reproof of the critics of His own time, uttered these words,—a crushing testimony Canon Farrar would take from the Lord's own mouth on the authority of two corrupted codices where the expression is omitted! That Daniel's book was a part of of the Old Testament *"Scriptures"* cannot be denied. Nor can it be denied that the Book of Daniel, as we have it, was the standard Palestinian and Temple text of the prophet, turned into Greek 250 years before Christ was born, and accepted by the Jews, Christ and His Apostles, as part of the God-breathed and closed canon of the Scriptures, authoritative in the mouth of Christ. Nor can the critics deny that the 70 weeks' prophecy is the *only* prophecy in that book which foretells that Messiah should be "cut off"—a Messiah the critics would make to be "Onias III., B. C. 170!" as Canon Farrar also does, as a matter of course. Dan. ix: 26. Nor will it be denied that the rubric, "the Psalms," because of their place at the head of this whole "Third Division" of the Jewish Scriptures, was a title given to the whole of that division, in which the "Book

of Daniel" stood prominent. The conclusion is irresistible that, since our Lord expounded ' in *all the Scriptures the things concerning Himself,"* He did not omit to refer to Dan. ix: 26, containing a signal prediction of His own death, and so did "appeal," "allude" and "point" to the 70 weeks' prophecy where that prediction occurs, and *only* there in Daniel's book. It is the companion-piece of Isa. liii: 4-13; Zech. xi: 10-13; xiii: 1, 7; Ps. xxii: 1-21. Had the Lord only "opened the understanding of the critics, their eyes would have seen things now forever hid from them.

4. But, more. Our Lord's answer as to the destruction of Jerusalem His Advent and the End of the Age is built, step by step, on the Book of Daniel, and appropriates even the terms used by the prophet in his prediction of the 70 weeks. He combines in His Olivet Discourse the events found in the closing parts, or Ends, of Daniel, Chapters ii., vii., ix., xi., and the whole of xii.—i. e., the events under the Roman Empire—in one connected prophecy, uses again the title "Son of Man," again confirming His claims by the Book of Daniel. It is His guide. In Matt. xxiii: 32, introducing that discourse, and taking leave of the Temple, the words "Fill ye up the measure of your fathers" are a direct allusion to the verb *"lecalle,"* to "fill up" or "complete the transgression" in Dan. ix: 24. He "points" to the "abomination of desolation spoken of by Daniel the prophet." Matt. xxiv: 15; Dan. ix: 27; xi: 31; xii: 11. He interprets Daniel's expression, "Unto the End, war," Dan. ix: 26, as "Until the times of the Gentiles be fulfilled," Luke xxi: 24, and in all shows that He is the Messiah of the 70 weeks' prophecy, and will come in the clouds of heaven, raise the dead, destroy the Antichrist, deliver Israel, judge the nations and bring His kingdom to victory. Thus did He "appeal" "allude" and "point" to Daniel's book, and affirm that it contained explicit prophecies of "Himself" and His "Kingdom," even of His "Messiahship." To those whose minds are warped by their prejudices, false theories and false science, no book is darker than the Sacred Scriptures.

Finally, here. It is from Dan. xii: 3 our Lord takes His illustration of the righteous "shining as the sun in the kingdom of their Father," when the "Son of Man" comes to reap the harvest. Matt. xiii: 44. His illustration of the "Stone" grinding to powder is from Dan. ii: 34. His "Times and Seasons" are Daniel's *"Iddanayya"* and *"Zimnayya,"* Dan. ii: 21; vii: 25; xii: 7; whose chronology it was not for His disciples, then to know. Acts i: 7; iii: 19-21. Was it from an uninspired novelist, a Maccabean romancer, a dreaming Haggadist or story-framer, our Lord quoted such expressions?

5. And did the "Apostles" never even "allude" to the Book of Daniel, or the 70 weeks' prophecy in confirmation of the Master's claims? Peter, in his second Pentecostal word, not only appeals to *"all the prophets,"* Acts iii: 18, and so to Daniel, concerning the sufferings of Christ, but expressly to the *"Iddanayya"* and *"Zimnayya"* of refreshing and restitution for Israel, in connection with the finishing of Israel's apostacy. Acts iii: 19-21; Dan. ix: 24. He boldly says that *"all the prophets, from Samuel and those that follow after"*—therefore Daniel—"have foretold these days." Acts iii: 24. In his first Epistle (1 Pet. i: 10, 11) he speaks of the prophets as *"searching* what and what manner of time" the Holy Ghost signified when He "foretestified the sufferings of Messiah and the glories after these," using the very verb *(binthi)* in Dan. ix: 2, and so "alludes" and "points" to the 70 weeks' prophecy. Dan. ix: 1-28. Paul's description of the "Man of Sin," in 2 Thess. ii: 3-8, is drawn from Dan. viii: 11, 12; xi: 36, 37; ix: 27; xii: 7. The special *"Iddanayya"* and *"Zimnayya,"* or *"Times and Seasons,"* in 1 Thess. v: 1, are those named by Daniel, and the scene at the close of the Tribulation (2 Thess. i: 7, 8)—the coming of the Lord with His mighty angels—is taken from Dan. vii: 13, and from its repetition in Matt. xxiv: 29-31; xxv: 31-46. Still more, he vouches for the truth of the historical parts of Daniel's book by "appeal," "allusion" and "pointing" to Daniel and his companions, who "stopped the mouths of lions," "quenched the violence of fire" and "escaped the edge of the sword" on the plains of Dura, to the brave Maccabees whose heroism Daniel foretold (Heb. xi: 33-35; Dan. vi: 22; iii: 25; ii: 13; xi: 32), and to the resurrection in Dan. xii: 23. In 1 Cor. xv: 41 he takes his star-illustration of the Resurrection-Glory from Dan. xii: 3. When, in Gal. iv: 4, he speaks of the "fullness of *the* time" when Messiah was born, he alludes directly to the close of the 69th week, and so "appeals and "points" to the 70 weeks' prophecy in confirmation of the Messiahship of Jesus.

And as to John's testimony to the "Book of Daniel" and the "70 weeks' prophecy," in connection with the Cloud-Comer and Destroyer of the Antichrist, it is simply overwhelming. His Apocalypse rests on "Daniel's Book," on the 70 weeks' prophecy," the interval between the 69th and 70th weeks, and the 70th week especially, and on the Olivet Discourse, as already has been shown in previous discussions. Especially in Rev. xiv: 14-20 does he use the title, the "Son of Man," and develops in 7 acts the scene in Dan. vii: 13.

Thus, both Jesus and His Apostles, notwithstanding Dean Farrar's provoking assumptions, did "appeal," "allude" and "point," many times and argumentatively, to the "Book of Daniel" and to the "70 weeks' prophecy" in direct confirmation of the Messianic claims of Jesus as the Great Sufferer, the Raiser of the dead, the Giver of Life and the Judge of all mankind. "I am the Resurrection and the Life." To deny this is to deny the New Testament. It is with Dean Farrar precisely, as with all perverters of the Truth, and all false interpreters of prophecy, whether evangelical or rationalistic. They commit themselves to error, then "stick to it," more anxious in regard to their own reputation than to the truth and the honor of Christ.

6. We have dwelt at some length on this matter here, because the "Book of Daniel" is one of the great battlefields of the Higher Criticism, so called. The critics assail its *Messianic* character with rare ferocity—*unguibus et rostris*. They bury talons and beak into its flesh, clawing its vitals, i. e., its genuineness and authenticity, its historic credibility, its miracles, its supernatural prophecies, its integrity, its Messianity, its eschatology, its reliability, its inspiration. The whole question, whether these peerless pages were written by an exilic Daniel, or are forged documents, compiled and redacted by a Maccabean novelist—a story book like Rasselas, or novel like Ivanhoe, Daniel Deronda or the Arabian Nights—lies here. The denial of their genuineness and authenticity is the denial of the "Book," and the conviction of New Testament eschatology as a dream suggested by fables. No appeal to certain evangelical scholars who allow a Maccabean origin, or partly so, and by their "typico-Messianic" theory seek to redeem themselves, can avail to vindicate for the book a divine authority. The same device might be applied to every apocryphal production. The book is a unit, and so confessed by all. Its author is one, and if its divine authority be denied, the "typico-Messianic" theory goes for nothing.

The *motive* of the crusade against the book is the same as that of their assault on every other book of the Bible. It is wholly in the interest of what they call their *"scientific method,"* whose first *"working-rule"* is the denial and exclusion of the supernatural. Once admit the genuineness and authenticity of the book, that it was written in exilic times by "the Prophet Daniel," and it is no longer possible to deny the reality of miracles and far-sighted prophecy which history has verified. The "scientific method" and the "working-rule" go to the "tomb of the Capulets." "Othello's occupation's gone!" Half-and-half expedients are alike exegetically and critically inadmissible. If genuine, it is authentic. If not authentic, it is not genuine. It is both. The proofs of its Messianity and of its fulfillment so largely already are legion,, and never can be sterilized by critical devices. Its language is a coin that can never be demonetized so long as the whole New Testament eschatology is of par value with its image and its superscription. The objective point of the whole criticism is the compromise of the character of Christ and his conviction, either as a politician knowing Daniel's book to be a fable, yet yielding to the popular belief that it was genuine, thus supporting his Messianic claims by fraud, or as a dupe, innocent and victimized by the Jewish Scribes and false traditions, and ignorant of its character. The outcome of the criticism is to undermine the authority of Christ in His person and prophetic office, extinguish His glory as the "Light of the World" and reduce the Gospel to a system of "Ethics," "Humanitarianism" and "Sociology." The evidence of this is manifold. The argument of the critics, that the Jewish belief in the divine authority of Daniel's book "proves *only* that it was in the Jewish canon, and is of no more value than the story of the sojourn of Jonah in the belly of the whale," is not only a bad logic and an empty sneer, but spins upon the pivot of the "working-rule," and hums and drones its old objections against the character of Jesus, whose belief was that of the Jews. And yet the sires and seed of such views as these are the authorities Dean Farrar cites as his supports, reckless of the consequences to all who are infected by them. It is a public disgrace to Christendom that any man should be accepted as a Christian teacher who instructs the Church that the Vision of the Son of Man in Clouds, Dan. vii., and the prophecy of "Messiah," Dan. ix., have nothing to do with Jesus Christ. t gives the lie to Christ Himself.

"Should a wise man utter vain knowledge and fill his belly with the east wind?" Job xv: 2. The flukes of the truth and divine authority of Daniel's book are too firmly anchored in the Rock of Ages to suffer the book to be endangered by the assumptions, conjectures, exclusions, illicit processes of the critics, and their scientific method. The inerrant "Teacher sent from God" stands before us as the *Interpreter* of the Old Testament. Beginning with Moses, He expounded the Law in His Sermon on the Mount, and its ceremonial teaching in His sacrifice upon the cross. Beginning with Isaiah, in the Synagogue, He expounded the prophets, showing that they spake of Him. Beginning with David, He expounded the Psalms down to His dying day. A Critic He was against the higher critics of His time who would deny to Daniel the rank of a "prophet," and against the critics of our time who do deny to Daniel and to Moses the authorship of "Scriptures" dictated by Himself. A critic He was against he lower critics who sought to break the Scripture and make vain the Word of God by their traditions; a Critic He was against Satan himself, who first redacted the xeth Psalm, then falsely quoted it. In all things, moral, religious, textual and critical, He asserted His superiority, and confounded the Scribes and the priests. From Him, and by His Spirit, the Apostles learned to read and understand the Old Testament, and for us, to-day, He is our Teacher, if we will but hear His voice. It is enough to know that the whole question of the supernatural—of miracles and prophecy—comes at last to be no less than one concerning the person and authority of Jesus Himself, a question whose solution depends upon the recognition of a personal God on the one hand, able to produce such a Person, and, on the other hand, upon the credibility of human testimony, which cannot be discredited by lack of this or that man's experience, or lack in this or that age, nor by any preconceived conclusions or assumptions built on sceptical grounds. To this it comes at last, *"Christ or the critics—which?"* and to a true believer the answer can neither be difficult nor doubtful. Each man must *choose* for himself, and with the full consciousness that "whosoever shall fall on this Stone shall be broken, but on whomsoever it shall fall it will *grind him to powder!"*

VIII.
CHILIASM.

The word *"Chiliasm"* means *"Millennialism,"* or the doctrine of *"the 1,000 years"* in Rev. xx: 1-6, the Greek terms for which are, in English letters, *"Chilia Etc"*—*"a thousand years."* It stands for *"Pre-*Millennialism," by which is meant that the Second Coming of Christ in Daniel and the Revelation, as in all the Scriptures, is *"Pre,"* or *before* the "thousand years"; i. e., the Advent comes before the kingdom in victory, and is, therefore, a *Pre*-Millennial Advent. This as an explanatory word.

An eminent Roman Catholic writer and post-millennialist has recently asked the question, "How do the Old Testament prophets relate themselves to Chiliasm?" With great frankness he says, "Many times their prophecies are so delivered that it would seem that an earthly kingdom restored to Israel shall follow the End of the Times of the Gentiles. Especially is that kingdom, which, according to Daniel, shall arise on the overthrow of the Colossus and destruction of the Fourth Beast, conceived of as the kingdom of the 1,000 years in John." Nothing is more true. His mode, however, of answering this clear revelation is the following—since he keeps his eye on the *"Roman Index,"* a sure reminder that he must teach the post-millennialism of the Roman Church, or find his book "prohibited." He replies, "But neither Daniel, nor any other prophet, knows of a kingdom *only* a 1,000 years long." He says, "The prophets *do not distinguish clearly* between the stages of the kingdom on earth and the eternal states beyond. They present the Messianic kingdom as at *the close* of the present age, *without any epochs or stages* in the same. When the prophets picture the future of the Kingdom of God, they insensibly pass from this side to beyond, *never designating* the temporal periods of the kingdom, or the order of their succession, definitely. *Only* the idea of the contrast between the humanity that is under the dominion of sin and the humanity redeemed from sin passes before their minds. Prof. Atzberger, University of Munich, "Eschatologie," p. 95.) I have italicised the words to be denied. Were the author's answer correct, no room would be left for his statement, that the prophets "do," and "many times," so deliver their prophecies that "it appears that an earthly kingdom restored to Israel shall follow the times of the Gentiles." He takes advantage of prophetic perspective in order to deny the clear teaching of the prophets, especially Isaiah, Daniel, Ezekiel and Zechariah, that there are "epochs and stages" in the development of the Kingdom of God on earth. He sees that the kingdom in Daniel is the 1,000 years in John, and "at the close of the present age," "and underneath the heavens." The answer rests (1) upon erroneous statements as to the laws of prophetic representation; (2) upon a spiritualization of the prophecies; (3) upon a confounding of the Ages and the Ends.

On the other hand, Dr. Paul Dornstetter, less regardful of the "Index," condemns the post-Nicene judgment of the Roman Church concerning Chiliasm, and its "spiritualizing methods." He says, "Not all Chiliasm was condemned by the early Church, but only that gross and sensuous conception of it which prophecy itself condemns. The highest moral ideal belongs to the Biblical Chiliasm. The conversion of Israel in the Time of the End is foretold by the prophets, and by Christ and His Apostles. The establishment of the Kingdom has, for its pre-supposition, the preaching of the Gospel, firstly, to all nations, the Antichrist, Israel's conversion and the coming of the Lord. Haupt spiritualizes the prophecies, and finds nowhere any concrete events of the future, but only moral and religious laws dressed up in Oriental drapery. Renan's idea that the Millennium is only "a little Paradise in the middle of the earth" is his conceit. The 1,000 years' kingdom is universal. When Reuss says that this kingdom is "a dogma peculiar to John," that statement is simply incorrect. The number, 1,000 years, was only an expression current in the Church for the temporal duration of the victory of the kingdom on earth, achieved at the Second Coming of Christ. It is untrue, moreover, when Mr. Carriere asserts "that, out of the disappointment felt at the long-continued absence of Christ, the idea gradually grew up that the 'Kingdom of Heaven' is exclusively an inner spiritual one, the same as life eternal beyond the grave." (Dornstetter, "Das end-zeitliche Gottesreich," pp. 141-144.)

Once more, another recent Roman Catholic author of the grandest ability, Dr. Franz Düsterwald, of Bonn, writes, "Antiochus Epiphanes was a type of the last personal Antichrist, who will be the soul of the Great Tribulation of the Time of the End, the head of the anti-Christian empire of the last times, and chief of a religious war and persecution of the people of God, and after whose annihilation the kingdom comes in triumph. Of this kingdom the Prophet Daniel speaks in ii: 44, and vii: 14, 27. This fifth kingdom is clearly set up in opposition to the kingdoms of this world. Already set up, spiritually, the kingdoms of this world stand beside it in conflict, but it comes to victory only with their overthrow. According to Daniel, it follows the Messianic Judgment, which is not the final or general Judgment of the world. Among the first Christian expositors of the Book of Daniel stands the holy Hippolytus, whose book is chiliastic. To him followed many in the first four centuries of the Church, and, indeed, not a few. The crass Chiliasm, which was the product of heretical sects, and awaited a kingdom of sensuous enjoyments, was rejected by the Church. Otherwise was it with the better Chiliasm. This a multitude of the fathers of the ancient Church advocated earnestly. When Jerome says, *"Cesset ergo mille annorum fabula,"* "Let the fable of the 1,000 years cease," so has he thereby condemned only the crass Chiliasm, since he remarks of the true, "which, although *we do not follow it, yet we dare not condemn, because a multitude of our ecclesiastical men, and the martyrs also, have believed it."* First in modern times, especially by the Protestants, was Chiliasm defended. Auberlen has remarked that 'Hengstenberg's defect was the lack of a Biblical Chiliasm.'" For the Roman Catholic Church, he adds, "If we remove from us all that is contrary to the true doctrine, then may the expositors of the Book of Daniel not merely admit it, but, in the words of Dan. xii: 12, find themselves among the 'Blessed who wait and come to the 1,335 days.'" (Düsterwald, "Die Weltreiche und das Gottesreich," pp. 279-280.)

Attempts have been made, since Mede published his great folio, to set aside his correction of the text of Justin, which the Roman church corrupted in the interest of Post-Millennialism, leaving Justin the victim of a self-contradiction, scarcely without a parallel. What Justin says is that the orthodox Christians, or "right-minded," who were "pure in pious faith," held with him the Chiliastic doctrine. He states also that there were " Many who are NOT of the pure and pious faith of the Christians, who do not confess this. They are called Christians, indeed, but are godless, impious heretics, because they teach doctrines in every respect blasphemous, atheistic, foolish. . . . They do not confess this, but dare to blaspheme the God of Abraham, Isaac and Jacob, and say there is *no resurrection* of the dead, but that, at death, *souls* are received up into heaven. Do not imagine that these are Christians" (Dialogue with Trypho. Caps. 80, 81). Mede restored the "NOT" before the words "of the pure and pious faith," and thus delivered Justin from the glaring self-contradiction that there were "many of the pure and pious faith of the Christians" who were "called Christians, but are godless, impious heretics, because they teach doctrines in every respect blasphemous, atheistic, foolish," etc. The restoration of the "*not*" justifies itself the moment the text and context of Justin are read. The "*not*" was erased, as Mede, and after him scores of others of the first eminence, have shown, like Chillingworth, Vint, Tillotson, Daillé, Volk, Christiani, Baur, Fehrmann, Wolff, Donaldson, that the erasure was made in order to compel Justin to say that there were "two classes of orthodox" in early times, one holding, the other denying, the pre-millennial doctrine, and that the deniers were the majority!—a device which would make Justin affirm that one class of the "orthodox" were "heretics!" It was natural that Kelly, the "*Any-Moment Adventist*," should, in the interest of his new doctrine, repel the early pre-millennialism of Justin, and Justin's testimony to the faith of the early church which excluded forever the modern invention. Others have in various ways, for various ends, assailed Mede's self-commending restoration of the true text, but in vain.

A recent able writer, Prof. MacDill, of Xenia, Ohio, in his "Pre-Millennialism Discussed," excludes all reference to Daniel Chapter VII., where the Coming of Christ and the *sequence* of the Kingdom "underneath all heavens" are so clearly stated—the culminating chapter of the whole book—and accepted by Justin and all pre-millennialists as the formal seat of John's doctrine of the 1,000 years. It is remarkable that, beginning the discussion with the statement that "the question concerning the *priority* of these two events"—Advent and Kingdom in victory—" is not of itself of much importance," yet fully one-half of the discussion is devoted to show that it is of prime importance, and that *Post*-Millennialism is the true doctrine. It is a vivid illustration that we cannot minimize the "importance" of *pre* or *post*. There lies the main question. Apart wholly from our personal interest in the coming of Christ, and viewed as a civil and political question in its relation to the nations and the term of Gentile sovereignty over Israel, just as Daniel viewed it, the vital question is, "How long shall the Colossus stand on nationally dead Israel in Israel's valley of Dry Bones?" It is the Eastern Question. By it all other question are decided in world-historical development. It is whether the vision of the Cloud-Comer in Daniel vii. means the literal Second Advent of Christ to bring His Kingdom to victory, or whether a Golden Age of universal righteousness and peace, when war shall be no more, can run parallel with the " Warfare Great " which that Advent terminates. To omit Dan. vii. in a discussion of PRE-MILLENNIALISM seems to intimate that the Coming of the Son of Man in clouds *"has nothing to do with the Second Advent!"* Criticising deservedly the inconsistencies of certain pre-millenarians—yet not himself free from the same defect—and justly repelling the modern "Any-Moment Adventism," the author has given us one more evidence of the indestructibility of the pre-millennial doctrine.

Nothing can break the consentient judgment of great scholars, historians and exegetes, as to the witness of the early church to the pre-millennial coming of Christ. " It was," says Gieseler, " the general belief of the apostolic age." " It was," says Mede, " the general belief of all Christians in the age next following the apostles, and none but heretics denied it." " It was," says Hase, " the old and popular faith." " The stream of all antiquity ran that way," says Homes. Muencher says, " It was almost universally held by all teachers." Rome wes never able to answer the sword-stroke of the great Chillingworth, that " the doctrine was taught and believed by the most eminent fathers of the Church in the age next after the Apostles, and by none of that age opposed or condemned." It is the scholarly Burton who affirms, in his Bampton Lectures, that "the early Church's faith in the pre-millennial Advent of the Lord is beyond successful denial." " The whole Church," says Alford, " for three hundred years held it, and it is the most cogent instance of unanimity which primitive antiquity presents. And such are the statements of Bindemann, Donaldson, Luthardt, Dorner, Volk, Christiani, and a hundred more that could be quoted. It is error to say that Justin taught that in his day any of the orthodox held the idea of a Millennium before Christ comes. It was simply an impossibility. Not till Dan. vii., and Matt. xxiv., and Rev. xix: 11-21, were "spiritualized" did the Church ever teach such a folly. It is incorrect to say that the majority of French and German scholars decide against Mede's correction of Justin's corrupted text. The fact is the other way, and immensely.

The latest method of vindicating the evaporation of the prophecies concerning the Jews is the effort of Professor D.

E. Haupt, of Halle, who announces, in his "Eschatology of the Gospels," as one of the recent "triumphs of scientific criticism," the "demonstration" that Jesus said one thing but meant another. In other words, the Lord made use of "Jewish *modes* of expression and *forms* of representation," but "put into them an entirely new and different meaning." The kingdom He preached was exclusively a spiritual one, inner, super-earthly, viz., our personal fellowship with God through Christ. Jesus was "not dependent on contemporary Judaism for His ideas, nor on ancient prophecy, but spake from his own self-consciousness as Messiah the Son of God." He thus poured the "New Wine" of a spiritual kingdom into the "Old Bottles" of the prophets, rejecting the literal interpretation. The prophecies do not really predict concrete historical events, but only set forth "moral laws and principles clothed in Jewish drapery." The conclusion is that Chiliasm is false, since the prophets, our Lord's own teaching, and the apocalypse, "must be interpreted spiritually!" Such the logic, the exegesis and the scientific method! The masterly manner in which Professor Schnedermann, of Leipzig, has demolished Haupt's idealism, in his "Announcement and Doctrine of the Kingdom of God, by Jesus," is at least known to all German scholars. He has shown conclusively that the denial of the Biblical Realism is the denial of a literal coming of Christ in the flesh, a literal resurrection of Christ, a literal resurrection of believers, a literal Second Coming of Christ, a literal restoration and conversion of the Jews, and a literal Kingdom of Glory on the earth; and that the critical separation of the "*thought*" from the "*form*" in which both the prophets and Jesus expressed themselves, amounts simply to a "denial of the Scriptures." No book of our times surpasses this for its thorough review of all the recent German writers on the kingdom of God. It defends triumphantly the Chiliasm of Moses and the Prophets, Jesus Christ and His Apostles. Beside it stand Yssel's work, "The Doctrine of the Kingdom of God in the New Testament," crowned by the Hague Society, also the special work of Schmoller, on "The Doctrine of the Kingdom of God," **both most thorough and exhaustive in exegesis and criticism, and both, like Schnedermann, maintaining the literal interpretation.** The defense of Chiliasm is complete, and vigorous **as it was** by the Swiss, Dutch, French and Russian Professors, Godet, Da Costa, De Sauley, Volck and Christiani, and is as victoriously defended by Wolff of Copenhagen, Krueger of Paris, by Cremer, **Wahnitz, and scores of scholars** of the first rank. The attitude of the Evangelical Churches in the United States, toward this doctrine, to-day, in view of the exegetical labor upon it in Continental Europe during the last thirty years, is no credit either to the Churches, or the Seminaries or the Ministry.

The words of Professor Reuss are supported by every deeper study of the pre-millennial question; viz., "The post-Nicene Fathers of the Church escaped the doctrine of the 1,000 years in John, only by substituting in the text a pretended spiritual interpretation altogether arbitrary, and condemned in advance by the author himself, who shows at every step that he will have his symbols understood literally and not as metaphors. It was by a system of allegories the Greek Fathers avoided the chiliastic consequences, until the Revelation was extended from the Canon. But for the Alexandrian school, which restored the book to its canonical authority, although spiritualizing its contents, it had altogether been rejected. This theory of interpretation continues in the Church until the time of the Great Reformation, at least among the so-called orthodox, and continues still even to our own day." (L'Apocalypse, pp. 40-44.

IX.
HOW NEAR TO THE END?

The only reliable *data* we have for the approximate determination of the question are (1) the Biblical and true distinction between the "End of the Age," and the common term the "End of the World;" (2) The doctrine of the Seventy Weeks in Daniel, with their included Intervals, the last our present age; (3) The Olivet Discourse, in which this Interval is defined as the Roman "Times of the Gentiles," and as followed by the Seventieth Week," at whose middle point the "abomination of desolation" is introduced; (4) The Thessalonian letters of Paul, whose eschatology rests on both Daniel and the Olivet Discourse; and (5) The Apocalypse by John, which again covers the same Interval, i. e., the period of Daniel's Fourth Empire, and at whose close the Seventieth Week is introduced the last time in Biblical prophecy. Here we have *chronological data* of definite measure, the Interval alone being undetermined. This chronological indeterminateness is, however, compensated for, in large degree, (6) by the predicted signs and events which "much needs" precede the Advent, and by the assignment of the Christian Church to her place alongside of Israel in unbelief, in the same perspective. Thus the Biblical *data* are exhausted. Daniel gives no "signs" preceding the Advent, but only the Seventieth Week and the Antichrist's career. Our Lord introduces the signs foretold by other prophets and amplifies by adding certain historical events, cosmical phenomena, and a moral condition of society corresponding to that in the days of Noah and of Lot. John still further amplifies, and arranges the whole in different series or groups of sevens.

We stand, to-day, with sixty-nine of the seventy weeks, and almost 1898 years of the Interval between the sixty-ninth and seventieth week, i. e., the Interval of the Roman Times of the Gentiles, behind us. How long this undetermined time may be, how much remains of it before the revelation of the Antichrist and opening of the seventieth week, none can tell. Manifestly, we are thrown upon the *Events* and *Signs* foretold in prophecy, as certain to occur anterior to the Advent. Only thus can we measure our probable nearness to the end. By no astronomical calculation can we fix the time-point of this event. Every effort so to do has been convicted of scientific error. By no Year-Day theory of reckoning can it be decided, since Daniel knows of none such. The series of precurrent events and signs were designed of Christ to be among the objects of the Church's *watching*, the special couriers in advance of his appearing. That Coming He has fixed in the most positive manner, as have the Prophets and His Apostles, at the "End" of the Church's Missionary Age, and given with great fidelity its unmistakable omens, "*Behold, I have told you before.*" These are political, civil, national, international, moral, social, religious, cosmical, i. e., terrestrial and celestial. Some enter singly, some contemporaneously, some successively, all increasingly. Some are nearer to us, i. e., remotest from the Advent; some are farther from us, i. e., nearest to the Advent; and as the end approaches are cumulative, more frequent, special, intense and universal. Some are mediate, some are common to all ages, but all together are peculiar to the "End." The earlier precursors do not retire from the field, but still continue. The heralds of the "Day of the Lord" persist and enter into the day itself. The last sign is "the Sign of the Son of Man in Heaven," that is, the Appearing of the Son of Man, who is Himself His own Sign, as Bengel beautifully says, "*Ipse Signum Sui.*"

Among the Events which portend the approaching End of the Age, are

I. Those given in the Old Testament, viz.:

1. The return of the Jews to their own land in numbers sufficient to satisfy the prophecy. Isa. xi: 11-16.

2. The covenant between the Antichrist and the Jewish masses, whereby they acquire a *modus vivendi* with the building of their temple, and revival of their ancient worship, the Lord reproving their unbelieving labor. Isa. lxvi: 1-4; Dan. ix: 27.

3. The conversion of the Remnant and their persecution by their apostate brethren. Isa. lvi. 5-9.

4. The breach of the covenant between the Antichrist and the Jews, followed by the Great Tribulation, Dan. ix. 27, beginning with the attack of certain Powers upon the Antichrist, and the Antichrist's Invasion of Palestine. Dan. xi: 40-45; xii: 1.

5. The gathering of the nations against Jerusalem, for the final conflict. Zeph. iii: 8; Zech. xiv: 2; Joel iii: 9-11.

6. The sanguinary action in the valley of Jehoshaphat and Valley of Decision. Joel iii: 12-14; Isa. lxvi: 15.

7. The Cosmic Signs—earthquake, the sundering of the Mount of Olives, the obscuration of the Heavenly Lights, and commotions in heaven and earth. Zech. xiv: 1-5; Joel iii: 15, 16; Hag. ii: 6, 7.

II. Those given in the New Testament. In the Olivet Discourse the Lord gives the Signs and Events for both the destruction of Jerusalem by Titus, and His Parousia, signs common to both, and signs special to the latter. Among the nearer signs are:

1. The appearing of False Christs, coming in His name. Matt. xxiv: 5.

2. Wars, civil and international, disrupting the bonds of amity and peace among nations. xxiv: 6, 7.

3. Cosmic Signs—earthquakes contemporaneous with sporadic famines and pestilence, in different places, xxiv: 7, these the signs and events nearest to us, as they were to the Jews before Jerusalem's destruction—"the beginning of sorrows."

Among the Middle Signs:

4. As to the External History of the Church, a universal hatred and bloody persecution of the saints by the nations. The extension of missions has for its pre-supposition not only the reception of the Gospel on the one hand, but its rejection on the other; the conflict of Christianity with the world-powers and the false systems of religion by which they are supported. xxiv: 9.

5. As to the Internal History of the Church. A Great Apostasy from the truth by unbelieving Christians, a departure from the true faith and life of the Gospel, and a practical return to a worldly and heathen walk and conversation, by means of false teachers themselves apostate from the truth—unbelief, lawlessness, pleasure, crime and declension of Christian love and vital godliness abounding in professing Christendom. xxiv: 10-12.

6. The Progress of Missions at the same time: a universal witness to the Gospel among all nations, during a condition of society such as was in the days of Noah and of Lot. xxiv. 14, 37; Luke xvii: 26-30. When these two contradictory yet concurrent facts meet in history, great missionary work and great apostasy, then the "End" shall come.

Among the signs remotest from us and nearest to the Advent, are:

7. The Antichrist, the Abomination of Desolation spoken of by "Daniel the prophet," the Great Tribulation, and false alarms as to the coming of Christ. The political dechristiani-

zation of the Christian powers, their subserviency to mammon and Antichristianity, will have advanced with the progress of Christendom in wealth, and its departure from the Gospel and the law of righteousness. What exists, save "Christ's elect," is a moral "carcass" fit only for the eagle's beak. xxiv: 15, 21-26, 28; Jas. i: 5-7. Christendom will be as morally corrupt as it will be architecturally splendid, and, save a faithful few, as dead to Christ and His Spirit, as it is alive to Mammon and the work of Satan, under the pretense of "Peace" and "Reform." "Money and Peace" will be its curse, all the time preparing for war,—Hypocrisy its policy, Unbelief its creed.

8. The culmination of the Apostacy, under the teachings of false Christs and false prophets, the frog-croaking ministers of the Antichrist and the False Prophet, deceiving the world by means of great signs and wonders, assailing the truth and proclaiming "the lie" that Christ and Christianity are a fraud. xxiv: 24; Rev. xiii: 5-18; xvi: 14.

9. The Conversion of the Jews and the Gathering of the Nations against Jerusalem. xxiii: 39; xxv: 32.

10. The Cosmic Signs next to the Advent, viz., Obscuration of the Heavenly Lights, Meteoric Showers, the Concussion of the Heavens, Earthquakes, Distress, Perplexity, Terror and Apprehension, the Sea roaring. xxiv: 29; Luke xxi: 25-26. Then the Son of Man Himself, His own Sign, in the clouds of heaven. xxiv: 30.

Such are the signs and events that "must needs come to pass" before the Second Coming of Christ. How many of these are in the field now is for the judgment of enlightened men to determine. As to the Nearer Signs, there can be no question. As to the Middle Signs, the only question is how long they will continue until the latest ones enter. That they are present in their measure is undeniable. That both the signs nearest to us and the middle signs contemporate and cumulate, in our day, cannot be disputed. The conversion of the world is nowhere a sign of the End in any book of Scripture, and any judgment based upon a presupposition so gratuitous is worthless. Nowhere has the Saviour said, "When the world is *universally converted*, then the End shall come," but this, "When the Gospel has been *testified* to all nations, *then* the End shall come." Nowhere is the Divine commission to witness to the Gospel in all lands, instructing all nations in the truth, and so discipling them, any pledge that the measure of true conversions will equal the universality of the command. It never has done so in any nation, city, town or village of the world, and never will in this present age. That vision is reserved for the future after the Antichrist is destroyed and Satan is bound. Only then "all nations shall come and worship before the Lord; because His judgments shall have been manifested," and that is when the Antichrist and his kingdom are destroyed, and the Colossus of Gentile politics and power has become as the "chaff of the summer threshing-floor." It is after Israel has been converted to the Lord, and their kingdom is restored. Dan. ix: 24; vii: 27; ii: 44.

The idea that the Lord may come any moment, and that, by a "special revelation to Paul in 1 Thess. iv: 14-17." He has subverted the whole body of Old and New Testament prophecy as to the time-point of His coming, its nature, and the order of events, and that "Signs" are only for the Jews—in a word, that He *might* have come before Peter had died, and Paul had borne witness at Rome, and Jerusalem had been destroyed, or any of the church been martyred, and that His intercession within the veil, the world's evangelization, and the fulness of the Gentiles, *might* have only required "a moment," a doctrine which makes Him a self-contradictory Teacher, in view of His assertion that He intended to "delay," "tarry," be gone "a long time," and only "after a long time" return to reckon with His servants—a doctrine, moreover, which deprives the believer of His place in that bright resurrection wherein the righteous shall shine as the sun in the Kingdom of their Father, may be allowed, here, to pass without comment.

On the other extreme are they who remove far into the future the hope of the believer by indulging the dream that the "Arbitration" of international disputes will introduce the universal reign of righteousness and peace before the Lord comes. This judgment is superficial. It is the honest but misguided view of many Christians. It is the scheme that Mammon will approve—the Stockholder's and the Bondholder's piety for the sake of money. The scheme was tried in ancient times. Argos, Lacedæmon and the Greek States had an "Arbitration Treaty" that lasted fifty years, then vanished away. The Italian republics of the Middle Age unsuccessfully attempted the same. All Europe, under the ægis of the Roman Church, had the "Truce of God" in the 10th century, which is broke in the 11th. When the "Crystal Palace" hove into view, at Sydenham, publicists announced that the "Era of Universal Peace" had come. International acquaintance and the spirit of Christianity were regarded as certain to bring speedily the long-desired result. More recent efforts among the most Christian nations have failed, for insuperable reasons. The ambitions of men, the rivalries of human governments, the power of sin and the unchained privilege of Satan defy a universal concert of the nations in terms of universal righteousness and peace. The diplomatic catch-word, "Peace with honor," beguiles only the sentimental and the inexperienced. A multitude of wars have crimsoned sea and land since Tennyson sang the time when:—

"The war-drum throbs no longer, and the battle-flags are furled
In the Parliament of man, the federation of the world."

Lord Russell, Chief Justice of England, calls it a "poetic dream" for this age, remarking that "Europe is pretty well *civilized* now, but all talk of a general disarmament is invariably received with a smile"—the smile of Christian Europe! The fact is that the nations cannot trust each other, and are confronted with conditions where "Peace with honor" cannot be maintained. Nor can the "Day of the Lord," that will "burn as an oven," be arbitrated away from the word and the purpose of God, with whom the judgment of the nations is a divine necessity. Peace with Shame, Disgrace, Dishonor, coffers filled with money,—Peace with oppression and injustice,—while guilty Christendom, unmoved, beholds massacre and murder by the Turk and the Spaniard, year after year, and the United States Government, ruled by the Money-Kings, under the plea of "Peace," withholds armed intervention in behalf of Justice, Humanity and Liberty, the blood of 600,000 starved and butchered Cuban men, women and children, crying to heaven for vengeance.

And far away from the heart of the Church, as a practical power, does the idea of the "universal conversion of the world" remove the hope of the coming of the Lord. Criminal Christendom, excusing its crimes by missionary contributions, preaches the conversion of the world before the Lord comes. Allusion to this has been made already. A close inspection of the facts—not to speak of the plain teaching of Scripture—will satisfy us that this also is a "poetic dream." If we consult the most reliable statistics as to the progress of Christian missions—furnished by Mullhall, Stundhall, Lavoisier, Fournier de Flaix, Pinkerton, Fabri, Vahl, the Royal Geographical Society, the Encyclopedia Britannica, Behm's Bureau of Statistics, in Berlin, and the A. B. C. F. M. Almanac for 1897—we shall get as correct a view as is possible in this branch of investigation. In 1800 the population of the globe was 700,000,000, the Christian population, including all the unconverted in Christendom, being 196,204,000, or 28 per cent. of the whole. In 1897, a century later, the population of the globe is 1,500,000,000, the Christian population, qualified as above, being 491,000,000, or 33 per cent. of the whole, the rate of increase of Christendom being relatively 5 per cent. in excess of the rate of increase for the total population of the globe. That is, nominal Christendom, including all infidels, criminals, unbelievers and rejecters of the Gospel, all corrupt forms of religion, and all its unbelief, is 2½ times greater to-day than in 1800, while yet the increase of Christendom relatively to that of the whole world's population is only 5 per cent. If, liberally, we estimate nominal Christianity, including all real converts, at 500,000,000, instead of 490,000,000, there remain still 1,000,000,000—a thousand millions—in heathendom not yet converted, even as there are millions in Christendom in the same condition.

And what have Continental Europe, Great Britain and Ireland, Canada, Australia, the United States, to show to-day as the converting result of their work in the foreign field? What the status now, after nearly 19 centuries, and the enormous wealth of modern times? In 1897 the statistics stand:

Missionaries on the field.. 11,659
Native helpers, also.. 64,220
Professing Christians..1,121,699
Under instruction.. 913,478

   Total number...2,111,065

Such the showing, the Turk still holding the fairest portions of the world which once were Christian. If we compare the 2,111,065 of Christians with the 1,000,000,000, what is the ratio of this Christian population, in heathen lands, to the unconverted 1,000,000,000 yet remaining there? This: 10,000,000 is 1 per cent. of 1,000,000,000, and 2,111,065 is but slightly more than one-fifth of this 1 per cent; that is, *the ratio of the Christian population to the non-Christian in heathendom is a trifle over one-fifth of 1 per cent. after nearly nineteen centuries.* Concede to the Church, liberally, all she claims, viz., the Bible translated, in whole or part, into 400 languages and dialects spoken by nine-tenths of the human race, religious books and tracts scattered by the million and increasingly, 280 missionary organizations, 25,000 auxiliary societies, 12,000 missionaries, 70,000 native helpers of every description, the occupation of vast regions in Asia and Africa, an ever-widening evangelization, and the number of actual additions in the foreign field, for 1897, as 780,858, *still the progress of Christendom, relatively to that of the population of the globe during 100 years save three is only 5 per cent., and the ratio of Christians in heathendom to the unconverted there is only a little over one-fifth of 1 per cent.*—the heathen population outrunning that of the civilized nations, Islam outrunning Christianity in many parts of Asia and Africa, new Hinduism resisting it, all the heathen religions still in force. If, after nearly 19 centuries, the most advanced stage of Christian civilization can show only one-fifth of 1 per cent. as the ratio between converted and unconverted heathendom, how long will it take to convert the heathen world so rapidly increasing, not to speak of the unconverted millions in Christendom? How long will it take, in face of the clear statements of the Lord that when He comes, it will be as it was in the days of Noah and Lot, and of Paul that Apostasy and Antichristianity will prevail, and of all the Prophets, Christ and His Apostles, that Christendom must be judged for its crimes?

But, when we remember that evangelization and conversion are not synonymous terms, and that of the 1,000,000,000 yet unconverted in heathendom vast multitudes have already been evangelized, though still rejecting the Gospel, even as in Christian lands, and that every day the missionary field is expanding through the steady toil of Christian men and women, and that when the Gospel has witnessed to "all nations " in the "whole creation," then the Lord will come, and in a time of deep apostasy and world-wide war, the case stands very different, and the hope of the believer brightens with every hour. The Lord does not expect the world to be converted when He comes. In the last prophecy of the New Testament, given by Himself to John, the last call of the Gospel, symbolized by the voice of the Zenith-Angel flying on the path of the sun, is to an unchristian world "ripe" for the Judgment. Rev. xiv: 6. But He does expect the world to be evangelized. The commission is to "disciple all nations," i. e., instruct them, in the Gospel—to preach the Gospel to "the whole creation." The Greek article placed in the original text, between "whole" and "creation," indicates the universality of the sphere of missionary labor, the geographical compass of the evangelization. Palestine was evangelized; yet all, save the "remnant of Israel," rejected the message of salvation. The Roman Empire was evangelized—the whole then civilized world, Col. i: 23—all adults and infants baptized, and Christianity made a state religion, and yet it was broken up under the judgment of God. The mediæval and modern kingdoms sprung from it, with others beside, all evangelized, will meet the same destruction. Heathendom evangelized will share the like fate.

The Church's missionary work goes on with a rapidity unparalleled before. Few sections in Africa have been unvisited. The Bible, whole or part, is found in every nation. Every province of China has been entered. Asia has missions in almost every region. India has heard the Gospel. The Pacific Islands are evangelized. Europe has grown gray under its sound. Both Americas are called Christian. Everywhere Christian and non-Christian nations are in contact, the same creeds, crimes, divisions and denominations found among the one seen also in the other. The message is rejected as well as accepted wherever it goes. A Mecca-programme unites the great chiefs of Islam in Turkey, Persia, and Afghanistan, in a common bond to resist the encroachments of "Christian Europe." The Madras and Calcutta journals scoff at European Christianity, and pronounce it "a plagiarism of the Persian and Egyptian religions," and the Mahdis and Mullahs of Asia and Africa, the Imaums and Sheiks of Islam but represent a force that Christendom must meet in final conflict. Evangelization indeed advances, but evokes resistance. All the world knows that Christianity in the East is defended solely by military force, and not by spiritual ideas, and that only in this way can the vantage ground already gained be preserved. Retreat of the nominally Christian powers of Europe means failure. Advance means collision. The whole East understands that the military conquest of their territory and its occupation by the powers of Europe, for the sake of trade and gain, means its subjection to that type of Christianity which makes aggressive war, not for the sake of justice and humanity, liberty and truth, but for selfish ends. Once more political Judaism and Mohammedanism seek to unite against the Gospel of Christ.

How soon the Gospel will be preached to the "whole creation," viz., "among all nations," is the undetermined point. The events and signs foretold in prophecy, and as seen in history, are now our only guide. If "the fullness of the nations" means, as the Greek term imports, the "full number of the nations," so that no others are to enter history, that number is now complete, and what remains before the Lord comes is their evangelization, the scenes attending the return of the Jews, their last struggle with the nations, and the trial of the faithful everywhere during the times of the last Antichrist. In this light the hope of the faithful is bright. The fact is that *the chief encouragement of the Church, externally, is found not in the meagre increment of 5 per cent., much less in one-fifth of 1 per cent., as the figures show, but in the conquest and occupation of heathendom by the European powers—notwithstanding their crimes—and the attending protection given to Christian missions.* The more rapid the invasion and partition of the East and South, the more rapid the evangelization, and the nearer the last collision and the solution of that great problem which expires with the end of the "Warfare Great."

We are left to our own judgment, enlightened by the "sure word of prophecy." All the phenomena now apparent in the social, political and religious world, in both hemispheres, indicate that we are now in a transition state. Of this no one doubts. Institutions, both secular and ecclesiastical, which, because of their long duration, have been regarded as imperishible, are being disestablished. Unbelief in Christendom threatens to sweep away the old faith. The spiritual life of the Church is in inverse proportion to her outward extension, wealth and worldliness. Political and international events, whose weight, multitude, rapid emergence and importance have never been surpassed, continue to crowd upon us. The outward push of a military Christendom, bent on the partition of two continents, is already a fact of daily observation, and threatens a collision, the greatest ever known in history. The Eastern Question, a dozen Western ones, the world's horrid armament, the antagonism between capital and labor, the greed of empires, and the struggle to survive, the restlessness and expectation everywhere, touch the deepest life of humanity, already strained with over-tension. The old question recurs, "How long shall it be to the end?" The answer can only be one of two alternatives. Either a new epoch for humanity—the forerunner of the end—stands in sight, or we rush to the proper end itself. Between these it might be difficult to choose, since the interval between the 69th and 70th weeks is undetermined. Yet 1897 years of it are gone, and the great prophetic heralds of the end are confronting us on every side. If Judaism and Mohammedanism shall combine in a treaty of mutual advantage, the "Christian powers" consenting for the sake of the "peace of Europe," no greater sign of the open political and moral apostasy of Christendom will ever have appeared in history. We lay no claim to the prophetic function. Rather, our claim is this, that the prophets, Christ and His Apostles have already pictured to us the very events our eyes are now beholding. If an opinion must be expressed in regard to a subject so vast, complicated and absorbing, it is both sober and justified to say that, viewing the state of Christendom and the world, as it is, in the clear light of prophecy, the remainder of the "Interval" must be relatively short, and the "End" not far away. In this judgment the best interpreters of prophecy agree. Many Swiss, German, Russian and Swedish universities now lecture statedly upon the Jewish problem, and the interest taken in the Eastern Question is phenomenal, as Daniel foretold. Some one is calling out of Seir, "Watchman! what of the night?"

As to the time required for the final arrangement of the ten kingdoms sprung from the old Roman territory, from the nature of modern warfare, though immense fighting must be done, it cannot be greatly protracted. If we take Van Kampen's and Kiepert's maps of the ancient world as it was in time following the prophecies of Daniel and Ezekiel, and compare them with a good modern atlas, we shall realize the situation. The line between the Eastern and Western foot of the Colossus runs from Belgrade, across the Mediterranean, to Tunis in Africa, losing itself in the desert. On each side in the last arrangement five kingdoms of imperial power must stand. Already six are on the Western and three on the Eastern side of the line. The dismemberment of Austro-Hungary, France going again to the Rhine, the smaller European states swallowed up by the greater, the rending of the Turkish empire, must certainly bring the last arrangement of the kingdoms. The Ottoman power holds the "bridge" (Asia Minor) between the West and East, and the "bridge" (Palestine) between the North and South. Here lies the storm-centre of the Eastern Question, nor can the nations have peace, nor can the kingdom of Christ enjoy a universal victory on earth, nor Israel be restored, until both are broken. That will break the rest. Here ends the Eastern Question, which began 2,200 years before Christ, when Eastern princes, with their Northern allies, invaded Palestine, and were pursued and slain by Abraham—his victory and recovery of their spoil a type of Israel's victory in the latter day. The evolution of this great question all believers will await with solemn interest. Prof. Sayce has clearly seen, and plainly said, that "whoever holds Palestine will control not only the Mediterranean and Constantinople, but the politics and commerce of the world." As to the completion of the evangelization of the nations, it occurs under the 7th trumpet, contemporates with the Great Tribulation, and is crowned with the Second Coming of the Son of Man, the resurrection of the holy dead, the rapture of the Church, the destruction of the Antichrist, the deliverance of new-born Israel, the judgment of the nations, and the kingdom. Until then the "Warfare Great" continues.

> *"Till He come"* so runs the line,
> Marking off the term of ill;
> Darkest hours of power malign
> Never more an hour to fill.
>
> *"Till He come"* the might of hell
> Still against the saints shall rage,
> And, beneath the Tempter's spell,
> Men in strifes and sins engage;
>
> *"Till He come,"* wrong will prevail,
> And the right be done in vain;
> Truth's confession still entail
> Toil, and obloquy, and pain;
> But *Our Hope* can brook delay,
> Waiting such a glorious day!

It is best not to dogmatise. The word from the watch-tower of the prophet is, "The vision is yet for an appointed time, but at the end it will speak, and not lie. Though it tarry, wait for it, because it will surely come; it will not tarry." Hab. ii: 3. This attitude of patient expectation is of divine commandment. Amid all vicissitudes the one abiding comfort is this, *"Jesus Christ, the Same, yesterday, to-day and forever."* Heb. xiii: 8. The Church's duty is clear: (1) To give the Gospel, at once, to the neglected parts of heathendom; (2) to work and pray for Israel's conversion; (3) to save all the souls she can and do all the good she can; (4) to bear a faithful witness to the truth; (5) to keep herself unspotted from the world; (6) to study earnestly the signs of the times, and (7) to wait, watch and pray, uttering back the promise of the Lord, "Amen! Even so, come, Lord Jesus!"

X.
DATES OF THE PROPHECIES OF DANIEL, AGE OF DANIEL, KINGS, THEME, PLACE, AND CHRONOLOGICAL ORDER OF THE CHAPTERS.

CHAP.	B.C.	KING.	AGE.	THEME.	PLACE.
I.	606	Neb.	15	Captivity.	Babylon.
II.	603	2nd Neb.	18	Colossus.	Babylon.
III.	586	19th Neb.	35	Furnace.	Babylon.
IV.	558	36th Neb.	63	Mania.	Babylon.
VII.	540	1st Belshazzar.	81	Four Beasts.	Babylon.
VIII.	538	3rd Belshazzar.	83	Antiochus.	Babylon.
V.	538	3rd Belshazzar.	83	Feast.	Babylon.
VI.	538	1st Darius.	83	Den.	Babylon.
IX.	538	1st Darius.	83	Seventy Weeks.	Babylon.
X-XII.	534	3rd Cyrus.	87	Warfare Great.	Persia.

That is, under Nebuchadnezzar's reign we have the biography of Daniel, the Colossus, the furnace and the King's mania; under Belshazzar, the Four Beasts, Antiochus and the Maccabean tribulation, the feast, and the fall of Babylon; under Darius the Mede, the lions' den and the 70 weeks' prophecy, and under Cyrus, the vision of the Warfare Great. The chronological order of the chapters is this: i., ii., iii., iv., vii., viii., v., vi., ix., x.-xii.; that is, after reading i.-iv., we omit v. and vi. and immediately go to vii. and viii., then return to v. and vi., and from vi., passing over vii. and viii., proceed to ix. and x.-xii. The reason of this is because the prophet has grouped the *historical* chapters together, viz., iii., iv., v., vi., between the two great prophecies concerning the World-Power, i. e., between ii. and vii., in order to relate them to both, and unveil between them the hostile character and deeds of the World-

Power toward the people of God, and also to give, in the victory of "God Most High" over it, and in the deliverance of His people, a practical pledge of the sure fulfillment of what is predicted in ii. and vii., and of which all the other predictions are only supplementation. All is written in the Chaldee or Aramæan language, and constitutes the first part of the book. By this means the rest of the prophecies, which unveil the long conflict of the Jews with the World-Power, are also grouped together, unbroken, in viii.-xii., and are written in Hebrew, the language of Israel.

XI.
CHRONOLOGY.

B. C. 621. Daniel born under the reign of Josiah.
B. C. 606. First capture of Jerusalem by Nebuchadnezzar; beginning of captivity; deportation of Daniel and his friends.
B. C. 603. Dream of the Colossus.
B. C. 598. Second capture of Jerusalem; Ezekiel deported, and others.
B. C. 586. Third capture of Jerusalem; burning of Temple; first destruction of the city; completed deportation.
B. C. 585. State-concert on the plains of Dura; anniversary of Jerusalem's fall; the fiery furnace.
B. C. 570. The girdled tree; King's mania.
B. C. 562. Nebuchadnezzar's death.
B. C. 561. Accession of Evil-Merodach.
B. C. 555. Accession of Nabonnaid, the father of Belshazzar.
B. C. 558. Accession of Neriglissar.
B. C. 549. Overthrow of the Median Empire of Cyrus.
B. C. 541. Co-regency of Belshazzar, son of Nabonnaid, and grandson of Nebuchadnezzar.
B. C. 541. Daniel's vision of the Great Tribulation and the Second Coming of Christ.
B. C. 538. Vision of the Maccabean persecution and profanation of the second Temple; Antiochus.
B. C. 538. Defeat of Nabonnaid in Accad by Cyrus.
B. C. 538. Fall of Babylon; death of Belshazzar; Gobryas.
B. C. 538. Accession of Darius the Mede, by authority of Cyrus.
B. C. 538. Prophecy of the 70 weeks.
B. C. 538. Daniel in the lions' den.
B. C. 536. Cyrus sole ruler of Babylon.
B. C. 536. Edict of Cyrus for Jewish liberation; end of captivity; beginning of the restoration; second Temple.
B. C. 534. Christophany, and vision of the Warfare Great.
B. C. 529. Death of Cyrus.
B. C. ? Death of Daniel.
B. C. 521. Accession of Darius Hystaspes.

APPENDIX. 289

B. C. 515. Completion of the second Temple.
B. C. 490. Battle of Marathon.
B. C. 485. Accession of Xerxes the Great.
B. C. 480. Invasion of Greece by Xerxes; Thermopylæ; Salamis.
B. C. 465. Accession of Artaxerxes I
B. C. 458. Ezra's commission.
B. C. 444. Nehemiah's commission.
B. C. 430. Close of Nehemiah's activity; end of the restoration.
B. C. 334. Alexander the Great invades Persia.
B. C. 334. Battle of Granicus.
B. C. 333. Battle of Issus.
B. C. 331. Battle of Arbela.
B. C. 325. Alexander at Shushan.
B. C. 323. Death of Alexander at Babylon.
B. C. 302. Partition of Alexander's empire.
B. C. 323. Ptolemy I., Soter.
B. C. 312. Seleucus I., Nicator.
B. C. 280. Antiochus I.
B. C. 285. Ptolemy II., Philadelphus.
B. C. 485. Accession of Xerxes the Great.
B. C. 285. Septuagint Version of the Old Testament.
B. C. 261. Antiochus II., Theos.
B. C. 247. Ptolemy III., Euergetes.
B. C. 246. Seleucus II., Kallinikos.
B. C. 226. Seleucus III., Keraunos.
B. C. 222. Antiochus III., the Great.
B. C. 221. Ptolemy IV., Philopator.
B. C. 205. Ptolemy V., Epiphanes.
B. C. 187. Seleucus IV.
B. C. 181. Ptolemy VI., Philometor.
B. C. 175. Antiochus IV., Epiphanes.
B. C. 173. First campaign of, against Egypt.
B. C. 170. Second campaign of, against Egypt.
B. C. 170. First campaign of, against Palestine.
B. C. 168. Third campaign of, against Egypt.
B. C. 168. Second campaign of, against Palestine.
B. C. 168. The Maccabean tribulation; profanation of the second Temple.
B. C. 165. End of the tribulation; cleansing of the second Temple.
B. C. 164. Death of Antiochus Epiphanes at Tabæ, in Persia.
B. C. 161. Death of Judas Maccabæus.
B. C. 64. Capture of Jerusalem by Pompey.

B. C. 48. Battle of Pharsalia.
B. C. 45. Debate on prophecy in the Senate House at Rome; the Sibyl; Cæsar.
B. C. 44. Assassination of Cæsar.
B. C. 42. Battle of Phillippi.
B. C. 28. Augustus Cæsar, first Emperor of Rome.
A. D. 1. BIRTH OF JESUS CHRIST, 538 years after the fall of Babylon by Cyrus, i. e., 538 years after Gabriel's prediction of His birth to occur at the close of the 69th week of the 70 weeks; and 536 years after the edict of Cyrus for the Jewish liberation; first Christmas.
A. D. 30. Baptism of Jesus—*common reckoning.*
A. D. 34. Crucifixion of Jesus.
A. D. 70. Second destruction of Jerusalem, by Titus; burning of the second Temple.

From B. C. 28 to A. D. 1898, so far, the Roman "Times of the Gentiles," or duration of the Fourth Prophetic Empire and its kingdoms, i. e., the legs, feet and toes of the Colossus. The Fourth Beast, out of whose horns the Little Horn, or last Antichrist, is yet to come, still exists. The Colossus still stands.

XII.
DANIEL'S GRAVE.

There need be no dispute as to the burial place of the great prophet. Eminent scholars have carefully investigated the whole question. Fabre d'Envieu of the Sorbonne (1888), Düsterwald of Bonn (1890) and Evetts of the British Museum 1897) alike reject the statement of the pseudo-Epiphanius, hat Daniel died at Babylon, and confirm the statement of Aboulfaradj, that he died at Shushan. Benjamin Tudela, the celebrated Spanish Rabbi and traveller, in the 12th century, narrates in his "Excursions" that when he visited Shushan the city had a population of 7,000 Jews, besides 14 synagogues. In front of one of these stood the tomb of Daniel, whom all the people held to be" the greatest satrap of Babylon and Persia, the most illustrious viceroy of Shushan under Cyrus the Great." This tradition they asserted to be a sacred and unbroken one. Some years ago the French explorers, under Dieulafoy, were driven away from the tomb by an armed band of Arabs, Persians and Jews, 800 in number, rushing to protect it from the "infidels" who sought to profane it "out of curiosity," as they did the tombs of the Pharaohs. The natives believed that "divine vengeance" would fall upon them, should they allow the French to violate the repose of "a man so beloved of God." The Sheik Mohammed-Tahir interfered to keep the peace. The Governor of Arabistan petitioned the Persian Government to guard the sacred spot. After protracted negotiations between Teheran and Paris the French withdrew. Interesting accounts concerning the tomb are given in Loftus' "Travels in Chaldea and Susiana," p. 317; in Fabre d'Envieu's "Le Prophète Daniel," i., p. 22; Düsterwald's "Weltreiche," p. 8, and in Haneberg's "Das Grab Daniel's" in "Geschichte der Bibl. Offenbarung," p. 414. In the Roman Martyrology Daniel's memorial day is July 21. Jew Moslem and Christian alike venerate that holy spot.

MILITARY CHRISTENDOM.

In Otto Hübner's "Statistische Tabellen" for 1897, Professor von Juraschek, Austrian Court Chancellor, and Fellow of the London Royal Statistical Society, gives the population of the globe, from the most recent official sources, as 1,535,000,000, or 23,000,000 more than in 1896. Of this increase, 7.5 per cent. belongs to Africa, 6.5 to Asia, 5.7 to Europe, 3.2 to the Americas. The population of Asia is 752,000,000, of Africa 265,000,000, of Europe 378,000,000, of the Americas 140,000,000. During 1896 the United States increased over 2,000,000; its population now 75,000,000. Russia increased over 8,000,000; its population now 135,000,000. The total European population is 378,000,000, or one-fourth that of the globe. Allowing 500,000,000 as nominally Christian, 1,035,000,000 remain for heathendom. China's population is 345,000,000, India's 296,000,000, Japan's 45,000,000. Great Britain rules over 382,000,000 of the human race.

The military aspect of Nineteenth Century Christendom is not without its significance for those who raise the question, "Is the world growing better?" If disorder, blood, murder, massacre, swords, bayonets, guns, torpedoes, dynamite, armies and navies are evidence of moral improvement, and the fruit of Christian civilization, the world is on the rapid road to perfection. Great Britain, population 39,000,000 at home, has an army of 220,000 men, besides an Indian army of 166,000, Volunteers 261,000, Militia 145,800, Reserves 76,800; total, 869,594, with a fleet of 854 war vessels carrying 2,564 guns. At the Victoria Jubilee her fleet extended 5 miles, four lines deep, not a vessel called in from any foreign station. Her naval expenditure, 1897, was $38,500,000, augmented for 1898 by $127,750,000. Russia, population 135,000,000, has a present army of 4,670,000, a "prospective" army of 12,000,000, a fleet of 265 vessels and 1,600 guns. France, population 38,520,000, ruling 80,000,000, has an army of 4,300,000 and a fleet of 135 vessels, 3,876 guns. The combined expenditure of Russia and France for naval purposes in 1897 was $26,055,000, augmented in 1897-'98 by $100,000,000, the budgets constantly increasing, as is the case with all the Powers. Germany, population 52,000,000, has an army of 4,300,000 and a fleet of 190 vessels, 1,460 guns. Austro-Hungary, population 44,900,000, has an army of 2,076,000, and a fleet of 142 vessels, guns 772. Spain, population 27,000,000, has an army of 600,000 men and a fleet of 130 vessels. 654 guns, both increasing. Portugal, population 19,320,000, has an army of 154,000 and a fleet of 34 vessels, 131 guns. Italy, population 31,290,000, has an army of 1,473,000 and a fleet of 341 vessels, guns 1,742. Holland, population 38,307,000, has an army of 888,000, a fleet of 130 vessels, 669 guns. Denmark, Sweden-Norway and Belgium, total population 15,670,000, have together an army of 857,000 men, with 146 vessels, guns 957. These nominally "Christian Powers," great and small, have together an army of 20,196,594 trained men, 2,187 ships of war, with 14,385 guns, all powerless by reason of their rivalries, greed, jealousies, mutual fear, international law, and "Concert of the Powers," to restrain the Turk from his atrocities, or compel Spain to desist from her even greater crimes. The United States, population 75,000,000, with an army not merely of 25,000, but capable of increase to 1,000,000 men in 30 days, and overflowing with money more than enough for all naval and army purposes, has witnessed, inactively, for 3 years past, the most inhuman cruelties, butchery, and extermination of 600,000 men, women and children struggling in Cuba against the tyranny of Spain,—the navy of the United States supporting in its crimes the bloodiest and most barbarous civilized Christian nation on the face of the earth. It is the "Monroe Doctrine." "It is Christian International Law!"—"Christian International Politics!"—the cry of the "Peace of the United States," even as the transatlantic cry was the "Peace of Europe." No prophet of ancient times could have witnessed such a condition of affairs among a people in a land called "Christian," and not proclaimed the "Day of the Lord" as "near," and the hypocritical catchword, "Peace with Honor," as an omen of judgment to avenge the blood of the innocent and the loss of righteousness, mercy and truth.

In face of the cries of outraged humanity, carnage, atrocities, and crimes whose mention makes the blood run cold, the governments of earth, ruled by the gangrened politicians of the day in league with Mammon, and hypocritically pleading "Peace," and "Christian Principles," refuse to intervene in behalf of the downtrodden and oppressed, unless their "business interests" are endangered, or the threatened loss of party and of power compels their action. The idol they worship is selfishness, their policy high treason to God, their country, and Humanity, to Righteousness and Truth, to Justice, Liberty, and Mercy.

The like excuse for inaction confronts the fearful situation in the Old World, and retards the deliverance of the Christian nationalities from the Ottoman yoke, and the repossession of his land by the Jews. Military Christendom stands powerless to execute justice and judgment, by reason of its selfishness and fear. England rules 290,000,000 of Asiatics, among which her sceptre covers 78,000,000 of Mohammedans, whose goodwill is important for her "business interests." Other powers are similarly related to the Moslem world, whose total population is 272,000,000, spread over India, China, Turkey, Egypt, Arabia, Africa and other places. Of these, 78,000,000 are under the British flag, bound together by an antichristian faith, all regarding England now as their foe, Russia and France as their friend. Under China there are 40,000,000; under Russia, 20,000,000; under Holland, 20,000,000; under France, 4,000,000. The Moslem knows that the "Concert of Europe" is a mere device to stave off the settlement of the Eastern Question, until the opportune moment arrives to divide his bankrupt estate among the "Powers," and that, while professing friendship for the Turk, Russia's aim is Constantinople, the revival of the old Eastern Empire, and the sway of Asia; England resisting the policy, yet nursing another, viz., the repossession of Palestine by the Jews, the defeat of Russian influence in the East, and the increase of her own empire. He knows that the "integrity of the Ottoman empire" is necessary to the "Peace of Europe" and the "Balance of Power," and plays off one Power against another, and, so, is master of the occasion, and occasion of the "deadlock" of the Powers in any movement for the liberation of peoples oppressed by his tyranny. He conciliates the Jew to strengthen his finances, and oppose the policy of "Christian Europe" in any attempt to crowd his empire. England, Queen of the Seas, and Russia, lord of the land, both bid for his sympathy and influence in the East, each opposing the other.

The object of Europe is the partition of Asia and Africa, each Power envious of the other. England stands alone in her "splendid isolation," checkmated in any movement for liberty, humanity and justice among the oppressed nations. She has lived to repent of the Crimean War, seen the Turk alienated from her and embraced by Russia, witnessed a "Triple Alliance" against her, the alliance also of Russia and France, the estrangement of Germany, the control of China by Russia, and the disapproval of her Egyptian and African policy. Germany hates France, as France hates Germany, and Russia dreads England, as England dreads Russia. The effect of the total situation is that "Christian Europe," so-called, maintains itself by force of arms, and not by spiritual ideas, nor by a law of righteousness, so that a military force of 20,196,594 trained soldiers and a navy of 2,187 vessels, guns 14,385, are impotent to suppress the Turk. Hence the revival and reunion of all Islam, and the projected combination of the Moslem and the Jew.

What changes in alliances will occur, he may tell who can trace the way of an eagle in the air, or of a serpent on a rock. The Russo-French alliance has a double face of war and peace; of peace as a counterpoise to the preponderance of German influence in Europe,—of war as a dream of the reconquest of the Rhine provinces by France. Germany, Austria and Russia stand for despotic rule, and the repression of democratic freedom. England, Italy and France stand for liberty; all pushing into the East and South for acquisition of wealth and power,—the Moslem and the Jew the ones with whom they all must reckon. The crisis cannot long be delayed. England, with all her faults, cannot long remain in isolation. Will the three great Northern military Powers stand pitted against the three Southern and Mediterranean naval Powers? Will France go to England, forsaking Russia? Will Greece go to Russia or to England, or to France, when the crisis comes? Three options remain to England: (1) To unite with the "Triple Alliance," (2) to unite with France and Russia, bringing in Japan as her ally, (3) to conciliate the Turk, break his alliance with Russia, unite with Japan and France, and, maintaining friendship with Persia and Afghanistan, seek the "Reform" of the Moslem, and promote the interest of the Jew. And the probability is that of a general break in the whole diplomacy of Europe, when the time comes for the last struggle, with the Turk ever irreformable, and alliances such as the shrewdest diplomats have deemed impossible;—a chaos of politics, Anti-Semitism here, Anti-Islam there, Anti-Slavism here, Anti-Hellenism there, Antichrist and Antichristianity everywhere! God alone can solve the World's Problem. Righteousness and Peace come only through the Judgment of the Nations.

As these lines go to press, the Congress of the United States is contending with the administration in reference to the course to be pursued toward Spain, for her brutal treatment of the Cubans and her treacherous nocturnal assassination of 266 American sailors in harbor of Havana, and her destruction of the battle-ship "Maine." All that the power of mammon and business interests can do, backed by the Presidential delay, and a score of expedients, even to mediation by the Pope and foreign powers, has been done to prevent the immediate execution of righteousness in the case, the vindication of national honor, and virtually to make the United States government guarantee the integrity of the Spanish empire, while proposing relief and reform for Cuba. It is the identical policy of the "Concert of Europe" in reference to the Turkish empire and the peoples under the Turkish yoke. It remains to be seen whether the Congress, waked to its duty by the voice of an outraged nation, will put an end to the Presidential "policy" of still further procrastination. Aggressive war for the sake of mammon, commerce, trade, wealth, territory, power, is a crime against God and humanity. Aggressive war in behalf of justice, liberty, humanity, mercy, righteousness, and truth, is a duty commanded of God, a sentiment of the heart, a dictate of conscience, a part of the international law, and is the uncorrupted voice of mankind. It belongs to the glory of Messiah, that He "delivers the poor and needy when he crieth, and him that hath no helper." "He breaks in pieces the rod of the oppressor." When there is "none to help," He chooses some nation as His instrument, and "puts on righteousness as a breastplate, and a helmet of salvation on His head. He puts on the garments of vengeance for clothing, and is clad with zeal as a cloak," Isa. lix: 16-18. "Righteousness exalteth a nation, but sin is a reproach to any people," Prov. xiv: 24. "In righteousness He doth judge and make war," Rev. xix: 11. It remains to be seen whether the United States shall at last coerce Cuba into submission, on terms proposed to her by the President or Congress, even as slaughtered Greece was "coerced," or, in good faith, be made "free and independent."

INDEX.

A.

Abolition of Jewish worship, 95, 96, 111, 118.
Abomination of desolation, 70, 72, 95, 111, 121, 162, 206, 207, 262.
Advent, the *First*, only in IX., 42, 43.
    the *Second*, in VII., 55, 57.
    not secret, 58, 198, 218.
    time-point of, 252, 253.
    precedes Millennium, 220-222.
    in John's Revelation, 252.
Ages, succession of the, 225.
    of Ages, 226, 227.
Age, character of the present, 192, 193, 283.
Allah Maozim, 176.
Alexander the Great, 93, 94, 156, 239.
Altar, Heathen, set up, 95.
Alliances, ancient and modern, 57, 58, 295.
Ancient of Days, 73.
Angels, in the judgment, 77, 78, 253.
    special ones, 253, 254.
Angelic Dialogue, 96, 203.
Antichrist, the, 169-175.
    photograph of, 175.
    types of, 63, 170, 171.
    is "the King," 175.
    sitting in the Temple, 181.
    last campaign of, 171-181.
Any-moment Adventism, 127-130.
Antiochus Epiphanes, 90, 94-99, 160.
    a type, 170, 171.
    last campaigns of, 161, 162.
    death of, 170.
Appearing of Christ, the, our hope, 128.
Apocalypse by John, 247-255.
Arbitration, 219, 279.
Armageddon, 258.
Armies, modern, 183, 293-295.

Ascension, not in VII., 81, 82.
Assize, the great, 53-56.

B.

Babylon, Lament by the rivers of, 21, 22.
    the fall of, 106, 109.
    and the Beast, 250.
Bar Enash, 79-81.
Battle, the coming great, 250.
Beast, the Four, 53.
Beasts, the Four, 53.
    identity with John's Beast, 251.
Books, The, opened, 78.
Book of Daniel, its canonicity, 16.
    its authenticity, 16.
    character and lesson of, 16.
    scope of the, 17, 21-23.
    central thesis of the, 25.
    the, is a "Scripture of Truth," 201, 202.
    critical questions as to, 49-51.
    completion of the, 201.
    predicted study of the, 201, 202.
    testimonies to the, 238.
    the, is Truth, 134, 145, 203, 204.
    chronology for the, 288-290.
    summation of the, 213-217.
Bridge between East and West, 284.
    North and South, 284.

C.

Chiliasm, 204, 227-232, 267, 269, 270, 271.
    science and, 225-227.
    objections to, 220.
    testimony to, 227-230.
    testimony to the writer, 227-232.
Christendom, Crimes of, 65-67.
    the judgment of, 78, 185.
    an apostatising, 181.
    military aspect of, 183, 215, 293-295.
    general aspect of, 283.
Christ, a Critic of the critics, 266.
Christophany, The great, 137.
Chronology, secular and biblical, 235, 236.
Chronological Table, 288-290.

Church, the, not in Daniel, 215.
    given her place in Olivet discourse, 247.
    her place in the Revelation, 216.
    duty of the, 216.
Coming, Appearing, and Revelation of Christ, at the same time-point, 128.
Coming for His saints, 197, 198. (See *"Thief-Time."*)
Conversion of the Jews, 106, 111, 112.
    of the world, 193.
    covenant with Antiochus, 95.
    Berenice, 158.
    Cleopatra, 159.
    Ptolemy, 160, 161.
    the Antichrist, 111.
Criticism, The Higher, 264-266.
Culture and Civilization, 190.
Cyrus the Great, 156.

D.

Daniel the prophet, his birth, 29, 288.
    his character, 29, 30.
    his mission, 22, 28.
    author of the book of, 201.
    three weeks' fast, 136, 137.
    prostration of, 140-142.
    recovery of, 142.
    comfort for, 143-146.
    depression of, 136, 137.
    perplexity of, 204.
    first dismissal of, 205.
    second dismissal of. 208.
    the grave of, 208, 291.
    the resurrection of, 208.
    father of universal history, 241.
Dates of Daniel's prophecies, 286.
Days, The 1,150. in VIII., 205.
    1,260, in VII., XII., 205.
    1,290, in XII., 205-208.
    1,335, in XII., 205-208.
Development, axioms of, 219.
    meaning of, 226.
Diadochian Kingdoms, 156.
Diagram of the 70 weeks, 115, 116.
    of the Time of the End, 173.
Dialogues, in VIII., X., XII., 96, 203.

Difference between Ezekiel's and Daniel's prophecies, 257.
Daniel's prophecies, 257.
Dream of Nebuchadnezzar, 31, 32.
    interpreted, 32, 33.

E.

Eastern Question, 92, 148.
    antiquity of the, 184.
    international politics of, 155.
    storm-centre of, 153-158.
    insoluble by the Powers, 189.
Empires, the Four, 53.
    must be judged, 185.
    duration of, 214.
    transient character of, 214-216.
End of the Age, how near, 131, 270-274.
    the Time of the, 100, 152, 220.
    the, "not yet," 250.
Episodes in the Revelation, 249.
Epiphany is the Parousia, 128.
Epilogue to Daniel's book, 133, 202.
Epitaph of the Nations, 24, 216.
Equation of Dan. vii: 13; Matt. xxiv: 29-31; 2 Thess. i: 6-10.
    1 Thess. iv: 14-17, Rev. xi: 15-17, xiv: 14, and xix: 11,
    as to their time-point.
Error of the writer corrected, 235.
Eschatology and Messiah, 219.
Evangelization not Conversion, 281.
Evolution, Development, 219, 225, 226.

F.

Farrar, on book of Daniel, 264.
Farewell to the prophet, 231.
First Resurrection, 197, 198.
Fulness of the Gentiles, 282, 283.

G.

Gabriel, 139.
Gladden Washington, 124.
Gobryas, General of Cyrus, 51.
Gog, and Magog, 178.
    and the Antichrist, 256.
    is pre-millennial, also, 257.
God, the ground of the universe, 24, 25.

ruler of the Nations, 24, 25.
name of, magnified and sanctified, 218, 219.
Grave of Daniel, 291.
    of Gog, 258.

H.

Harvest, the,. 253, 254.
Hiddekel, the, 135.
Higher Criticism, the, Pref. 7-9, 264-266.
History, Difference between the prophetic and the ordinary, 157.
    does not end with the Advent, 123.
    the laws of, 186.
    Daniel, father of universal, 241.
Historical narratives in Daniel, 31.
    Situation, time of Daniel, 30, 31.
Horns, the Ten, 55.
    identity with the Toes, 42.
    discovered, 63.
    they are Christians, 65.
    final arrangement of, 62, 63, 284.
    retribution upon the, 71.
    the Two Little, not the same Horn. the Little Horn, 53, 55, 69, 70, 71, 101.
Hope of Israel, 208, 229.
    of Believers, 229, 230.
    of the Nations and World, 230.

I.

Image of Nebuchadnezzar, 21.
    of the Antichrist, 207.
Interpretation, the spiritualizing, 43, 123, 268, 271, 272.
Intervals in prophecy, 113, 217.
    in Dan. ix., 114, 117.
    in Dan. xi., 157.
    proof of supernatural, 157.
Interval between 3d and 4th week, 217.
    46th and 70th week, 217.
    69th and 70th week, 217.
Israel's place in history, 29.
    apostasy from God, 29, 30.
    great tribulation, 192.
    help in the final crisis, 133, 134.
    deliverance, 189, 194-196.
        place in the Revelation, 195.

J.

Jehovah, how viewed by the heathen, 30.
Jerusalem, all nations against, 218, 219.
    final siege of, 181, 182.
    sunrise over, 207.
    centre of Millennial age, 214-223.
    called "Jehovah-Shammah," 223.
    and Rome, 250.
Jesus Christ, the Stone, 32, 41.
    the Son of Man, 79.
    the Wonderful Numberer, 96.
    that "Certain Saint," 96.
    the Cloud-Comer, 80.
    the Linen-Clothed Man, 137, 138, 139.
    the Birth of, 111.
    the Crucifixion of, 111.
    the Second Coming of, 81.
    the Critic of the Critics, 266.
    the Monarch of the Fifth Empire, 83.
Jews, the return of the, 111, 112, 28.
    the Tribulation of the, 73-75, 94-96, 177-180, 192.
    the Conversion of the, 111, 112, 194-196, 106.
    the Deliverance of, 194-196.
    the Restoration of the, 83-86.
    the modern interest in the, 185.
    powerless in the last crisis, 189.
Joel's great prophecy, 181, 182.
Judgment, The vision of, 53-56.
    time of the, 57, 58.
    place of the, 59.
    parties in the, 61.
    duration of the, 64.
    design of the, 218.
    books opened in the, 78.
Justin Martyr and Chiliasm, 269, 270.

K.

"King *the*," Antichrist, 175.
    of the North, 171.
    of the South, 171.
Kingdom, the, not in VIII., 89.
    the goal of prophecy, 25.
    set up in conflict, 224, 225.
    universal and indesctructible, 216.

is a reign and a realm, 31, 223.
various forms and spheres of, 225.
to be "underneath all heavens," 38, 39, 83, 213.
to be given to the Saints, 83-86.
time-point of victory of, 216.
character of, 223, 225.
Kingdoms and Kings, synonymous, 33.

M.

MacDill, Professor D., and Chiliasm, 270, 271.
Maccabean tribulation, 163.
    war-cry, 165.
    heroism, 165.
"Man of Sin," 176.
Martyrs of the Law, 163-165, 200.
    of the Gospel, 166.
Median empire, overthrown, 98.
Megiddo, Armageddon, 256, 258.
Merriam, Professor Geo. B., correcting the writer's error, 235
Michael standing up, 179, 180, 190, 191.
Millennium, not in this age, 204, 214, 215, 227.
    its sequence in Dan. VII.
    its sequence in Zech. XIV.
    its sequence in Isa. XXIV., XXVI.
    its sequence in Rev. xx.
Military statistics, 185, 215, 292-294.
    Christendom, 215, 293-295.
Missionary statistics, 280.
Mendelsohn, Judith, 208.
Montefiore, Sir Moses, 208.
Mohammedan power, overthrown, 86, 87.
    Antiochus, type of, 98.
Moslem, and Crusades, 184.
    prayer of the, 185.
    and the Jew, 283.
    statistics of the, 294.

N.

Nations, must be judged, 183.
    gathered at Jerusalem, 182.
    not wholly destroyed, 217.
    judgment in order to save the, 218.
Nearness to the End, 131, 270-274.
New, the something new, in prophecy, 31.

"Nihtak," the determined, 113, 120.
Numbers, the prophetic, 237.

O.

Oath of the Linen-Clothed Man, 203.
Olivet, Mount, sundered.
    throne of glory over, 79.
Olivet Discourse, 247, 262.
Omar, Caliph, 181.
Optimism, modern, refuted, 192.
Order of Chapters in Daniel, 286.
    of Events, 77.
Outlook of Christ and Apostles, 192, 193.

P.

Palmoni, Wonderful Numberer, 96.
Parousia. (See Advent.)
    no secret, 198.
People of the Saints, 83, 84.
    their victory, 85-87.
Political ethics, 20.
Population of the globe, 292.
    of Christendom, 280.
    of Europe, Asia and Africa, 292.
Post-Millennialism, 257, 269-271.
Pride, the heathen, abased, 22, 23.
Prince, the, that shall come, 72, 111, 121.
Powers, attitude of the, 295.
Prayer, the Lord's, 218.
Prologue to Daniel's last prophecy, 133.
Pronouns, the, "He," "His," "Him," 171.
Prophecy is unerring, 26.
    the fundamental, 31, 36.
    symbols changed in, 31.
    the something new in, 31.
    the cyclic law of, 31.
    advance in, 52.
    debate in Roman Senate on, 126.
    how much of Daniel's fulfilled, 180.
    abuse of, 226, 227.
    a peculiarity of, 250.
Prophetic numbers, 237.
Prophets, all look to the End, 218, 219.
    all predict the World's last battle, 219.

R.

Rationalism, 33, 146.
Reaping of the living saints, 254.
Reckoning, different modes of, 120, 134, 135.
Relation of Book of Daniel to Olivet Discourse and the Revelation, 247.
Remnant, the, 194.
Reservation, God's, 187.
Resurrection, of the Holy Dead, 77, 197, 251, 253.
    Israel's and ours, one, 199.
    time-point of the, 77, 197, 198.
    no simultaneous and universal, of the good and evil, 197
    splendor of the, of believers, 199.
Resurrections, two distinct, and separated by time, 197.
Revelation, the, of Christ, identical with His Parousia and Appearing, and at the same time-point, 128.
Revelation, the, by John, 247.
Rome and Jerusalem, 250.
"Run to and fro," 202.

S.

Saints of the Most High, 83-87.
Satan, the god of this age, 191.
    cast out from the air, 191.
"Scripture of Truth," 228.
Science and the Ages, 219, 225.
Second Coming of Christ, 128. (See "Coming," "Advent.")
Seleucids, the, 156.
Senate of Rome, debate in, 126.
"Sepher" and "Sepharim," 145.
Sequence of kingdom on Advent, 220-222, 228.
Seventy Weeks, the. (See "Weeks.")
Signs of the End, 275-277.
Sociologists and World-Reformers, 229.
Son of Man, a Person, 79, 80.
    is Messiah, 80, 81.
    (See "Jesus Christ.")
Sovereignty, taken from Israel, 213.
    restored to Israel, 217-219.
    of Jesus Christ, 217.
Splendor of the Risen Saints, 199, 200.
Statue of Jupiter, 175.

"Stone," the, not a "rolling" one, 37.
    impact of the, on the toes of the Colossus, 34-46.
    time-point of the impact, 40.
    common interpretation of the, 38.
    Irenæus and Hippolytus on, 41.
Succession of the Ages, 226.
Suffering and Glory, 200.
Suffix, the important Hebrew, 121.
Sultanate of the Horn, 12.

T.

Testimonies to Daniel and his book, 238.
Testimony of the writer to Chiliasm, 227-232.
Temple, the Jewish, to be built, 113.
    Antichrist sitting in, 181, 194.
Thessalonian error corrected, 130.
Thief-Time, 249.
Time of the End, 100, 152, 177, 178, 220.
    vision of the, 133.
    miracles in the, 136.
    the twofold, 149.
    extension of the, 205.
    events in the, 220.
    is not the End of Time, 123.
Time-Point of the Advent and the Resurrection of Believers, 197-199.
Times and Seasons, What, 241-243.
Transition-Section, the, 169.
Tribulation, the Great, 73, 119, 192.
Tribulation, the Maccabean, 163-165.
Truth, Daniel's book is, 134, 145, 203, 204.
"Tsaba Gadol," 142, 169.
Type and Antitype, 170.

V.

Valley of Decision, 182.
    Jehoshaphat, 182.
Vine of the earth, 254.
Vintage of the earth, 182, 254.
Vials, special introduction to the, 249, 254.
Vial of the Consummation, 255.

W.

War, the Lord's summons to the nations to prepare for, the modern war-preparation, 183.

Wars of Syria and Egypt, 158.
Warfare Great, the, 133, 134, 142, 169.
   Geographical theatre of, 155.
Weeks, The Seventy, 110, 112.
   false translation of, 121, 122.
   the 7 weeks, 114.
   the 62 weeks, 114.
   the 1 week, 117, 118.
   beginning of, 113.
   intervals between, 114, 185.
   the many calculations of, 120, 217.
   confirmation of, 120-126.
   jurisdiction of, 127-129.
   dominate the New Testament, 129.
   determine the time-point of both Advents, 127, 131.
   prove Messiahship of Jesus, 259-264.
   the Church-Fathers on, 122, 123.
   diagram of, 115, 116.
   the one undetermined point, 120.
Week, the Seventieth, 237, 252.
Wicked and Wise, in the End-Time, 205.
Winepress of Wrath, 182, 250, 254.
World, not converted in this Age, 193.
   Coming of Christ the only Hope of the, 215.

X.

Xerxes the Great, 156.

Y.

Year-Day theory not in Daniel, 118, 119.
Years, the Thousand, 224, 225.
Yeor, the River Nile, 136, 202.

Z.

Zionism, modern political, 229.

STUDIES IN ESCHATOLOGY.

The Thousand Years

(MILLENNIAL AGE.)

WITH SUPPLEMENTARY DISCUSSIONS UPON THE OLD AND NEW TESTAMENT APOCALYPSES.

By REV. NATHANIEL WEST, D.D

TESTIMONIALS

UNITED PRESBYTERIAN: "The author of this book has given us a book of profound erudition and research. The style often rises to the loftiest strains of eloquence. The chapter on "Our Present Age" stirs the reader like the sound of a trumpet."

EPISCOPAL RECORDER: "This book is a work of profound scholarship, by one who is deservedly recognized as an able interpreter of the Word of God, and will be read by many who are honestly seeking the light, and be found wonderfully instructive. We thank the author for it, and pray that it may have access to multitudes of readers."

PHILADELPHIA PRESBYTERIAN: "The author of this book has given us the fruit of his long-continued studies in eschatology, and no one is more competent to speak on this subject. No one can peruse its pages and not receive light and comfort from them. It uses ungloved hands toward post-millennianism."

THE CHRISTIAN CYNOSURE: "Dr. West handles his subject like a diligent and patient student, and in a manner sufficiently erudite and critical without passing beyond the comprehension of the ordinary reader. This volume marks the high-tide, in this country, in prophetic study, and will not be omitted from those works which the students of prophecy regard as a necessity."

DER CHRISTLICHE APOLOGETE: "The volume breathes an almost inspired love for the Word of God by one who is no stranger to its power. The gifted author demolishes the fond theories of men who negate the contents of prophecy by their spiritualistic interpretations of it. He indulges in no dreams. His exegetical power in both Testaments is wonderful. Every friend of prophetic study will thank Dr. West for the invaluable help he has brought to support a great truth hid from so many eyes."

JAEKEL'S U. CRAMER'S VIERTELJAHRSCHRIFT: "Dr. West treats his subject exegetically, and it is impossible to deny that he puts into the clearest light many portions of the Old Testament, and of the Apocalypse, which hitherto have been obscure. His masterpiece is the Seventy Weeks of Daniel, nor can we see how it can be answered. The exegesis pleases us exceedingly. It is fundamental study and fundamental exposition. The style is captivating and incisive as well. We bid it a hearty welcome and commend it earnestly to all sincere investigators of the Word of God."

DER SENDBOTE: "The work of Dr. West will stand the test of genuine criticism. It is a triumphant defense of the pre-millennial doctrine grounded in both the Old and New Testaments. It is a work of fundamental eschatological study of the highest value."

THE METHODIST REVIEW: "The work before us bears on every page the marks of intense and patient study, elaborate scholarship, and exhaustive research. The author is at home in the Scriptures. The book is packed with learning and shows familiarity with the writings of the ablest scholars in Christendom, both German and English. In his treatment of the Seventy Weeks he solves a problem which for eighteen hundred years has baffled all interpreters. We know of nothing to be compared with it."

PRINCETON REVIEW: "The work of a patient scholar, yet aglow with the fire of genius, brilliant erudition, and deep knowledge of the Scriptures. On several points we reserve our judgment."

PRESBYTERIAN JOURNAL: "Every friend of prophetic truth will thank Dr. West for the labor and pains he has endured in their behalf in the preparation of this remarkable work. It is no ordinary book."

THE TRUTH: "This book is the result of twenty years of devout study; and if brilliant scholarship, profound research, a trenchant style, and a masterly exposition can make a work attractive, Dr. West will not lack readers who will be exceedingly profited by his able presentation of the truth."

THE ADVANCE: "The confidence of the writer may, at times, be objectionable to some of his readers, but it must be confessed that the task the writer proposed to himself, so wide and deep, has been performed with a thoroughness and zeal, and exhaustive research to which every page bears witness."

RELIGIOUS TELESCOPE: "This book of Dr. West illustrates the organism of all prophecy, and perfect unity of God's Word, and the realistic meaning of the lively oracles, in remarkable manner. It illuminates. We commend it to every student."

FAITHFUL WITNESS: "We hail this volume. Those who love to dig deep will find abundant help here; a light such as not yet has dawned on many minds. Its exegesis, expositions, summaries, arguments and focalizing of Bible-light on prophetic themes, command our admiration."

CONGREGATIONALIST: "The author has given us the results of a life-long study on the subjects of prophecy and eschatology. The work is elaborate and appeals especially to scholars."

THE NEW YORK TRIBUNE: "Every page of this rare book bears evidence that the author is a master of interpretation and a scholar whose eye has not suffered to escape from him any writer on the subject of which he treats, at home or abroad. It is no mere index-learning we have here. The book will rank high among evangelical scholars and divines."

PITTSBURG TIMES: "The book is no ordinary book. The chapters that handle the Seventy Weeks of Daniel will, doubtless, be regarded as the most attractive. We cannot so effectively commend the book, as by assuring the public that they will find not only a very complete and masterly, but absolutely novel solution of a problem which, already, specialists have noted as a discovery that effaces a whole library of abortive speculations."

COURIER-JOURNAL, LOUISVILLE: "Solid learning, energetic style, deep conviction, prolonged study, and a wide research entitle the author of this book to speak confidently. He never indulges in over-statement. Trained skill in exegesis, power of argument, grave satire of ecclesiastical optimism, are among the weapons wielded against the corruptions and errors of the times."

FREE PRESS, DETROIT: "No one can read the pages of Dr. West's book, so free from the feverish fanaticism and excitements of modern Second Adventism and the recklessness of mere time-reckoners, and not see, even in a casual glance, that he has made an unexceptionally strong case in defense of the primitive church view of the millennium. The book is not only one of superior scholarship, but of profound reverence for the Bible."

INTER-OCEAN, CHICAGO: "There is more sound, Scriptural truth in this book, more of a well-trained mind, deep in the love of the Bible, and more real scholarship than can be found in a hundred others on the same subject."

THE CHRISTIAN UNION: "We do not believe the subject is more thoroughly or ably discussed in any volume of our acquaintance."

THE CHRISTIAN, LONDON, ENGLAND: "The book is one of the ablest that has appeared in our day; deep in its reverence for the Word of God, powerful in exegesis and in argument, and must be hailed with delight by students of prophetic truth."

For sale by all booksellers, or sent post free on receipt of price by the publishers.

THE PRINCIPLES OF THE HOPE OF ISRAEL MOVEMENT

The Hope of Israel Movement aims to bring the fullness of the Gospel of Jesus Christ to His brethren according to the flesh. We hold that Scripture—not Talmudic or Rabbinical, still less Reformed—Judaism is as much a divine revelation as Christianity. The canon of the New Testament has no higher divine authority than has that of the Old. Neither is complete without the other. Salvation is from the Jews, John iv: 22. And the Gospel is "to the Jew first," Rom. 1: 18. The Jew is not a Gentile. The term "proselyte," therefore, can never apply to the Jew. The promises of God are Israel's, Rom. ix: 4, 5. Gentile believers are the real "proselytes," once far off, now made nigh. Eph. ii: 12, 13. The root of God's good olive tree, Israel, bears us; not we the root. Rom. xi: 17, 18. To "proselyte" the Jew, then, is to ignore and to reverse the divine order.

The Jew has no need whatever of the organizations or institutions of historical (i. e., Gentile and denominational) Christianity. All he needs is personal, saving faith in his own Jewish Messiah, the Christ of God, nothing more. And all that was divinely given him through Moses he has full liberty to retain and uphold as far as possible when he becomes a believer in Jesus Christ. This to us clearly follows from these Scriptural considerations:

1. Abraham—the divine pattern of the true Jew, as well as of the believing Gentile, Rom. iv: 11, 12—received circumcision as an everlasting covenant after he had believed God unto justification. Gen. xvii: 9-14. God Himself added circumcision to Abraham's faith. And thus Paul writes: "Is any man called being circumcised? Let him not become uncircumcised." 1 Cor. vii: 18. This was the ruling of the Apostle to the Gentiles in all the churches. (Compare Ezek. xliv: 7, 9.)

2. The natural seed of Jacob shall not cease to be a nation before the Lord forever. Jer. xxx: 11; xxxi: 35, 37; xlvi: 28; Rom. xi: 1, 29. This is God's eternal purpose and the secret of Israel's preservation. Even so at this present time—through the Gospel— a remnant of the nation is being saved, according to the election of grace. Rom. xi: 5. These saved Jews, to be a remnant, should not surrender any of the divinely appointed marks of the nation Israel. They should not be taught to un-Jew themselves.

3. The Lord Jesus Christ was a minister of the circumcision for the truth of God. (Israel's national election.) Rom. xv: 8. He came not to destroy, but to fulfill, the law. Jewish disciples of Christ, by the word of the Lord Himself, should not be taught to break or disregard one of these commandments. Matt. v: 17, 19. They should walk and live even as He lived among His own people, i. e., as true, conforming Jews (barring, of course, mere traditions of the elders and the commandments of men). 1 John ii: 6.

4. On and from the Day of Pentecost myriads of Jewish believers were by the Holy Spirit baptized into fellowship with the glorified Christ. He did not cause or direct either the Apostles or other Jewish believers to "forsake Moses." Apostolic teaching and practice throughout the New Testament only show Jewish Christians "walking orderly and keeping the law." Acts ii: 46, 47; iii: 1; vi: 7; x: 9 (Chap. xv: 28, 29, by implication, clearly makes observance of all the laws and ordinances of Moses for Jewish believers a matter pleasing to the Holy Ghost); xvi: 3; xviii: 18; xx: 16; xxi: 17-26; xxiii: 1; xxv: 8.

5. Jesus Christ, the Son of God, is also Son of Abraham and Son of David. He is at once Head over all things to the Church (built up of Jews and Gentiles), and the rightful and coming heir of David's throne, which He will restore and occupy at His return from heaven. Luke i: 32, 33; Acts xv: 16; iii: 21. Jesus has not surrendered or forfeited His distinctive claim to the throne of His (Jewish) ancestor, David, by ascending on high and becoming the glorified Head of His body, the Church. No more should Jewish believers in Christ, being living members of His body, be made or taught to surrender anything which is divinely ordered and appointed for Israel as God's and Christ's age-lasting and peculiar people.

...Hope of Israel Movement...

A. C. GAEBELEIN, Superintendent,
E. F. STROETER, Secretary.

Headquarters 128 2nd Street, New York City.

The Hope of Israel Movement aims to bring the fullness of the Gospel of Jesus Christ to the seed of Abraham. The leaders of the movement are Gentiles. Our principles are found on the next page. They are non proselyting and non-denominational.

....Our Hope....

A Christian Monthly devoted to the study of Prophecy and organ of the Hope of Israel Movement.

Subscription for 1 year, $1.00. Special rates for larger quantities. Sample copies sent free on application.

Jewish, Hebrew and German Publications.

The Hope of Israel publishes large quantities of tracts in different languages for free distribution among the Jews in this and other lands. Any quantity of tracts will be sent to Christian people who desire to distribute this literature. Postage must be sent with the order.

"*TIQWETH ISRAEL,*" a *12-page Christian Monthly in the Jewish language.*

OTHER PAMPHLETS IN ENGLISH:
Life from the Dead, by E. F. Stroeter.
Does Christianity Annul Judaism? by Dr. J. M. Stifler.
A Strange Inconsistency.
Israel's Awakening, by A. C. Gaebelein.
No Millennium Before Christ Comes, by W. J. Erdman, etc., etc.

ADDRESS,

HOPE OF ISRAEL,

No. 128 2nd St., - - - New York City.

www.ingramcontent.com/pod-product-compliance
Lightning Source LLC
Chambersburg PA
CBHW030812230426
43667CB00008B/1185